Becoming
PALESTINE

GIL Z. HOCHBERG

Becoming
PALESTINE

TOWARD AN ARCHIVAL IMAGINATION

OF THE FUTURE

DUKE UNIVERSITY PRESS | DURHAM AND LONDON | 2021

Cover designed by Aimee C. Harrison
Text designed by Matthew Tauch
Typeset in Portrait Text Regular by Westchester Publishing
Services

Library of Congress Cataloging-in-Publication Data
Names: Hochberg, Gil Z., [date] author.
Title: Becoming Palestine: toward an archival imagination of the
future / Gil Z. Hochberg.
Description: Durham: Duke University Press, 2021. | Includes
bibliographical references and index.
Identifiers: LCCN 2021005977 (print)
LCCN 2021005978 (ebook)
ISBN 9781478013884 (hardcover)
ISBN 9781478014829 (paperback)
ISBN 9781478022138 (ebook)
Subjects: LCSH: Visual communication—Political aspects—
Palestine. | Archival materials—Palestine. | Ethnomusicology—
Palestine. | Arab-Israeli conflict—Mass media and the conflict. |
Palestine—In motion pictures. | BISAC: ART / Middle Eastern |
ART / History / Contemporary (1945–)
Classification: LCC P95.82. P19 H634 2021 (print) | LCC P95.82. P19
(ebook) | DDC 302.2095694—dc23
LC recordavailableathttps:/ /lccn.loc.gov/2021005977
LC ebookrec ordavailableathttps:/ /lccn.loc.gov/2021005978

Cover art: Steve Sabella, *38 Days of Re-Collection*, 2014. B&W
film negatives (generated from digital images), printed with
B&W photo emulsion spread on paint fragments peeled off
Jerusalem's Old City house walls. The photograph was taken
in a Palestinian home occupied by Israelis since 1948.

CONTENTS

Might we understand ourselves as always in the
process of becoming Palestinian? | SOPHIA AZEB,
"Who Will We Be When We Are Free?"

Becoming Palestine is a book about archival imagination *of* and *for*
the future. While much has been written about Palestine and
archives, the investment in the archive has been past-oriented—
centered on quests to open a gateway to the past (*or the past before
the past*) to discover "proof" or to recover "the stuff" with which
to heal the present (or at least identify the sites of loss to initiate
just reparation). Some look to the archives to prove that the *Nakba*
(Catastrophe) happened, and provide us with details of the atrocities (this is the "New Historians" line of inquiry as practiced by
Benny Morris, Ilan Pappé, and others).[1] Others turn to the archive
to show that Israel looted Palestinian archival material; like detec-
tives, they scour the Israeli archives to find the stolen goods.[2] Then
there are those who create their own alternative archives to prove
that there were better times and options in the past, in which Jews
and Arabs lived—or *could have potentially lived*—peacefully and hap-
pily together. This last type of archival work I call looking for "the
moment before the moment."[3] While these and others comprise
important archival efforts,[4] I fear that so long as the archive remains a portal to pasts both known and unknown, both actual
and potential, the sensation of discovery is bound to fade quickly
and the political impact of the intervention will be short-lived. In
Becoming Palestine, archival returns are oriented more toward the
present and the future, and less so the past.

The book suggests that little remains that is redemptive or
promising about the archive as a source of historical knowledge.
There is nothing left to find or prove. Secrets have been exposed
and more will still be unveiled, but these archival efforts, important as they are, result in little political change and bring about
minimal if any new configurations of future potentiality. "It is

striking to see how little our understanding has changed following the release of state documents," writes historian Efraim Karsh in his review of the work of the New Historians.[5] Karsh does not deny the archival findings, but rather simply argues that they reveal nothing new, nothing previously unknown.

Historians look for historical facts in archives, and we have all grown accustomed to the promise of the archive in revealing and affirming truths. The idea, the illusion, is that if only we find a record (a written document, perhaps some photographs), we will then *know* the truth (what *really* happened) and can finally set the record clear. We continue to believe that archival knowledge of who did what—who are the perpetrators; who are the victims; and what were the deeds—can be transformative. *Becoming Palestine* is significantly less optimistic about this perception of the archive's promise. While I restrain from making a general observation about the role of archival findings in providing justice in other historical cases, I feel quite confident to suggest that in the case of Israel/Palestine, archival findings (if they are approached in a limited historical manner, which is to say, as long as the archive is considered a gate to the past) make little to no impact on the shaping of the present and future. At this point in time, we are already saturated with archival information about "what happened," and there is hardly any denial of Palestinian expulsion and ruination. The historical facts are all known, documented, and publicized. Since the Israel State Archives were opened in the 1980s (or perhaps even earlier), there have been no more secrets to be found there—historians were able to document the full range of atrocities involved in the Nakba, yet the revelations amount to little ethical and political change. The problem we face is one of denial on the part of Israel and its allies, of course, but *not* a denial of "facts" (hence no additional archival revelations are necessary)—it is rather a denial of the moral, ethical, and political implications and significance *of* these facts. This particular problem of the archive cannot be solved with a historical methodology that continues to see in the archive a source of historical facts, data, and information. A different approach to the archive is needed here. It is indeed time to realize that archives hide very little, and that the secrets of the archive are usually *open secrets*, and hence hardly secrets at all. Thus, for example, sixteen years and two Palestinian Intifadas after Benny Morris first published his groundbreaking account of the horrors of the Nakba based entirely on findings from the Israeli state and military archive,[6] he stated:

In certain conditions, expulsion is not a war crime. I don't think that the expulsions of 1948 were war crimes. You can't make an omelet without breaking eggs. You have to dirty your hands. . . . A society that aims to kill you forces you to destroy it. When the choice is between destroying or being destroyed, it's better to destroy. . . . *There are circumstances in history that justify ethnic cleansing.* I know that this term is completely negative in the discourse of the 21st century, but when the choice is between ethnic cleansing and genocide—the annihilation of your people—I prefer ethnic cleansing.[7]

Archival findings may prove guilt beyond all doubt, but they easily lose their political impact when reread through and into a pregiven Darwinian ideology (call it a meta-archive) of "us versus them," which shamelessly justifies even the crime of ethnic cleansing.

This ethical collapse is further aggravated by what I call "archive fatigue": the fact that what is found in the archive, despite its claim to novelty, is never actually "new." Palestinians have been testifying to this violence and ethnic cleansing since 1948. In short, there was never a real breakthrough; nothing truly "new" has ever been revealed. What the archives "revealed" is what Palestinians already knew, and what most Israelis knew but chose to deny. Archival findings in this context, and perhaps in many others too, are less about new findings and more about the repeated affirmation of already known historical information. Finding, exposing, sharing the same information and the same facts, time and time again—the same atrocities, the same numbers (more or less), the same unveiling of open secrets—can be numbing. To fight this archival fatigue and make archives actually matter, we need to develop an altogether different approach—one that builds on imagination, future vision, playfulness, creativity, speculation, and *fabulation*, to borrow Saidiya Hartman's term.[8]

The archival imagination I find in the artworks I engage with throughout the book is no longer about providing proofs of past deeds, documenting loss, or witnessing past trauma. This archival imagination upturns the temporality of the archive to find traces of the future in the present. When reading the present itself as an archive, the point is not only or mainly to look backward to find traces of the past, but also, and perhaps more significantly, to find traces of the future "not as a promise to come but as immanent within the setter colonial present."[9]

I find this future-oriented archival imagination at the heart of many contemporary Palestinian artistic projects. This archival imagination underlines the recognition of the fact that historical Palestine has already been destroyed and that whatever this means for any future claim of repair, return, and change is something that needs to be invented and constructed—quite literally beyond the limits imposed by the archive as a historical source of factual information to which we owe our future. Documentation and witnessing are thus replaced in these artistic works with the incentive to approach the present as an archive for imagining otherwise. In a broader sense, I think this archival imagination has to do with many Palestinian artists and writers' movement away from a historical investment in the archive (searching for facts, documenting atrocities) and toward a more experimental approach. This approach reflects a shift from earlier modes of expression, following Edward Said's call for the "permission to narrate,"[10] to a new mode of artistic expression and political intervention that can be described as a permission to *refuse narrative*. This refusal of narrative is largely a refusal of familiar discursive frames (for example, "the nation," "the people") and genealogical narratives of origins, loss, and recovery, in which the future is tautologically predestined. There are some good historical reasons for why we may be witnessing this shift as an aesthetic response to the teleology of revolution (loss, return, and recovery).[11] Most of the artists I interviewed during the process of writing this book expressed discomfort with national politics; some even spoke about "the collapse of the national project" and the need to move away from aesthetic modes of expression that suggest nostalgic, even romantic, frames of narrative that link future to past, and link revolution to retreating to a time in history *before* the rupture of 1948. But another aspect of this new trend or aesthetic lingo conversely has to do with the move away from the "permission" aspect of the initial mode of expression. The works I discuss in this book, like many other works of young Palestinian artists, are less concerned with the need to make the case of Palestine known (that work has already been achieved) and accordingly seem also less concerned with appearing in legible ways, or being recognized and transposed into preexisting narrative forms, not least of which is the nation.[12]

This new archival imagination approaches the archive not by following the imperial desire to unearth hidden moments (there are no such hidden things or histories, only open secrets), but by challenging the very identification of the archive with the past. The archive's assumed role as the past guardian is replaced with an understanding of the archive as the guardian of the present as we know it. My focus on artworks and artistic imagination aims at highlighting the critical potential involved in activating the archive in experimental and playful ways that defy the monopoly and power of the

more common and authoritative historical engagements. Artistic activizations of the archive thus provide, among other things, alternatives to the
tendency of historical engagements to separate past from present, and facts
from imagination and to leave future out of the equation. Art, in its artistic engagement with the *figure of the archive* as a structure of thought and
a mode of knowledge production, is particularly productive in helping us
(1) break apart the teleological view of history and open up unpredicted
configurations of the future; and (2) expand our experience of the present
to remind us that there is always more than one present.

Becoming Palestine thus joins the call to move away from the main
downfall of today's Left, as Wendy Brown, following Walter Benjamin's
original critique of "Left-Wing Melancholy" (1931), identifies it: "It is a Left
that has become more attached to its impossibility than to its potential
fruitfulness . . . [it is] caught in a structure of melancholic attachment to
a strain of its own dead past" (26).[13] To move away from wounded attachments, loss, and impossibility, and toward a politics invested in future
potentiality, is the ability to imagine otherwise—to take a risk and let go
of the investment in predefined collectives configured in familiar political
categories (nation-state, ethnicity, nativity, etc.), and in favor of new and
still unrecognizable collectives of/for the future.

The book critically engages *both* the politics of archival knowledge production in Israel/Palestine *and* the general tendency of most theories of
the archive to follow a Benjaminian messianic logic of material historicity.
I claim that to archive for the future we must abandon our attachment to
history and the redemptive hopes of messianic delivery in favor of a more
radical imagination that breaks away from the past toward new becomings:
unknown, uncertain, but potentially more just. I find such radical imagination in artistic activations of the archive. Through them, I show how the
archive can be activated to rethink the concept of potentiality. Liberated
from the grips of history, the archive can join, in turn, a future-oriented
social force connected to a moment of political becoming. As long as we
approach archives in search of "what really happened" or "what could have
happened," we will continue to deal with closed frameworks and even dead
ends. The archive should instead become a platform for building a just society as a process of becoming rather than as a stagnant rearticulation of
past collectivities, victories, losses, atrocities, and gains. *Becoming Palestine*
suggests that the political potentiality of the archive depends on its ability
to serve as a source of imagining a (still-unknown) future by returning to
the present with all its visible and invisible potentialities.

Becoming Palestine is a labor of love and deep personal and political investment. It is a book about culture, imagination, and politics—about imaginary configurations of the political and about the politics of imagination. The artworks are my main theoretical informants and inspiration, following a similar methodology of close readings that informed my earlier two books. Only very late in the process of completing this book did I realize that *Becoming Palestine* was a third installation in a trilogy about Palestine. This trilogy follows an unplanned sequential order. My first book, *In Spite of Partition* (2007), is about the past and about what we have lost to history (the Arab-Jew "we were"). My second book, *Visual Occupations* (2015), focuses on the political contours of the present and studies the visual politics that allow for present Palestine to appear as it does. With *Becoming Palestine*, I shift my attention to the future. This is a book about a future that may be—a future that we must first learn to imagine.

I owe my most profound gratitude to the artists and writers who inhabit this book. I thank each one of them for their inspiration, for sharing their work with me, for their trust, for spending so much time talking to me, and for patiently addressing my questions. This book is about their work and is informed by their work and visions. If there is to be found here a "theory of the archive," it is an outcome of a collective effort that springs from the artists and writers with whose works I have been fortunate to engage. In this sense, these individuals I thank are really my coauthors: Jumana Manna, Basal Abbas, Ruanne Abou-Rahme, Umar al-Ghubari, Shuruq Harb, Arkadi Zaides, Emily Jacir, Sami Michael, Kamal Aljafari, Larissa Sansour, Farah Saleh, Azza El-Hassan, and Basma Alsharif.

In January 2020, the Center for Palestine Studies (CPS) at Columbia University hosted a workshop in which participants read an earlier draft of this manuscript. I cannot overstate the profound contribution this workshop made in improving this project. I am forever grateful for having had such a supportive group of brilliant friends and colleagues who willingly and generously read the entire manuscript and provided me with immensely helpful comments, suggestions, and critique—and in the most collaborative and supportive manner possible. I thank each of you deeply: Lana Tatour, Nayrouz Abu Hatoum, Ella Shohat, Simone Ilana Rutkowitz, Brian Boyd, Marianne Hirsch, Claudia Breger, Lila Abu-Lughod, Nadia L. Abu El-Haj, Nadia Yaqub, Nasser Abourahme, Brinkley M. Messick, and Nasreen Brooks Abd Elal. You will surely find your fingerprints all over this book.

I also thank the following individuals for an ongoing exchange about many of the ideas articulated in the book and for dialogues that extend over years: Galit Eilat, Ariella Azoulay, Ayelet Ben Yishai, Reem Fadda, Gayatri Gopinath, Saidiya Hartman, Mana Kia, Stephen Sheehi, and Debashree Mukherjee. I extend my gratitude to my editor, Courtney Berger, who made working on this book a truly pleasant experience. I also which to thanks Susan Albury and Sandra Korn at Duke University Press. A very special thankfulness to Colleen Jankovic, who also worked with me as an editor on my previous book—she remains my harshest critic who always makes me work more than I want to. I thank her for her dedication, support, patience, and intellectual engagement.

I extend my gratitude to the following dear friends and family, whose love and support sustain me. When in doubt, I turn to them, and they always guide me back on track. Thank you, Tamar Assal, Naomi Kaniuk, S. A. Bachman, Sarah Gualtierri, Yonit Efron, Mel Chen, Jack Halberstan, Daniel Tsur, Itamar Tsur, my mother Ruth Ramot, and my partner in crime Keri Kanetsky. A special thanks to Ariel Seroussi for teaching me the importance of sometimes doubting my own self-doubt and to Kathleen McIntyre for teaching me the power of fearless curiosity. Finally, Eli Kanetsky and Omri Kanetsky, my kids: I thank you both for reminding me time and again that my books "are boring." It helps lower expectations.

Archival Imagination
of/for the Future

To turn the archive into something living is to
fundamentally connect to a moment of political
becoming. | BASAL ABBAS AND RUANNE ABOU-
RAHEM, "The Archival Multitude"

> And if there was no past? And if the past was
> the invention of the imperial archive? And if the
> keepers at its gate are guarding something else?
> | ARIELLA AZOULAY, *Potential History*

In 2013 Umar al-Ghubari and Tomer Gardi edited and published a
bilingual (Arabic and Hebrew) book of twelve short stories, written by various Palestinian and Israeli writers, under the title *Awda*
(Arabic for "return") and the subtitle "Imagined Testimonies from
Potential Futures." Each story weaves an imagined future set after
the return of the Palestinian refugees and the replacement of the
Zionist regime with a new sociopolitical arrangement. Each story
imagines a different future, with some portraying a democratic
postnational society; some depicting a Palestinian revival without
a historical trace of Zionists; some describing a Palestinian Arab
society with a well-integrated Jewish minority; and still others set
in a metahistorical time where "return as a dream" freely flows
as "the eternity of return," unfettered by state bureaucracy. No
political agenda is outlined or advanced in the book as a whole;
rather, these fictional testimonies come together as opening *the
very possibility* of envisioning different futures in a current reality

hemmed down by ongoing violence, stagnation, and hopelessness. The reader is invited to witness testimonies that are ahead of time—that help her imagine the unimaginable *as already* a possible reality.

These *parafictions*, to borrow Carrie Lambert-Beatty's term,[1] amount to a new archive: an archive of/for the future. These imagined testimonies for potential futures maintain a plurality invested in the very possibility to imagine, thereby avoiding a restricted and dogmatic utopian vision of the future. Dogma and doctrine are replaced with what Avery Gordon has recently called "utopian margins"—"a poetic knowledge: ex-centric, queer, and scandalous . . . in which ideas and actions in the-yet-to-come are articulated in the present tense, as if they [had already] acquired the power of a narrated story told urgently."[2] *Awda* demands of us to witness "a yet-to-come" that the present has not yet caught up with, and to read this potential future (urgently!) in the present tense.

The introduction to *Awda* is written by Umar Al-Ghubari. It is dated a decade *after* the book's publication, when the imagined testimonies have become reality, and when the time gap between imagination and realization has already closed. The Palestinian refugees have long returned, and the introduction describes the twelve writers taking a train together to Beirut for a conference. They are invited to discuss their project and talk about how they were able to imagine and predict the future at a time when it was still an unthinkable possibility: "You were like prophets, you foresaw the impossible," the host from Beirut comments. "We want to understand how you came up with such an idea and what were the responses to your book at the time."[3] The introduction to *Awda* functions as a metacommentary on both the potentiality and the limits of the poetic knowledge produced by the project. Al-Ghubari's words, which frame the book as a whole, achieve two things at once: first, they demand we continue to imagine and project into an unrealized future (in which the imagined futures accounted for in the twelve stories collected in the book have already become part of a political reality and a verified past), and second they authoritatively guide us in understanding "how to read the book" not as a dreamy utopian recovery or political plan but as a *disturbance*: an archive of unarchivable speculative testimonies of/for the future that the present keeps failing to catch up with.

Like several other artistic engagements with archives, this alternative collection (a book of imagination presented to us as an already existing archive of testimonies) draws political inspiration from defying the limits that the present political order places on what can and cannot be foreseen,

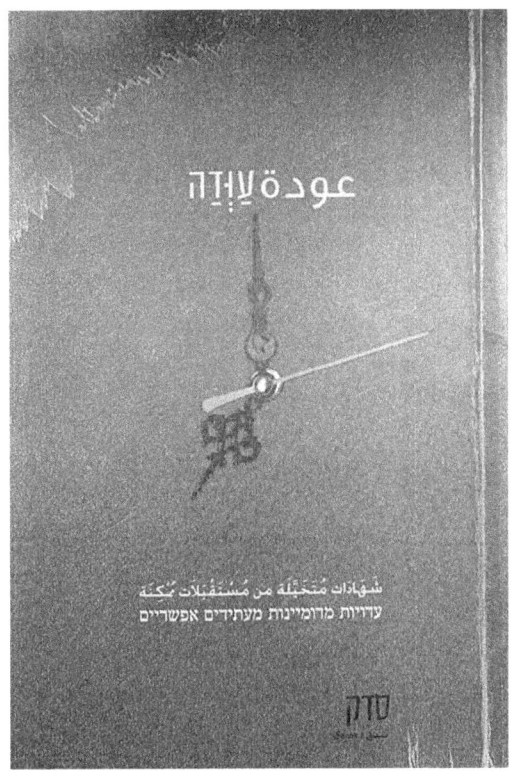

1.1 Cover of the book *Awda: Imagined Testimonies from Potential Futures* (Tel Aviv: Zochrot, 2013), edited by Umar al-Ghubari and Tomer Gardi.

and what can or cannot be imagined as a possible future. This archive of testimonies opens up an alternative future not dominated by Zionism and its aftermath (occupation, apartheid, refugees) by positing a fictional future as already a past. We are invited on a time leap journey—first entering a future (presented in the introduction) in which the speculations collected in the book have already and miraculously come true. This future, attested to as reality, never forms a coherent vision. Rather, we are continuously reading ahead of ourselves, catching up, as it were, with the past and with a future that is becoming the present as we read, becoming and unbecoming as we move from one story to another.

I open with *Awda* because the collection of stories exemplifies what I mean by an archival imagination that operates in the service of the future and advances a temporality that exceeds historical causality. The archival imagination I trace throughout this book blurs the distinction between official archives and recognized archival documents on the one hand, and alternative, impossible, or imaginary archives on the other. If *Awda* has one imperative message, it is that future aspirations, communities, and solidarities cannot be found in preexisting archives and must be created through speculative ones.[4] It is worth mentioning in this regard other important speculative interventions that increasingly have been taking place in Palestine/Israel since the early 2000s. The first is the ongoing project by DAAR, "Decolonizing Architecture Art Residency,"[5] while the second is a related ongoing online project called "Arena of Speculation."[6] In both cases, architectural and spatial imagination serve as key elements for creating a new speculative political space that derives its force from imagination just as much as from the "factual." These are projects that focus on finding practical solutions to the ongoing Palestinian refugee problem, but do so by searching for radically creative and speculative ways for rethinking the ontology of the present and the relationship between history and futurity, as well as the factual and the imaginary.[7] In *Awda*, the act of return is featured in all these projects as both the most urgent act of restoration and the most important component for imagining a radically different, better future that goes beyond the knee-jerk solution of limiting our political imagination to the framework of the nation-state.

In a moving personal account, Marianne Hirsch describes the terror of being a "stateless" refugee after she and her parents left communist Romania in 1961, lost their citizenship, and decided not to accept the Israeli agency's invitation to become Israeli citizens. Instead, they stayed paperless in Australia, and "the term *stateless* came to encompass this sense of dispossession and negation, this loss of identity. It connects the hiding and lying, the fear of discovery, the feeling . . . of being tolerated but unwanted, of being other . . . and it brings back yearning for belonging, for the legitimation of citizenship and a passport."[8] Having lived as a refugee and a stateless person, Hirsch is not shy about finding comfort in her American citizenship: "Every time I open my US passport at an immigration counter, my body relaxes and I am so grateful to have a valid one."[9] Hirsch is writing her memories at a time when the number of refugees and stateless people across the globe is multiplying—in Palestine, across the Mediterranean in South Asia, Mexico, the United States, across Africa, across Europe. No one could possibly think these stateless people should remain in this state of un-belonging, without rights, without even "the right to have rights" to borrow Hannah Arendt's famous expression.

And yet, as Hirsch writes, "Statelessness could be claimed as a space of openness and potentiality, rather than merely a blockage to be overcome."[10] Consider in this regard DAAR's innovative *Refugee Heritage* project from 2017.

DAAR carefully followed the criteria of the United Nations Educational, Scientific and Cultural Organization (UNESCO) to nominate the Dheisheh Refugee Camp in the West Bank as a heritage site for the UNESCO World Heritage List.[11] The act of compliance itself calls upon us to revisit the idea of cultural heritage as centered on the nation-state. *Refugee Heritage* entails more than the idea of turning a refugee camp into a heritage site, which is a proposition already radical insofar as it dramatically alters the way we think about refugee-ness. The proposal requires that we also rethink the concept of heritage, in terms that are not dominated by the geopolitics of the modern nation-state. Nominating the Dheisheh Refugee Camp to the UNESCO World Heritage List, DAAR maps heritage onto an "illegitimate" site: a Palestinian refugee camp that is meant to be temporary, and a site that is an outcome of political failure and a mark of political crisis. In marking the refugee camp as a heritage site, the temporality of the camp as a state that must be overcome is replaced with the idea of the camp as an ongoing state of being. The project further invites us to consider the state of refugee-ness and statelessness not only as a humanitarian crisis but also as a productive possibility and a position from which to rethink the dominance of nation-state order as the only legitimate and desired political horizon.

In nominating Dheisheh for the UNESCO World Heritage List and providing all the required criteria in the application, *Refugee Heritage* renders the trauma of refugee-ness an important, legitimate part of Palestinian heritage. Refugee-ness thus becomes not just a condition of crisis and loss but also an opportunity for rethinking cultural heritage, or what counts as such. In short: it is an attempt to move the burden of crisis from the refugee to heritage. *Refugee Heritage* is heritage in crisis. I read it as a refusal to "take refuge" in current modalities of heritage (pregiven and static notions of cultural possession, authenticity, ownership, national identity) and as an effort to rethink cultural heritage beyond the nation-state, beyond narratives of victory and glory, and beyond melancholic attachments, but also beyond the fictive and inherently colonial ideas of "mankind heritage" and "cultural heritage of universal value."[12]

What does it mean to think about the space of a refugee camp in terms of heritage? To think of the temporality of the refugee camp in terms of heritage? In the case of Palestine, this is a particularly tricky question, as it involves recognizing refugee-ness as an ongoing state and historical condition—a permanent condition that threatens to override the demand of Palestinian refugees to return to their original stolen lands, refusing their current living conditions as the basis for a future solution. As

Alessandro Petti of DAAR writes, "Refugee camps should not exist in the first place: they represent a crime and a political failure."[13] What does it mean, then, to claim political failure as cultural heritage?

Perhaps the most important aspect of DAAR's project is found in shifting the locality of failure from the refugees themselves to the political circumstances that brought Palestinians into refugee camps. *Refugee Heritage*, at least as I understand it, is preoccupied neither with celebrating refugeeness nor with the refugees' success in building a life under the hard conditions of exile. It is not a project that seeks to create a new site for "heritage tourism." What would the tourists see when they visit the camp? There are no tents or fragile structures in the camps, which look like many other urban centers and small cities. In short, the project is not invested in heritage as a source of generating capital or celebrating national legacies. In what then is it invested? I believe it is about finding a way to frame historical injustice, resistance, and perseverance as heritage to bring the concept of heritage itself (and the civil game of UNESCO's nomination) into crisis.

As stated by DAAR, the point of the project is not to actually convince UNESCO to add the Dheisheh refugee camp to the World Heritage List (a very unlikely scenario). More than anything, *Refuge Heritage* is a performative intervention, like earlier projects by DAAR. It is a provocation as a way to begin a conversation about both the "permanent temporariness of camps"[14] and the criteria by which heritage sites are selected, nominated, and registered as carrying universal value.

Dheisheh refugee camp is not a holy site, nor a site of great archaeological importance. It is not in Hebron or in Jerusalem, nor is it particularly old or made of interesting architectural structures. It hosts no natural wonders, lakes, waterfalls, or canyons. It is not, in short, made of the stuff of heritage. The camp was established in 1949 with 3,400 people. By now, seven decades later, it has a population of approximately fifteen thousand residents. Tents have been replaced with cement urban structures. The camp hardly even looks like a camp. It doesn't carry the aura of an unchangeable past. It is fairly modern. *Refugee Heritage* is not a fetishization of the past, of exile, of the refugee. It celebrates the mundane: daily life in a refugee camp that is already seventy years old. The project suggests that refugee history, the history of this camp, for example, is important and cannot be written out of history as temporary or as only a humanitarian crisis. It suggests that refugees are part of our cultural heritage and that if heritage wants to remain relevant as a concept and a practice, it needs to find articulation in new modalities and new understandings of our times.

UNESCO's World Heritage List may be fiction, nothing but a diplomatic Monopoly board game, but DAAR's *Refugee Heritage* quite seriously engages with this fiction. Playing by the rules and making its own nomination to UNESCO, DAAR's proposal affirms UNESCO's position and status as the authority on all things heritage, but also undermines it by turning the application itself into an exhibit and part of an art show: a political nomination that takes the form of an art exhibit. Politics or art? Reality or fiction? These are some of the questions DAAR's project raises in its unique format, but these are also the questions we can direct back at UNESCO's World Heritage Project: is this real or fictional?

Refugee Heritage is not simply an attempt to "take refuge in heritage" by joining an already powerful, if fictional, apparatus of the symbolic international distribution of power and recognition. It is, rather, an attempt to destabilize this mechanism while taking it seriously—an attempt to alter the conditions of the game called cultural heritage by asking: what constitutes heritage? Is there really a point in having UNESCO continue to map World Heritage Sites nominated by, and attributed to, nation-states in a world where millions of people live as refugees? Is it not time to rethink the logic and criteria by which we identify, classify, nominate, and locate sites of heritage? Is it not time for refugees to replace the nation-state as the central agency through which we distribute the "spiritual heritage of mankind"?

The performative and strategic nature of the *Refugee Heritage* project ties to other attempts by artists and scholars who use art, writing, and architecture as a platform for rethinking history-as-crime and for investigating the often complex and messy relationship between memorialization, archivization, responsibility, and complicity. "An intellectual must try to restore memory, restore some sense of the landscapes of destruction," Edward Said tells us.[15] Restoring some sense of a landscape of destruction is not an easy task. It is not the same as restoring the memory of something *before* it is lost or destroyed. Nor is it the same as restoring the destruction or proving a crime has taken place (the work of forensic architecture, for example). The task presented before us is to restore the magnitude of a historical event of destruction, and the long-lasting impact of such an event on the present, where visible or audio traces of violence are not necessarily immediately or accessibly present. The refugee camp as a site of heritage is precisely such an attempt at restoring a landscape of destruction: restoring a history of crime, not as an event of the past, but as a feature of the present. DAAR's political and artistic intervention reminds us of other projects. I am thinking in particular about Emily Jacir's installation "ex libris"

(2010–12), a documentation of the thirty thousand books looted from Palestinian homes, libraries, and institutions by Israeli authorities in 1948. Six thousand of these books were archived in the National Library of Israel in Jerusalem, where over a span of two years Jacir photographed them using her cell phone. Presenting the images alongside some books, Jacir draws attention to the absence of the books, which are visible before us only as digital copies. These are the traces of stolen objects. Their present-absence stands for a history of destruction and erasure. But at least the photographs prevent the erasure of the erasure. They document the absence, the detraction, the loss. And this documentation in turn becomes a presence in its own right. A book, a scrap of paper, a photograph, a building. These are the making of refugee heritage. Whether or not UNESCO will change its criteria for nominating World Heritage Sites to include the Dheisheh refugee camp is a different question, but certainly not the most important one.

Becoming Palestine is a book about such artistic speculative political interventions. I use the term *becoming* to account for such open-ended futures, invoking Gilles Deleuze's distinction between poetic-political intervention on the one hand and a mode of historical investigation on the other. For Deleuze, art captures possible universes as pure events that escape history: "What History grasps of the event is its effectuation in states of affairs or in lived experience, but the event in its becoming, in its specific consistency, in its self-positing as concept, escapes History."[16] Becoming requires a certain "leaving behind" of historical preconditions "in order to become, that is, to create something new." It requires speculating beyond the narrative comfort zone of history's "actuality," which is held in place by preexisting, recognizable political terms (state, empire, nation, or people). This is where art comes in. Art creates possible universes that escape the limits of history: "The artist intervenes in the possible universe in ways resistant to time . . . art opens history onto the ahistorical, and resistant to space, art opens the actual universe onto new universes or lands."[17]

The bulk of this book, then, turns to recent artistic interventions—essay film, video art, dance, literature, performance—to open history to potentiality, imagination, and speculation. I search for ways that both historical Palestine and today's Israel might undergo a process of "becoming": to cease to be in their actuality and become something radically new. I nevertheless call this "becoming Palestine" because the name *Palestine* marks more than a place or a history. It carries within it a certain productive ambiguity and uncertainty. Patrick William and Anna Ball ask, "Where is Palestine?" in their introduction to a special issue about the (missing) place of Palestine in postcolonial studies.[18] This seemingly straightforward question cannot simply be answered with "nowhere." While the nowhere of Palestine is affirmed time and time again (it prevented Elia Suleiman's film *Divine Intervention* from being nominated for an Academy Award in 2004, citing its lack of an acknowledged nominating nation-state),[19] this "nowhere" takes a much more complex form, given that even though it is not a current nation-state, "Palestine" exists in cultural memory, both as a past and as a desired future. It also exists as a "question,"[20] and as a metaphor, as the late poet Mahmoud Darwish frequently has reminded us.[21] As a concrete political vision, some consider Palestine to be "the idea of a secular democratic state in Palestine for Arabs and Jews."[22] Whether this particular political vision or another is the answer goes beyond the scope of my interests here. While this book is about potentiality, it refrains from promoting any concrete "solution" (one state, two state, no state) or outlining a specific political vision for the future. In the spirit of the texts I analyze, the book follows a "pessoptimist" approach, advancing a pessimistic optimism: pessimistic about current politics, it remains optimistic about the power of imagination.[23]

In a political reality dominated by the incentive to be realistic, I advocate for the place of imagination. While "dreaming is often suppressed and policed not only by our enemies but by leaders of social moments themselves,"[24] it is important to remember that significant political change has never been possible without imagination. "Palestine" as a horizon of change and potentiality is an explosive term because it is the biggest threat to Zionism and Israel (as a place, an idea, an ethno-national movement, a settler colonial paradigm) but also to the broader understanding of politics as a "realistic response" and a dismissal of the emancipatory potential of imagination.

Becoming Palestine obviously requires the un-becoming of Israel as we know it, but it must also be distinguished from Palestine as a preexisting territorial, historical, spatial, and national configuration. Becoming Palestine, in this sense, is not becoming Palestine *again*. It is not a move backward toward a fantastic vision of past revival, nor is it an anachronistic call to do away with the tremendous historical and political impact of the past seventy years of Israeli existence on local, regional, and global politics. It is not a resurrection of Palestinian nationhood before the fact, nor a flexing of Jewish nationalism after the fact. At stake is not a utopic vision of justice, either, as "becoming" can only suggest potentiality as a direction, not a predetermined end result. Rather, it is an attempt to imagine a livable life made of new collectives yet to become: beyond the limits of national imagination; beyond partition; beyond Zionism; and beyond any other ethnic, religious, national, or territorial divisions.

Archival imagination is central to the process of becoming precisely because its temporality exceeds that of the historical causal narrative. "Something is wrong with the temporality of the archive and with its announced mission to serve as a guardian of the past," Ariella Azoulay writes.[25] Archives are charged with creating a clear and archived past from which to understand the present as a logical and inevitable outcome and the future as a projected extension of this teleological order. But the archive nevertheless holds a potentiality that refuses the closure of historical time. It can always be read, as Jacques Derrida reminds us, as "a promise" and "a responsibility for tomorrow."[26] Unlike Derrida and his followers, however, I do not think the archive intrinsically generates such a promise. On the contrary, I find nothing promising in the archive as such. Accordingly, *Becoming Palestine* does not join the efforts to define the nature of the archive per se, or to advance a theory of the archive's emancipatory qualities. Instead I argue that there are multiple, diverse, and variously productive archival imaginations—only some of which successfully challenge the limits of historical reasoning in activating the archive as a future-oriented social force ("a responsibility for tomorrow") that is "fundamentally connected to a moment of political becoming."[27] In short, there is nothing intrinsically promising about the archive, only in various activizations of the archive.

Perhaps precisely because archives, particularly state archives, tend to arrest sociopolitical potentialities, limiting political imagination by ordering facts, narratives, identities, and time along preexisting borders and within the time frame of the nation, many artists, filmmakers, performers, and writers are drawn to them. They turn to the archive not simply as a gateway to the past or as a way to uncover what "really happened," but rather, as *Becoming Palestine* suggests, as a means for setting free potential elements of the present that are held hostage behind the archives' gates and guarded by gatekeepers of the past. "To succumb to realism is to give up hope"[28] because "reality" is never the sum of our present; rather, it is politics that make some elements of the present visible ("reality") while rendering others unseen ("fiction"). *Awda*, for example, advances an archival imagination that shakes up the present's suffocating political contours by staging several meeting points where the recorded past (pre-1948, the Nakba, the years following the Nakba) and the projected future (after the return of the Palestinian refugees) meet in new figurations. The collection of stories situates its impetus to archive (to collect witness accounts of a future-past) as a force of imagination that works not in the service of history, but in the service of potentiality, in turn producing future memories. *Becoming Palestine* is a process of activating archives that returns us to the present, reminding us that the fictive, imaginative, utopian vision for the future is in fact *already* part of our present, albeit well guarded and hidden behind the politics of the status quo.

What Is an Archive?

The archive has long been the center of critical investigation. Since Michel Foucault's early writings in *The Archaeology of Knowledge* (1969), the archive has been approached with great analytical suspicion. No longer, if ever, considered simply as a source of scholarship and knowledge, the archive has gradually become a subject of investigation, to paraphrase Ann Stoler.[29] With particular intensity since the mid-1990s, scholars, artists, archivists, curators, and data specialists have been defining, condemning, rescuing, defending, performing, questioning, queering, creating, negating, restaging, reclaiming, and debating the archive. What was once an underinvestigated source of historical authority has become a tantalizing enigma. "Nothing is less clear today than the word 'archive,'" Derrida wrote in 1995.[30] In many ways, academic discourse, beginning with historians, and leading up to anthropologists and critical theorists, invented the fiction we call "the archive." It is an entity or term open to critical speculations and debates in the most universal and general terms. We read that the archive dies in this or that way, or that we should read the archive in this or that manner. But the very idea that there is a thing we can call "the archive" is itself a fiction. There are only, and always already, many different kinds of archives, and as many different potential archival imaginations.

Today, more than in past decades, we can surely agree that the institution we call "the archive" has undergone a vital process of democratization—as partial as it may be. We can no longer say that the archive only, or mainly, consolidates power (the power of the archons, the state, the scholars). Archives also contest power, as in the case of nonnational/nonstate archives, including refugee archives, diaspora archives, queer archives, etc.[31] While in many places archives are still hard to enter and documents are guarded under tight surveillance, digitalization means that we are living in, and are part of, an *archive-saturated era*. Everyone everywhere is archiving. Everyone everywhere is questioning the impetus to archive and its value.[32] What once was the territory of the state, and before that of the masters and mega-stars (the archons of ancient Greece), and what once was the "stuff" of official history written by trained historians, has slowly been undone and redone. Many more individuals are creating archives as well as questioning the authority of preexisting ones.

This relative democratization also means that we have today many different *kinds of archives:* state archives, private archives, museum archives, "archives of feelings."[33] The importance of this expansion of the archive from a relatively hegemonic and centralized site of power with limited access and great supervision to a reality in which even private photo collections or collections of ephemeral objects "count" as an archive is not to be underestimated. Digitalization has eased how documents, material, images, and footage are collected and stored, but even more significantly how they are shared, circulated, and manipulated. One is reminded of Walter Benjamin's ambivalent relationship to film and the technological advantages of mechanical reproduction, which he considered as an important democratization of art, but harmful to art's auratic status: "That which withers in the age of mechanical reproduction is the aura of the work of art."[34] Along the same lines, we can say that the "archive in the age of *digital* reproduction" is both more democratic, and less auratic. This loss in aura also means that earlier theoretical concerns with the authoritative status of the archive and its policing nature, beginning with Foucault and developed by Derrida, must be replaced with more nuanced accounts that consider how those in marginal positions can use the power of the archive differently—to build, create, and express alternative collectivities, interests, and desires.

Along these lines, Arjun Appadurai argues that the archive's *generative power* for counterhegemonic future aspirations is oft overlooked. Commending Foucault for his early intervention and critical account of the archive as a state-policing apparatus and a gatekeeper of knowledge production, Appadurai notes that while Foucault successfully "destroyed the innocence of the archive," he nevertheless "had too dark a vision of the panoptical functions of the archive, of its roles as an accessory to policing, surveillance, and governmentality."[35] Appadurai emphasizes in his short essay that "the archive" cannot possibly be analyzed only or mainly as a policing device, and certainly not in this day and age when archives are everywhere. Given its multiplicities, the archive can be activated in many ways, and, as we shall see in the following chapters, what I call "archival imagination" often takes the form and content of social anticipation. Archives for the future are, in this sense, counterhegemonic meta-interventions into the political status quo.

For Foucault, the archive is "the law of what can be said, the system that governs the appearance of statements as unique events";[36] that is to say, it is the law that frames that which can be articulated or even thought. More recently, Ariella Azoulay has called this "the archival condition."[37] But, as Appadurai makes clear, the archive is also a practice of everyday life and a tool open to imagination, manipulation, and future creation. Without overlooking the disciplinary dangers of the archive, we must also recognize its potential to anticipate and advance social change.

To activate the archive as a future-oriented social force that is still firmly grounded in the present is to "fundamentally connect to a moment of political becoming," write the Palestinian artists and collaborators Basel Abbas and Ruanne Abou-Rahme,[38] whose work I explore in the fourth chapter. For Abbas and Abou-Rahme the archive offers an opportunity to access the present as a juncture—a tensed configuration of time that holds within it access to possibilities of unattainable pasts and glimpses of poten-tial futures. Their own engagement with various archives is never "histori-cal" in the sense of using archives to study the past or past events. Archives that are approached as documents of "what really happened," they argue, remain "closed, static, even dead."[39] Such an approach to archives can yield nothing but already familiar narratives. The political promise of the ar-chive depends on the ability to make the archive an integral part of the present, rather than a record of the past. To borrow Walter Benjamin's seductive words, I would rephrase this proposal as one that associates the political significance of the archive with its ability to *crystalize* "the time of the now."[40]

In Walter Benjamin's compelling and poetic rendition of dialectic material historical time, the linear progression of time from past to present to future is interrupted by the various densities of the present in relation to the past. The past as chronology carries little meaning or political significance. The past matters when it manifests in the present: "For every image of the past that is not recognized by the present as one of its own concerns threatens to disappear irretrievably."[41] The only historical time that matters, then, is the present—a "time filled by the presence of the now [*jetztzeit*]." This dense present marks the collapse of the linear progress between the past and the present, given that the present already includes within it the "tiger's leap into the past."[42] For Benjamin, it is from this dense present, this "time of the now," that an opening toward a (messianic) future is enabled—not as a predicted agenda or a planned futurity or progress, but as a messianic leap: "Every second of time was the strait gate through which Messiah might enter."[43]

While I am less invested in messianic arrivals (Derrida's writings on the archive's futurity, following Benjamin, are steeped in this rhetoric of messianism),[44] I nevertheless find productive the move away from thinking about the past (and the archive) as the cause, origin, or key for understanding the present in tautological terms. Here and throughout the book, the archive is used as a source of a *yet-to-come* future, and not as an explanation of the present (how we have arrived at where we are). In this sense, the archive is never "found." It is always made and remade. This making and remaking, this activization, tells us something about the present in relation to both potential histories (histories that did not come about, but could have) and potential futures (becomings that *in the present* exist only in the form of a fantasy or science fiction). These potential futures are the mark of collective aspirations to live otherwise.

In their "10 Theses on the Archive," the collective Pad.ma suggest that there are two approaches to the archive: the first involves minorities, whether ethnic, sexual, religious, or otherwise, who are "waiting for the archive," by which they mean: waiting to become part of the hegemonic, usually state, archive and the legitimate narrative. The second involves a riskier position, which replaces the "waiting" with a "making": this approach replaces the plea for recognition and inclusion with an effort to create alternative archives for often still "radically incomplete" collectivities.[45] There remains today a strong discursive preoccupation with redemption and recovery as the incentive to find or enter the archive. But, subjecting archival imagination to this task of recovery does little in terms of generating new (if radically incomplete) collectivities or new potential futures. On the contrary, these recovery projects tend to reinforce the status of the archive as a tomb—a temple of the past and a source for cultivating limited and highly restricted identities based on a "shared past." As convincingly argued by Stephen Best, the "repeated returns to [the archive as] the scene of a crime, a crime imagined as the archive itself, in practice have mirrored the orientation that Sigmund Freud called 'melancholy.'"[46] If recovery projects suffer from melancholic historicism,[47] the center of this melancholic attachment is the lost object of a predetermined "we" that is continually lost and found in the archive. It is also the center of the plea "to be found" in the archive and of the quest to take one's (historically predetermined) place.

Indeed, to borrow Best's words again, "Forensic imagination is directed toward *the recovery of a 'we' at the point of 'our' violent origins.*"[48] This does not mean that archival imagination, which is directed at a future, turns its back onto the past. Nor does it mean that archival imagination contains no elements of recovery or an engagement with a lost (unarchivable) past toward the building of a new cultural memory and collective. But it means that such engagement must be based more on speculation than on a factual historical methodology. Saidiya Hartman's methodology of engaging with the archive of the Atlantic slave trade offers a useful example:

> I have attempted to jeopardize the status of the event, to displace the received or authorized account, and to imagine what might have happened or might have been said or might have been done. By throwing into crisis "what happened when" and by exploiting the "transparency of sources" as fictions of history, I wanted to make visible the production of disposable lives (in the Atlantic slave trade and, as well, in the discipline of history), to describe "the resistance of the object."[49]

The "archival imagination" I describe and promote in this book is based on fabulation, manipulation, reproduction, and often experimental and playful alterations of pregiven state and personal archives. The works I engage with advance a futuristic imagination by replacing the impulse to trace evidence of familiar historical narratives with the impetus to imagine potentialities not yet fully identifiable. As Appadurai reminds us, "The archive is itself an aspiration rather than a recollection," a "work of imagination," and a "conscious site of debate and desire."[50] *Awda* demonstrates this by breaking down the division between fiction (imagination) and history, the past and the future, and testimony and aspiration. The story collection suggests that the act of imagination ("imagined testimonies") and the production of "memories for the future" can bring about political change. "How is it possible to foresee the impossible?" *Awda* asks in its first pages. Its answer appears unequivocal: it is not possible, and yet it remains a necessity. Imagination must always precede political change. Our task is to imagine.

The Art of Imagining Otherwise

> Ghosts are hovering all over towns. Refugee ghosts, returning to claim their homes. | YEHUDA SHENHAV-SHA'HARABANI, "Reference" in *Awda: Imagined Testimonies from Potential Futures*

Archival imagination involves imagined archives: imagining existing archives differently as well as creating new archival effects and affects.[51] It is archival in that it is citational, mimetic, intertextual, and often mobilized by archival fever: it cites, recites, and revisits archives new and old, creating new archival sites and undoing others. It is often playful and mischievous, but it never takes the archive lightly. It is drawn to footage, documents, and photographs of the past, but it mixes and remixes toward potential futures. Archival imagination returns to the archival drive to preserve, collect, store, and document, but also to the equally powerful drive to destroy, displace, manipulate, and radically alter.[52] The archival imagination I am speaking about blurs the distinction between "archival" and "found" documents as well as between "official archive" and "private collection." With the spread of online archives and increasingly open access to a multitude of archival documentation, the distinctions between "archive," "collection," "data," and "footage" begin to dissolve. Holding onto them would be theoretically anachronistic and politically not particularly useful. Following film theorist and media scholar Jaimie Baron, I refer to "archives" and "archival" primarily in terms of their *effect*. The archival is constituted only insofar as it is experienced as such: "As coming from another time or from another context of use or intended use . . . the archival depends on the effects it produces."[53]

A remarkable short film by the Ramallah-based director Shuruq Harb, entitled *The White Elephant* (2018, 12 min.), demonstrates what I mean by archival effects. The film is made entirely from recycled video footage that Harb found online in various Israeli sources during the "golden days" of the Oslo peace negotiations in the early to mid-1990s. Posted and reposted, the video footage appears in Harb's film without any framing, explanation, or archival annotations. The film begins with a mishmash of images: signs in Hebrew announcing the first Gulf war "alert," footage of Palestinian youth demonstrating during the First Intifada, a young man with a gas mask, and panoramic images of Tel Aviv. Soon after, the narrator's voiceover and background music begin. The narrator, a young Palestinian woman, recounts her personal story of growing up as a teen in Ramallah: she talks about dating a young guy who participated in the First Intifada and died after throwing a Molotov bottle on an Israeli bus; sneaking out to dance parties in Tel Aviv; "passing" as an Israeli girl; attending rave parties on Tel Aviv beaches; meeting a new boyfriend who steals Israeli cars; and loving Dana International, the Israeli singer of Yemeni origin who was the first trans person to win the Eurovision contest. This semi-autobiographical narrative about a young Palestinian teen who "just wants to have fun" is visualized in its entirety through Israeli footage collected by browsing social media—youth dancing and drinking and Israeli soldiers praising trance music ("Trance music makes me high!" "This is the biggest ever historical event!").

As this mix of vivid images and upbeat music passes by us, the narrator's memories unfold like a stream of consciousness. She too was there at the raves, but her images are not found in the archive: "We were making history [but] you couldn't guess who we are." The narrator's absent-presence in the online archive is haunting. She is there, she tells us, but we cannot see her. She escapes the archive. Bringing the footage and her voice together, the narrator creates an alternative archive: one in which her "absence" is marked and visualized. The last sequence of images, with which the film closes, mixes footage from the Israeli pop star Dana International's first recorded performance with video-recorded images of the narrator's sister dressed like Dana and imitating her singing and dancing. Dana International is singing her first hit in broken Arabic, "My name is not Saida," in which she first "came out" as both a trans woman and an Arab-Jew. The narrator's sister is imitating Dana's performance and her broken Arabic. The images of the two women overlap to produce a new montage. This layered footage makes for a personal archive of memories. What kind of an archive is this? It is an archive made of online "found footage," circulating on social media. This footage, belonging to the public domain, is activated, however, through its use to tell a personal coming-of-age narrative. This diverse footage becomes an archive precisely thanks to its archival effect, which depends, here and elsewhere, on the viewer's recognition of the contrast between the original context of the footage (the Israeli raves, Dana International's performance and her status as an Israeli pop icon) and the context in which the footage is now used to tell a personal Palestinian narrative. Between the original context and the new one, the archival effect is produced.[54] In this case the effect is profound: a young Palestinian woman tells her personal story by mixing and rearranging video footage she finds in Israeli sources. To choose to tell the story of the self this way requires both imagination and the willingness to look in less obvious archives, not simply to find one's missing image, but to tell one's own story through and in relation to the other.

By speaking of archival effects, I am referring to a practice of working with and in relation to the figure of the archive perceived as *first and foremost* a political force that depends on activization: citation, repetition, mimicry,

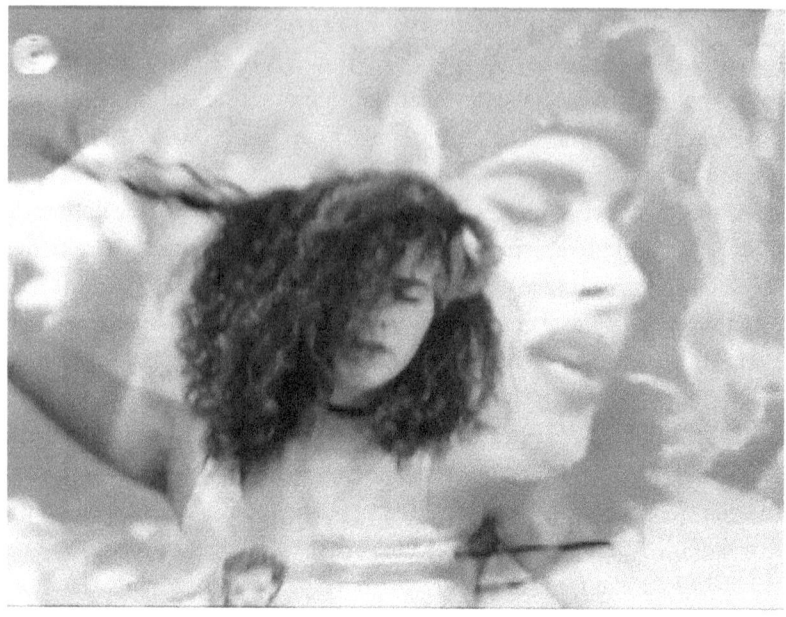

I.2   Still from Shuruq Harb's *The White Elephant* (2018). Courtesy of Shuruq Harb.

and revisitation, for its archival affectivity and effectiveness. Such archival imagination works through the assumption that, as Derrida writes, "There is no political power without control of the archive," but it attributes more flexibility and mobility to the archive and assumes a more democratic distribution of its potential effects.[55]

....

One of the most original and influential critical engagements with the figure of the archive in the context of the modern Middle East is the decades-long project by the Lebanese artist Walid Raad, "The Atlas Group Project."[56] The project, a product of Raad's imagination that also includes actual historical documents such as newspapers and images documenting the Lebanese Civil War, is presented as an "official archive" created between 1975 and 1996 by cofounders Maha Traboulsi and Zeinab Fakhouri. Both are figures of Raad's imagination. Raad thus created the archive and the archivists, and then went a step further, using his own imaginary archive both as an art display in museums and as part of a performance in which he plays the part of the scholar lecturing about the archival materials. The rich archive made of found documents Raad collected (press photographs, interview transcripts, video footage, graphics, texts, and video art) is available online, but also serves as the raw data for Raad's artistic projects presented in various museums over several years. The archival effect achieved here has to do with the blurring of the line between real (serious, scientific, rigorous) academic presentations about real historical archives and mock presentation (performance) that nods to the self-importance of both the archive and the academic presentations about it.[57]

The center of Raad's artistic intervention is his mimetic presentation of the conventional archival display *both* as a historical document *and* as a collection of artistic artifacts. The collection is similar to those often captured in the conventional museum setting. The circulation of the archive or of "archival goods" in museums and academic presentations is the reference doubled and revisited in Raad's creation of an archive that feeds itself, doubles itself, and produces and reproduces its own archival effects.

Raad's maverick work has influenced many artists, particularly in the Middle East. Among them is the Lebanese artist Akram Zaatari, whose work engages photographic archives and who is best known for his series of photographs titled "Hashem El Madani: Studio Practice." Palestinian artist Khalil Rabah, creator of (the imaginary) "Palestinian Museum of Natural History and Humankind," is another. If the first engages in the creation

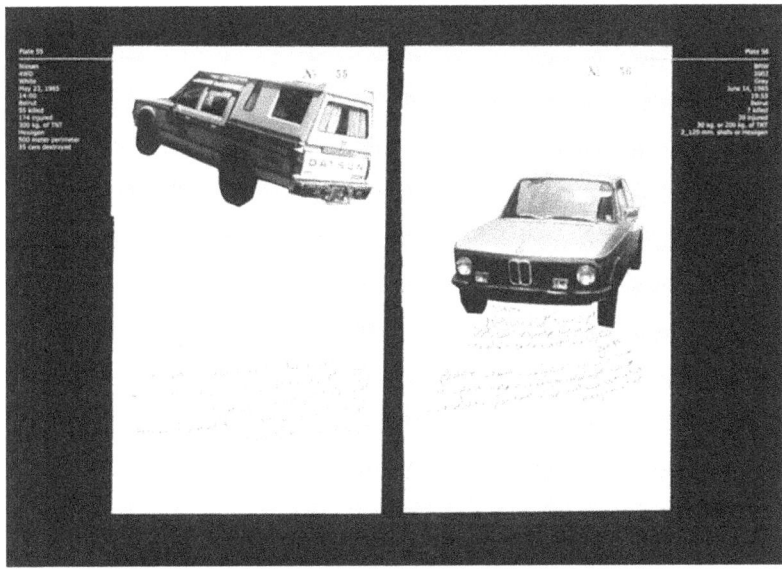

I.3 From Walid Raad's "The Atlas Group Project" (1989–2004).

of what Gayatri Gopinath, following artists Chitra Ganesh and Mariam Ghani, calls a "parasitic archive"[58]—the curatorial reframing and restaging of historical archives in radically new ways—the latter constructs an altogether fictive museum with a fictive editorial board, publications, and sponsors.[59]

These examples (and many others) are suggestive of the wide range of artistic practices and modalities of archival imagination. Some of these works emphasize recontextualizing and restaging historical documents (footage, photographs, texts) in new settings. Others focus on creating para-fictions as alternative archives. And still others center on generating archival affects and effects by mobilizing an archival aesthetic and/or opening the figure of the archive to include *more than* the familiar term by directing attention to archival drives, principles, and aspirations. The model of artistic intervention that has gained the most critical recognition and has come to be most closely identified with what we call "archivist art" today involves, as in the case of Raad or Rabah, the construction of an (imaginary) archive.[60] However, this represents just one artistic approach and preoccupation with "the question of the archive." Archival imagination does not necessarily produce imaginary archives or try "to make historical information [physically] present" in order to restore historical loss.[61] Indeed, most of the works

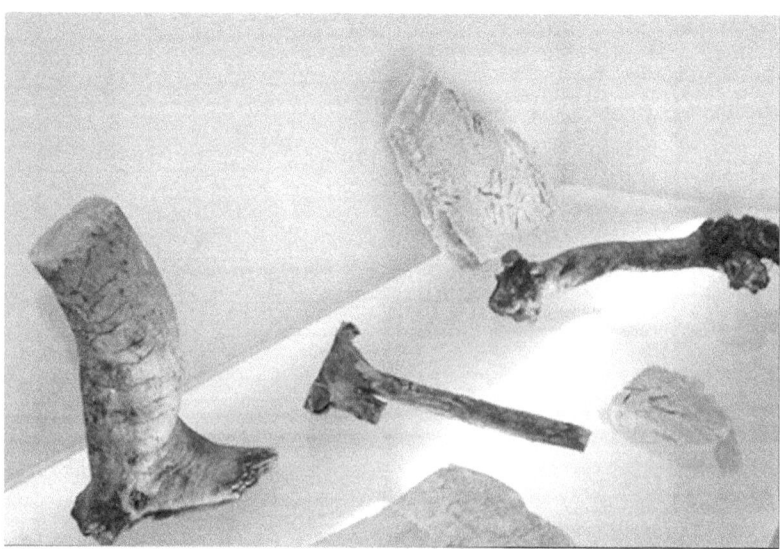

I.4 From Khalil Rabah's fictive museum project, "Palestinian Museum of Natural History and Humankind" (2003).

I discuss in the book have a more complex relation to the archive as an apparatus of selective remembering and forgetting, preserving and destroying. Work such as Emily Jacir's artistic oeuvre has greatly contributed to the creation of an alternative counterdominant Palestinian archive. Jacir repeatedly uses art to ensure the archivization of oral history, common memory, and the salvation of otherwise lost, damaged, or stolen archival material, which was confiscated by the Israeli state. Jacir's work often takes on the autobiographic form to assert an "I" (the "I" of the artist who is also an archivist and an information transmitter) that speaks from *within* and *for* a collective. Her 2001 *Memorial to 418 Palestinian Villages Destroyed, Depopulated and Occupied by Israeli in 1948*, for example, is emblematic of her artistic and political commitment to preserving and creating the otherwise missing centralized archive of Palestinian modern history. Working with Walid Khalidi's book *All That Remains: The Palestinian Villages Occupied and Depopulated by Israel in 1948*, Jacir erected a refugee tent in her New York studio and invited friends and colleagues to embroider the names of the villages that Khalidi researched to create an artistic, communal, and affective archive of this historical loss. In this early work, as in many that followed, Jacir incorporated elements of activism and sociohistorical reconstruction to transmit the otherwise disappearing Palestinian archive. A related act of salvation, transmission, and repair is found in her 2005 work *Material for a Film*, and in her 2010–12 projects "ex libris." Both are dedicated to the transmission and documentation of otherwise looted, erased, and destroyed Palestinian property, history, and cultural memory.[62] But the majority of the works I discuss in the following chapters do something quite different. Less invested in the creation of archives, or even in the act of recovery and salvation of archival material, these works, I suggest, are engaged in an explicitly *theoretical* meta-artistic commentary about what it means to create an archive. They ask, what does it mean to be invested in archives? What does it mean to draw on archival material to generate (historical or otherwise) knowledge? Immanently speculative and self-reflexive, these works engage with archives, create alternative archives, but above all, they invite a critical preoccupation with the archive by raising questions about the relationship between archives, narratives of origins, points of departure, points of arrival, temporality, and collectivity. For example: when we create an archive, alternative as it may be to state politics, do we assume a point of origin? Do we start with a pregiven "we" whose collective past, memory, and history we seek to revive or restore? Or, can the "we" serve as the "end goal" of archival creation? Can we create archives not only or mainly of past communities but also for a collective *in becoming* and for a future to-be-archived? These are the questions that read with and through the artworks in the following chapters. Reading these works together can indeed create an archive in and of itself, with each of these works referencing and citing other sources and works, gestures, images, affects, sounds; however, the outcome of this archive and my own goal is less about creating a new stable and recognizable (alternative) archive. My engagement with artistic activizations of archives is in close dialogue with structural and poststructural theories of intertextuality and citationality.

Roland Barthes, who developed Julia Kristeva's theory of intertextuality, distinguishes between two types of readers: there are "consumers" who read the work for stable meaning (we can equate them to those who read the archive for historical indexicality), and there are readers who are "writers of the text" and engage in intertextual activity, breaking open the closeness of any given text to a larger web of citations and intertextual references. "Any text is a new tissue of past citations," Barthes reminds us, as "there is always language before and around the text."[63] To think of the archive in terms of intertextuality, then, is to think about it as a *tissue of citations*, rather than a source of direct and unmediated indexicality or a window to a better understanding of "reality." If we understand the working of archives as Barthes understood the working of texts, and realize that at least in *certain textual traditions* (Hebrew and Arabic literatures most notably) citationality and intertextuality function as *the* archival modality, we arrive at a much more elastic definition of the archive as, above all, a mode of reading, writing, rereading, and rewriting. "Archives are made, not found."[64] This is the premise of my own investment in the archive as a figure of political change modeled on citationality, recontextualization, and the generated visions of potential futures based on old-new collectivities. The following concrete example I provide is a literary one.

In 2005, the Israeli writer of Iraqi descent Sami Michael (born Kamal Salah) wrote his sixth novel *Yonim be'Trafalgar* (*Doves in Trafalgar*). At this point, Michael was already well known for his writings about the plight of Arab Jews in Israel and about Israel's internal racism. There was nothing surprising, therefore, to find in his new novel a protagonist struggling between his "Israeli Jewish part" and his "Arab part." This time, however, the "Arab part" was not an Arab Jew but a Palestinian adopted and raised as a Jewish-Israeli by a Holocaust survivor who was given the house of his biological parents—a Palestinian couple that fled Haifa in 1948, leaving behind a baby. This plot undoubtedly sounds familiar to some readers, and not to others. Evidently it was not immediately recognized by many Israeli readers, including the editor and publisher of the novel, who simply failed to recognize its overt intertextuality. Moreover, once this intertextuality was "revealed," it was read by some as a "literary scandal." Michael was even accused of dishonesty for not acknowledging his main textual inspiration: Ghassan Kanafani's celebrated novella ʿĀʾid ilā Ḥayfā (The Return[ed] to Haifa, 1969).[65]

In his defense, Michael has claimed that Kanafani's text was never hidden; quite on the contrary, it was openly and explicitly displayed in his novel, which not only includes direct allusions to the novella but also models the Palestinian father of the protagonist on Kanafani's own well-known public life as the spokesperson for George Habash's Popular Front for the Liberation of Palestine (PFLP). Michael's character, like Kanafani himself, is said to be killed in a car bomb in Beirut in 1972, allegedly set up by the Israeli Mossad. These allusions to Kanafani's biography and text are so overt and easily recognizable in the novel, Michael suggested, that disclosing this intertextuality seems not just unnecessary, but altogether ludicrous.[66]

By the second edition of Michael's novel, the publisher already included a line, under the title: "A dialogue with Ghassan Kanafani." But calling this textual intertextuality "a dialogue" is already undoing the archival effects of Michael's text. Intertextuality is not simply a dialogue, but rather, and more accurately, as Daniel Boyarin suggests, "the way that history, understood as cultural and ideological change and conflict, records itself within textuality. . . . The fragments of the previous system and the fissures they create on the surface of the text reveal conflictual dynamics which led to the present textual system."[67] Michael's narrative, I argue, is not "in dialogue with" Kanafani's, but rather is enmeshed with it; intertwined such that it creates a new archival imagination in which the impact of past traumatic events, to paraphrase Wendy Chun, finds its force not only from recalling the event itself, but from "the citation of other such events." This citationality exposes the "larger social implications" of trauma as an archive of intertextual references.[68]

Some may consider such intertextuality a form of colonial appropriation, but a more careful reading of Michael's text suggests a much more nuanced engagement not only with Kanafani's text, but also with the figure of the Arab Jew as a key figure around which to produce a new archival imagination (we shall see a similar investment in the Arab Jew in Jumana Manna's film discussed in detail in the following chapter). Responding to a question by an Israeli interviewer about why he chose Kanafani's novella as a pretext to his own, Michael responded: "The idea fascinated me. If I look at myself, I am like [Kanafani's] abandoned boy. I grew up in an Arab country, my mother tongue is Arabic, and after a flight that lasted a few hours, I found myself in Israel with a different identity. I belong here, and the Arabs regard me as an Israeli Zionist, whereas the Israelis regard me as someone who comes from there—with the heritage, language and customs of the enemy. So I saw myself in his story."[69]

A Palestinian literary narrative of return and resistance, Kanafani's novel is written after the 1967 war (the *Naksa*), at a moment of great defeat for Arab states and as the hopes of Palestinian refugees to return to their homes in Palestine became the heart of the forming revolution. But the narrative "of return" in this case is in fact a narrative of a failed return: at best a "visit" and a vow to continue the fight for a future return. Return, impossible return, failed return, promise of return, future return, fight for return—these are all positions outlined in Kanafani's novella. To enter an intertextual relationship with Kanafani's text is to open anew the question of return. And, in the context of the Second Palestinian Intifada, which is when Michael's novel is written, it is to encourage Israeli readers not only to become familiar with Kanafani's text (translated into Hebrew just four years earlier), but also to confront the question of return that unsettles the well-guarded borders of Israeli Zionist cultural imagination.

To read *Doves at Trafalgar* as a product of new archival imagination, then, is to realize that one cannot simply read Kanafani's novella as a pretext to Michael's novel, or Michael's novel as an expansion of the novella. The reading of the text requires an intertextual activity of reading back and forth, together and apart as a multilayered reality made of intertextual connections that undermine the radical separation of Israeli and Palestinian, past and present, Jewish and Arab, Kanafani and Michael. It is this reading back and forth that amounts to a new archive that breaks the political contours that allow "for collectivities and narratives to appear and be recognized as a *fait accompli*."[70]

Hannah Arendt has famously written that "refugees [would become] the most symptomatic group in contemporary politics."[71] Kanafani's texts ask us to consider this seriously in reimagining Palestine as a site of symptomatic agony, where one refugee (Jewish) finds a home in the home lost to another (Palestinian). Michael returns to Kanafani, reminding us that a home made through the creation of new refugees can never really be a home. It alerts us to the urgency of breaking the chain of ongoing trauma. If Kanafani's novella asks us to imagine Palestine in view of the trauma (the 1948 Nakba, the 1967 Naksa), Michael's novel asks us to revisit Kanafani's narrative of return and read it as a promise: an archive of/for the future.

Between *Awda*, as a project that seeks to create an archive of a future in which the return of Palestinian refugees *already* took place, and *Doves in Trafalgar*, in which the vision of such return remains (as it travels from Kanafani's text to Michael's), the core element of a new shared Israeli and Palestinian literary archive of mourning and loss, there are many other articulations of future-oriented archival imaginations and archival practices, some of which I will analyze in depth in the following chapters. While some of the projects discussed in this book are more overtly optimistic than others, all of them, in their multiplicities, take part in the poetic and political drive I call *Becoming Palestine*.

The Question of Palestine as a Question of the Archive

"What archives are or should be in this case of a dispersed people with no state archive, no less a state, a majority of whom live in exile or under occupation and have had their 'proper' archive destroyed, seized, or sealed in inaccessible colonial archives belonging to those who dispossessed them and still rule over them with force, are tough questions."[72]

Palestine "as a question," seen through the framework of Edward Said's *The Question of Palestine*, is not only a matter of land ownership, national self-determination, colonial violence, and historical injustice. It is also a question of narrative and memory—the stuff of archives. Whose memories gain the status of a recognizable historical narrative? Whose memories, in turn, are unarchived, deleted, erased from the global stage? Raising these questions, Said's *Question of Palestine* makes it clear that the political role played by the archive and archivization in this contested context is key.

What violence, what memories, and what histories escape the archive— are written out of it in line with the archive's internal logic of order, selection, collection, and classification? Who has access to the archive and who has the right and ability to archive? Said emphasizes the right to narrate and highlights the question of Palestine as one of dispossessed memory.[73] Such questions address the archive as a site of power—often state power. Israel has notoriously, and from very early on, seized the power of the archive: collecting, documenting, and archiving the modern history of the newly established state. It simultaneously invested in creating an elaborate archive of archaeological findings meant to prove the historical ties of Jews to the land, and hence to affirm that the establishment of Israel was unlike other cases of modern settler colonies. Rather, these findings aim to support a national narrative of *return* and nativity: a modern revival of an ancient people reuniting with their long-lost native land. With a frenzy that matches perhaps only modern Greece, Israel set up well-organized national state archives and classified military archives hosting generations of historians dedicated to telling the story of the nation. Meanwhile, as more recent studies have shown, Israel has also confiscated, looted, and absorbed into its various archives collections of Palestinian books, films, photographs, and other documents, further subjecting them to the logic of the Zionist archive and rendering Palestinian archives invisible, "missing," or nonexistent. Stolen books found in private Palestinian homes after 1948 were archived under the "AP" ("abandoned property") section in the Israel State Archive, thus serving not only as worthy, authentic historical documents (mostly in Arabic), but more significantly as items that reinforce the uncritical (and by now hardly believable even among Zionists) historical account that Palestinians were not expelled in 1948, but rather voluntarily abandoned their homes and property in the haste of an escape.

Thanks to the historical research of Gish Amit, we have recently learned about the scope of such looting, which included books, newspapers, and textbooks from Palestinian homes in Jerusalem, Jaffa, Haifa, Tiberius, Nazareth, and other places. This looting and archiving demonstrates, as Amit puts it, "how occupation and colonization is not limited to the taking over of physical space. Rather, it achieves its fulfillment by occupying cultural space as well, and by turning the cultural artifacts of the victims into ownerless objects with no past that can therefore become new items in the Israeli national archive."[74] Other scholars, among them Rona Sela, Ariella Azoulay, and Aron Shai, have documented the Israeli looting of Palestinian photography, film, and antiquities, creating together a vast and detailed account of historical erasure and colonial depletion.[75]

In essence, the question of the archive in the context of Palestine is similar to other colonial contexts where looting and transforming living aspects of the colonized society into archival (dead) objects is a common feature.[76] The work of Palestinian artists is often in direct dialogue with that of indigenous artists and activists across the globe, whose fights to alter national archives and inscribe the memory of their ancestral past result in significant changes in teaching curricula and commemoration ceremonies, and lead to important conversations about reparation and collective memory. The shared underlying goal is decolonization—a radical shift in political formation and collective way of life that undoes the settler colonial nation. I would venture to say that what may offer Palestine an advantage in this regard is the fact that the colonial reality we face here is a belated one, emerging, as it did, in a global postcolonial era. "The Zionist project is anachronistic" to paraphrase Tony Judt. Perhaps this makes the Zionist settler colonial project more vulnerable,[77] presenting us with an opportunity to enact here something seemingly impossible: a full political *undoing* of the colonial order and its replacement with an altogether different future.

The question of the archive in this context, then, is a question of phantasmal power. Remarking on Palestine's unique position in today's world politics, Sophia Azeb notes, "If there is anything unusual about Palestine or the Palestinian case, it is the fact that Palestine presents a potential to introduce new ideas about sovereignty and liberation into practice. This is why imagination is so important here."[78] I share this conviction, which is why *Becoming Palestine* is above all an urgent call to imagine. What future aspirations, communities, and solidarities the archive holds are a matter of engagement: our job is to imagine.

....

In general, the artistic interventions I discuss in the following chapters are less concerned with questions of historical liability or acts of repair, such as the return of archival goods to their lawful owners or the centralization of scattered and looted Palestinian archival materials and documents. Instead, I read them as attempts to rewrite, expand, circulate, and alter the archival conditions that currently limit our political imagination. While not the focus of this study, there is a recent important and influential development in the creation of new Palestinian archives aiming to battle historical amnesia and the Israeli singular control over the historical narrative of Palestine. Among these important initiatives are the Palestinian Archive at the Ibrahim Abu-Lughod Institute of International Studies (IALIIS) at Birzeit University and the more recently initiated Palestinian Museum Digital Archive (PMDA) at the Palestinian Museum in Birzeit. Another significant online archival initiative has recently become available through the Palestinian Museum, entitled "Palestinian Journeys." Smaller and lesser-known archival projects include Dor Guez, Christian Palestinian Archive (CPA), and Emily Jacir's inspirational transformation of her family's house in Bethlehem into an art institution and an archive of rare visual and textual documents from late-nineteenth and early twentieth centuries' Ottoman Palestine.[79] Finally, the grassroots project, Khazaaen, centered in East Jerusalem, has created a societal archive (operating since 2016) through gathering ephemeral material such as newspapers, magazines, films, photo-graphs, posters, brochures, commercial and cultural ads, business cards, and wedding invitations.[80]

Such actualization and institutionalization of alternative archives through which Palestinian history becomes visible and expandable *beyond* the tragic encounter with Zionism and its aftermaths in 1948 certainly opens the possibility for imagining the past differently. Yet, even these in-terventions risk not advancing a flexible enough archival imagination from which one could eventually revisit the question of Palestine *as* a question of the future. To do so we must go beyond questions of possessions (who owns the archive, who are the archive's patrons, who has the right to nar-rate) and matters of inclusion (whose stories do the archives tell) to in-vite and encourage the creation of archival imagination that fosters "new solidarities" and "new memories."[81] This is the additional and necessary aspect of archival imagination on which this book focuses. It centers on certain artistic activations of the archive that both scrutinize the archive as an authoritative source of knowledge production and at the same time take advantage of the archival drive to preserve, collect, trace, store, and classify in order to generate new remixes, new intertextual connections, and new reencounters with the past toward the anticipation of still becoming and of not-yet-determined potential futures.

The idea, however, is not to establish a neutral "ground zero" from which to create new solidarities out of nowhere and imagine new futures out of a fantastic archival imagination. Far from it, *Becoming Palestine* situ-ates future potentiality from *within* the archival condition of state violence. The works discussed in the book all operate *within and under* the inescapable current hegemonic archive, that is to say, *already within* the economy of par-tition, colonial appropriation, and erasure. In this sense, potentiality, while directed at the future, is also a matter of how we read the past—discovering traces of potentiality in the archive. But this is not the same as seeking to fill archival gaps. A good example that demonstrates the potentiality lost to the past, awaiting to be activated, is Ariella Azoulay's film *Civil Alliances* (2012, 52 min.), which centers on the transformative year of 1947, when his-torical Palestine *was becoming* Israel. The film is an attempt to overcome what Azoulay calls "the archival condition," by exposing a potentiality associated with "what [history] could have been" and what it could have looked like *if* the archival condition did not already dominate the ways we recognize history: one history for the Jews, another for the Arabs. The archival principle, she argues, condemns Jews and Arabs "to mutual enmity" and rests upon the "basic division of history, as though the history of the Jews and the state of Israel could be told apart from the history of the Palestinians."[82] *Civil Alliances*, then, seeks to restore the lost historical potentiality that cannot appear in the state archive, but that precedes *the becoming* of Israeli and the Palestinian subjects by exposing the violence of the archive itself: the making of the Israeli Jew and the Palestinian as two separate political agencies.

Staged and filmed as an overtly theatrical performance, the film depicts a group of Israelis and Palestinians gathered around a map of historical Palestine and reading out loud, in Arabic and Hebrew, archival cases that Azoulay describes as cases of "civil alliances." These cases took place from early 1947 until close to the declaration of the state of Israel in May 1948. The testimonies were collected from archival documents found in the Israel State Archive, but the reenactment of the documents—the reading in both languages and the performance of the collective united around the map—tells a different story from the one found in the archive. If the latter is at best a story of "collaboration" of Palestinians with the new Jewish forces, the reenactment and the creating of this alternative performative archive escapes the national archive: a story that chronicles a togetherness *before* the fact—before the (state) archive makes it disappear. The past is envisioned, performed, and filmed. This potentiality is not found in history as we know it, but in history as it could have been. This potentiality cannot be found in the (state) archive because the latter is already organized along the archival condition of partition, which divides the history of 1948 into two separate narratives: the history of the Jews (a history of victory) and the history of Palestinians (a history of loss). To imagine the past *outside of* or *before* the archival condition, then, is to think beyond "the perspective of the ruling discourse—sovereign nationality."[83]

The question of potentiality, then, is a question about the past (What could have been? What could have happened?) as much as it is about the future (What may become?). Above all, it is a question of imagination: How and what can we imagine? How and what are we *compelled* to imagine? I address these questions in the following chapters by engaging with various attempts by artists, writers, and filmmakers to imagine otherwise by reordering, restaging, remixing, expanding, revising, and rewriting existing archives. These attempts to generate new horizons of potential futures do not bypass the violent history of colonialism, partition, military occupation, and nationalism. They are by no means escapist. On the contrary, these attempts all spring from the site of violence, and as a response to it.

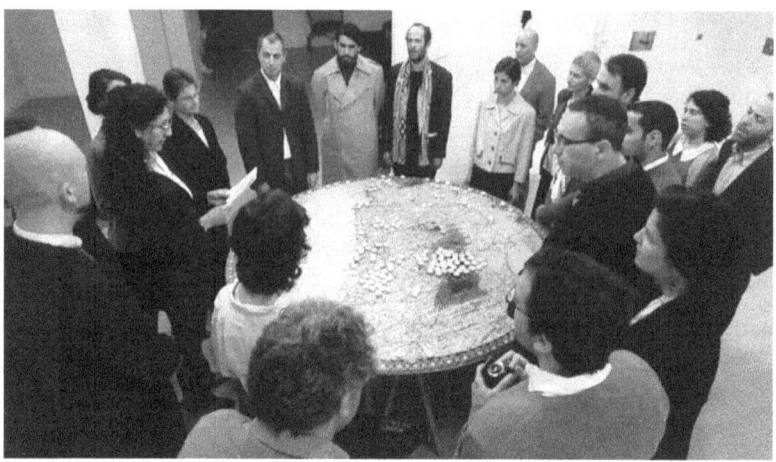

I.5   From Ariella Azoulay's *Civil Alliances* (2012). Courtesy of Ariella Azoulay.

Becoming

In an interview with Antonio Negri (1990), Gilles Deleuze provides a useful explanation for the difference between (his concept of) becoming as a political project/poetics and history or historical investigation. I find this distinction incredibly helpful. Deleuze notes that "what history grasps in an event is the way it's actualized in particular circumstances; the event's becoming is beyond the scope of history." The becoming of any given event, then, is never about an actualized event or even a "set of preconditions, however recent." Becoming requires a certain "leaving behind" of such preconditions "in order to become, that is, to create something new."[84] Perhaps the simplest way to say this is to highlight the difference between actuality and potentiality. If we understand history as a narrative, we can recognize it as actual because it is rendered in already recognizable political terms (state, empire, nation, a people, etc.); becoming, or thinking in terms of becoming, requires thinking in terms of potentiality, beyond the comfort zone of preexisting (political) terms and modalities. This difference maintains a gap between potentiality as we know it (from history) and potentiality as still unknown, still in becoming. There is, no doubt, a danger in using such open-ended terms that enjoy (at least in theory) relative freedom from historical confinement and preexisting political arrangements. One could already hear the expected critique: "Everything can be *becoming*." Yes. And no.

In an essay published in 2006, Laurence J. Silberstein, professor of Jewish Studies and an expert on "post-Zionism," engages Deleuze's philosophy to defend post-Zionists' refusal to "provide a detailed programme for the future." He thus writes: "Postzionism cannot but refrain from proposing specific programmes. Instead it invests its energies in making visible the ongoing processes of deterritorialisation and the lines of flight that continue to redefine and transform Israel socius."[85] Silberstein applies Deleuze's concept of becoming to stretch open the horizon of Zionism, but not to do away with it. Hence, he concludes the essay with the following: "Postzionism helps to move these processes beyond the current majority imposed limits" (which, according to him, exclude Palestinian Israelis, Mizrahi Jews, women, and gay Jews) to "open new and productive avenues of *becoming Israeli, of Israeli Becoming*."[86] "Israeli becoming" is modeled on the expansion of the Zionist principle to include a broader population within it, but as such, it is not a rejection of the Zionist principle or a reversal of its settler colonial logic. "Israeli becoming" builds on Zionism and goes beyond it ("post") to include the state's minorities, but it avoids accountability for colonial violence or a radical change through future reparation and remodeling of society. This "becoming" remains confined to an extension of a preexisting political model: Zionism becomes post-Zionism. But "post" can never fully provide a radical alternative, only an expansion: more people, more minorities, will be included in the future nation-state. What has not yet become and still awaits *becoming* in the true sense is not a post-Zionist Israel, but an anti-Zionist (and anti- any other ethno-national separatist ideology, for that matter) society.

For Israel and for Palestine as we know them, pre- and post-1948, to go through a process of becoming, both entities must cease to be in their actuality and must become something radically different. I call it *becoming Palestine*. Becoming Palestine is not becoming Palestine *again*. At stake is not a break from the past or the present but a *return to the present*, with the recognition that the Nakba is not a traumatic rapture or "event" in the past, but an ongoing condition that still creates refugees.

Our task, politically and ethically, is to replace this actuality of becoming refugees with a different potentiality and a different political imagination, which I call "becoming Palestine." This potential becoming does not involve a redistribution of suffering, expulsion, and uprooting, but a radical break from the economy of refugee-ness. Kanafani, in his novella mentioned above, warns us against any simplistic solution of replacing one refugee with another, reminding us of the importance to center the figure of the refugee at the heart of any political fight for justice. A solution for one refugee should never be the creation of a refugee condition for another.

At stake is not a utopic vision of justice either (and utopia is always about exclusion, Jameson reminds us),[87] but an attempt to institute justice and create a livable life by building new collectives that exist beyond the logistics of nationality and the naturalization of citizenship as the only ticket to belonging.

The chapters of this book highlight several different aspects of this potentiality by elaborating an alternative archival imagination. Some chapters (mainly the first two) are primarily preoccupied with the poetics of archival citationality and mimicry. Chapter 1, "Revisiting the Orientalist Archive: Jumana Manna's Re-Mapped Musical Archive of Palestine," explores the appeal and limits of the Orientalist archival impetus and reconsiders it as a source of articulating a potentiality for a future yet to come. The chapter follows the meeting between a young Palestinian artist and filmmaker (Jumana Manna) and a musical archive she finds, explores, follows, mimics, and takes apart: that of the once-famed German-Jewish ethnomusicologist and Orientalist, Robert Lachmann. Attending to Manna's film *A Magical Substance Flows into Me* (2015), in which she travels throughout Israel and the West Bank exploring various Palestinian musical traditions, modeling her cinematic journey on Lachmann's musical archive, this chapter looks closely at the frictions between the Orientalist archive Lachmann produced during his short years of living in Palestine (1936–1939) and the new archive Manna creates by circumventing his Orientalist modality. Finally, the chapter highlights *A Magical Substance*'s meta-cinematic *preoccupation* with questions of mastery and ownership over the archive. What might have been a naïve (if well-intended and certainly well-informed) Orientalist fantasy on the part of Lachmann, to "use music" to promote cultural understanding between local Jews and Arabs in Mandate Palestine, becomes in Manna's hands, I suggest, a much more subversive project of outlining a potential futurity. To paraphrase Manna's words: revisiting Lachmann's archive "provides a space from which another Palestine can be[come]."[88]

Chapter 2, "Lost and Found in Israeli Footage: Kamal Aljafari's 'Jaffa Trilogy' and the Productive Violation of the Colonial Visual Archive," is dedicated to the cinematic oeuvre of Palestinian director Kamal Aljafari. While the first chapter focuses on the ambiguities of the Orientalist archive, the second chapter draws attention to the structural and historical raptures of the Israeli visual colonial archive. The chapter explores Aljafari's mimetic archival imagination, focusing on the futuristic vision of his hometown, Jaffa. The "Jaffa Trilogy" is made almost in its entirety from footage he collected from various Israeli archival sources: films, videos, and photographs. I explore Aljafari's unique cinematic endeavor and his insistence on *recycling* and manipulating Israeli footage rather than creating images of his own. I show how Aljafari's digital cinematic practices center on the ultimate failure of the Israeli settler colonial archive to do away with the Palestinian natives, or keep them outside of the cinematic frame. Aljafari's film trilogy highlights the potentiality inherent within the colonial archive, which inevitably already includes its failures. What his mesmerizing and ghostly films make visible is that even if the Israeli visual archive was partially successful in pushing Palestinians to the margins of the frame, their presence nevertheless is invasive and inescapable. A blurry face, a side vision of a turning body, a small figure hiding behind a closed window—Aljafari brings these images to the forefront, reminding us that every archive is haunted by its exclusions, and such hauntings are the visual testimony and reminder of a potential future to become.

The following two chapters, 3 and 4, share an interest in archaeology and specifically biblical-Israeli archaeology as the archive (understood in Foucault's terms as "the law of what can be said, the system that governs the appearance of statements as unique events")[89] that dominates the local and international political discourse about Israel/Palestine. The metaphor and practice of archaeology enables a certain materialization of the archive and a certain imagination of materiality. Often this is the most important underlying archive of a nation and a people, which is so profound that it must not *appear* manmade but must emerge as a miracle: a past coming alive in the present. Naturalized as discovery, and emerged (actual, material, Real) traces of the past, archaeological findings form a base archive for national imagination by seeming to exceed the confining borders of any given institutionalized archive. Creating, marking, and guarding the counters of national imagination, archaeology provides both the logic and the content of presumably unachievable archives: the ethos, the evidence, the proof of peoplehood. If this is the case in general, it is most certainly and exceptionally so in the case of Zionism.[90] Chapter 3, "'Suspended between Past and Future': Larissa Sansour's Sci-Fi Archaeological Archive in the Past-Future Tense," is dedicated to Larissa Sansour's twenty-nine-minute-long essay film *In the Future They Ate from the Finest Porcelain* (2016). The film, a mesmerizing sci-fi tale, unfolds a story of a self-identified "narrator-terrorist" through a conversation between her and her psychoanalyst. Both narrator and therapist, I argue, speak the language of archaeology, but while the therapist seeks to heal her patient's scars of past traumas through the archaeological modality of psychoanalysis, the narrator wishes to mobilize archaeology for "terror attacks" on history. This chapter explores the role of archaeology in the formation of national imagination and its function as a constituting apparatus of order that can nevertheless be defeated with similar means.[91] The seeming embrace of the archaeological drive in the film, I suggest, must be read as a radical critique of the archival aura of archaeology, which is mobilized by Zionism to argue for the historical rights of Jews to resettle in Palestine. But beyond this astute critique of Zionism and its reliance on the archaeological archive, *In the Future* advances a broader critique of archaeology as the modality for understanding peoplehood in terms of a shared historical legacy upon which rights of land ownership are established. Accordingly, my reading focuses on the replacement of "digging" (the archaeological defining activity) with "burying" in Sansour's film: the burial of fake archaeological findings for future discoveries. Such a reversal of activity and temporality offers a radical departure from myths of authenticity and origins along the lines outlined by Laura Marks in her definition of "cinematic archaeology": a mode of inquiry that replaces the search for an "authentic voice" with the evocation of "the myth of culture as a necessary fiction."[92]

Chapter 4, "'Face to Face with the Ancestors of Civilization': Ruanne Abou-Rahme and Basel Abbas's Archive of the Copy," is dedicated to the multimedia work of the duo Palestinian artists Ruanne Abou-Rahme and Basel Abbas, *And Yet My Mask Is Powerful* (2016–2019). The chapter returns to the status of archaeology as a national archive (in the Israeli case, *the* national archive) by exploring the use of archaeological findings (both artifact and ruins) in a new, counterarchaeological manner. I read Abou-Rahme and Abbas's work as a critique of archaeology that targets both the manipulative role it plays in Israeli politics and the methodology itself as a broader principle of historical reasoning. *And Yet My Mask Is Powerful* returns to sites of Palestinian ruins, where the artists perform tours and fictional rituals with groups of young Palestinians. These tours function not only as an act of reclaiming place but also as an act of reclaiming time: replacing the temporality of the colonial nation with a radically different temporality in which the "ruins" are no longer sites of destruction, or indexes of a long-gone past, but rather opportunities "from which to think about the incomplete nature of the colonial project" and through which "to activate a potentiality to become unbound from colonial time" to borrow the artists' own words. The critique of archaeology is further enhanced by the artists' creation of a 3D print of an original Neolithic mask housed in the Israeli Museum in Jerusalem. *And Yet My Mask Is Powerful* traces the logic of the copy and the fake as a mimetic shadow of the colonial totem. While the latter carries the promise of originality, the former evokes an economy of becoming that is free from the fetish of any narrative of origins and hence of the aura associated with the archaeological archive.

The fifth and last chapter, "Gesturing toward Resistance: Farah Saleh's Archive of Gestures," centers on the role of the body-as-archive and the possibility of body movement—dance, particularly—to undo the archival focus on documentation and recording (the past) through enactment and speculative performative variations directed at a future imagination. The chapter engages with the work of Palestinian dancer, choreographer, per-former, archivist, and activist Farah Saleh to suggest that her work, which bridges between the studio, the stage, and the street, as well as between art and activism and between preexisting archival materials and new embodied performances, successfully creates alternative "archives of gestures." Hers are archives that document gestures and that simultaneously also gesture toward the ability to revise, recirculate, and reinvigorate, as well as trans-form and deform, preexisting archives. If the archive is seductive by nature, as Derrida and many others have suggested, Saleh's work highlights the fact that the archive's seductive nature emanates not from the allure of power and authority, but rather from its ability to spark and elicit an *affective* reac-tion. Saleh's dance work often springs from her initial meeting with archi-val material, while the choreography centers on and explores the impact of *the meeting* between the past and the present, the archival document and the body of the dancer, and one's own body and the bodies of others. In-deed, her work foregrounds the archive's seductive propulsion but turns it from malice and fever (*mal d'archive*) to imaginative elaboration and *critical fabulation*, to borrow Saidiya Hartman's term.[93] Focusing on Saleh's video-dance installation and film *C.I.E.* (2016, 12.29 min.), this chapter focuses on Saleh's *affective* archives to suggest that they transmit knowledge through a corporeal experience that reshapes archival material from their historical function as visual documentation toward political activism by exploring through the archive a question of great political importance: How can we learn to move politically?

....

In a short essay entitled "Palestine as Archive," Sherene Seikaly notes that the ongoing violence and destruction in Gaza must be understood as an "instance of the Palestinian condition," rather than as an exceptional state of emergency. "Gaza today belongs to the archive of colonialism," she rightly comments, folding Gaza into a long history of imperial and colonial violence and rejecting the idea of it as an incident of rare, sudden, and exceptional atrocity. But "Palestine as archive" is not only made of records of colonialism. It is also an archive of decolonization.[94] Read together, the following chapters create an archive of sorts—an archive of decolonization that brings together a rich body of art that is already operating in a "time of becoming." Read it, if you will, as an archive of a collective endeavor to imagine what others insist is impossible: the becoming of Palestine.

ONE

Revisiting the Orientalist Archive

JUMANA MANNA'S RE-MAPPED MUSICAL ARCHIVE OF PALESTINE

Archive fever is spreading among Palestinians everywhere. Whether in Ramallah or London, Haifa or San Francisco, Beirut or Riyad . . . and this is just the tip of an iceberg, whose full dimensions can hardly be imagined. | BESHARA DOUMANI, "Archiving Palestine and the Palestinians: The Patrimony of Ihsan Nimr"

I am haunted by the past, but allergic to nostalgia. | JUMANA MANNA, in an interview with Omar Kholeif

There is a certain irony, indeed a bitter irony, that for a young Palestinian filmmaker the path to recovering early twentieth-century Palestinian music begins with a visit to the Israeli State Archives. But the irony only begins here. When the young artist Jumana Manna[1] wishes to recuperate, as it were, a cultural moment preceding the *Nakba*, the Palestinian Catastrophe—preceding that is the displacement and forced exile of Palestinians and the establishment of a Jewish state in Palestine in 1948—to recuperate perhaps something more whole, more lively, more natural, less tragic, less arrested, and less destroyed, she is directly led into a small archive of a German-Jewish ethnomusicologist by the

name of Robert Lachmann. The archive, held in the larger Israel State Archives, comprises a relatively small collection of written documents, including the musicologist's lectures from a radio show he used to host on the
British radio channel in Palestine from 1936 to 1938, a few other lecturers
and written notes he took, and a rich collection of sound recordings he
made in Palestine between 1935 and 1939. The recordings primarily feature
musicians from Jerusalem and its surrounding areas, including Kurdish
Jews, Samarians, Yemenite Jews, Bedouins, Coptic Christians, Muslim and
Christian Palestinians, and more. A German Jewish archive held in the Israeli national archive offers the Palestinian artist and filmmaker a gate into
a past she wishes to explore. Armed with the collection of recordings and
Lachmann's notes, Jumana Manna resumes her initial plan and original
interest to make a film about local music in pre-1948 Palestine. But the
archive Manna finds preserves the past through an Orientalist lens, that of
a German ethnomusicologist who is considered among the fathers of ethnomusicology and as a world expert of oriental Arab music. The frame of
the archive, and its classification principles, presents the young artist with
a challenge: How can she engage this material from Lachmann's archive,
but differently?

Drawing from Lachmann's musical archive and notes, Manna's film,
A Magical Substance Flows into Me (2015), follows the director as she traces

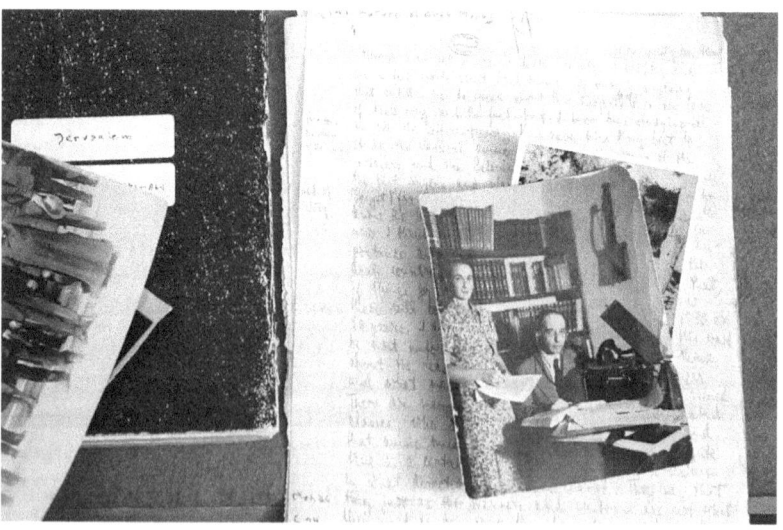

1.1 From Jumana Manna's *A Magical Substance Flows into Me* (2015). Courtesy of
Jumana Manna.

Lachmann's footsteps across present-day Israel and the West Bank to visit the communities where he made his original recordings. This act of following and mimicry is not simply a duplication. As Manna traces Lachmann's path and engages with his archive, she further investigates the limits of the Orientalist archive upon which she models her own cinematic tour and exposé. Sharing some of the recordings with family members of the musicians Lachmann recorded in the 1930s, Manna makes new musical recordings using her iPhone, in turn creating a new, contemporary, and digital musical archive that is modeled on the old, while also clearly differentiated from it. In some ways, Manna's cinematic journey revives Lachmann's archive and rescues it from its status as a dead archive: a body of work comprising folders of writings and CDs sealed away, buried in the archival tomb in Jerusalem.[2]

The Specter of Robert Lachmann: On the Generative Temporality of the Archive

Well known to musicologists, particularly those immersed in the history of German comparative musicology and its origins in the late nineteenth century through the mid-twentieth century, Robert Lachmann remains a mostly unknown figure among historians and other scholars specializing in Palestine during the British Mandate Period.[3] A prominent scholar in Germany and one of the pioneers in the formation of ethnomusicology in the first decades of the twentieth century, Lachmann became a marginal figure in Palestine. Like many of his Jewish colleagues, Lachmann was fired in 1935 from his position as the chief music librarian at the Berlin Staatsbibliothek. Hoping to be integrated into Jewish academic circles in Palestine, he spent several years trying to secure an academic position at the newly established Hebrew University of Jerusalem, but was never granted one. Instead, he died young, four years later, from an illness. It is possible that Lachmann's scholarly agenda was incompatible with the vision of the majority of his colleagues at the Hebrew University. While they sought to create a (Jewish) secular and European-like university in a future Jewish national home in Palestine, Lachmann's research interest and archival drive aimed at emphasizing the local Arab musical traditions *across* the Zionist divisions and between the liturgical and the secular, as well as between the Arab and the Jew.[4] Lachmann's ideas about musical connectivity across national, religious, and linguistic divisions in Palestine not only clashed with the agenda of the newly established Hebrew University but also were at odds with the official policy of the British-operated radio station where he worked during his few years in Palestine. A state-owned station operating from Jerusalem, Palestine Broadcasting Service (PBS) broadcasted programs in English, Arabic, and Hebrew with the assumption that "community would follow language: Arabs would listen to the Arabic sections, Jewish would listen to the Hebrew section and everyone would enjoy light classical music."[5] Lachmann's music program directly opposed this separatist principle, promoting instead the development of interconnected communities. Lachmann, whose radio show was delivered in English with a thick German accent, saw Arab music as key to the creation of a new, cross-ethnic, cross-religious society in Palestine.

In Manna's film Lachmann emerges as a tragic protagonist and a failed prophet: a man whose vision of musical outreach across ethno-national divisions was unwelcome in late 1930s Palestine—and ever since. But it is Lachmann's failure and missed opportunity that Manna finds most appealing: "I was amazed to see what Lachmann envisioned already in the 1930s as a shared (musical) tradition for oriental Jews and Palestinians and a potential for fostering coexistence. It was a vision that was totally opposed to the Zionist ideology of most of his Jewish colleagues, who artificially separated 'Arab' and 'Jew.' In revisiting this history I saw a rare opportunity to open anew and talk about the relationship between Mizrahi Jews and Palestinians in the present."[6]

With no financial support from the university, no publication opportunities, and without the scholarly audience he had in Germany, Lachmann's "voice" in Palestine was restricted to his PBS weekly radio show. A Magical Substance opens with his voice as radio broadcaster, played over a dark screen. He speaks in English with a thick German accent: "Gentlemen, I have invited you because of the shocking attacks and protests directed against our programs and especially the musical program, both by the Arab and Hebrew newspapers. You know that we have spared no trouble in securing the very best and noblest representants of music to be found in Palestine. Still our ardent efforts have been met with ill feeling and insulting criticism. I would ask you now to give me your most valuable advice as to possible changes in our program and method." Robert Lachmann is speaking in December 1936 in front of the advisory committee of the PBS.[7] The voice of a dead man addresses us across time, projecting as it were the urgency of his plea in the past onto the present. This man who never appears before us in the film carries a strong ghostly presence in it nevertheless: his voice, handwriting, and original recordings accompany the director on her journey from one community to another, from one musician to another, in present-day Israel and the Palestinian territories. As the director films herself and the musicians she meets, Lachmann remains a specter, without whom the film has no anchor.

The temporal relationships between the director and her subject of investigation, between the director and the archive she consults, and between the past and the present, remains suggestively ambiguous. While Lachmann serves as the tour guide, leading the director through the past (via archival files and recordings), he also becomes a ghostly tourist: a specter brought back to life and taken along a cinematic journey, in which he is introduced to a country he would no longer recognize. This is a country today divided by walls, fences, and checkpoints, where his cultural vision of coexistence could not hardly be grasped.

Opening the film with Lachmann's plea, "I would ask you now to give me your most valuable advice as to possible changes in our program and method," *A Magical Substance* turns us, the viewers, into the recipients of this desperate message from the past. This mode of temporality bypasses the chronology of time and renews the urgency of Lachmann's plea. Accordingly, the historical failure of Lachmann's cultural vision to take root in Palestine in turn becomes the preface and motivation for Manna's own cinematic journey:

> Lachmann realized that from a scholarly perspective, the distinction between Arab and Jew, which was already ubiquitous in Jerusalem at that time, was false and detrimental to the study of Oriental music. His refusal to recognize this divide made it difficult for him to raise funds for his research. . . . My film is based on [Lachmann's radio] program, which was a failure in certain ways. I aim to question why it failed, and I ask what the stakes of such a project might be in the present. . . . There is a kind of potentiality within the film [although] I'm also addressing the . . . impossibility of reconstituting the space of Mandate Palestine in the present day. [The film] does not idealize this time and the Mandate, but [uses the past] to provide a space from which another Palestine can be.[8]

A European ethnomusicologist and a prototype German Orientalist for whom, as noted by Ruth Davis, "the oral musical traditions of rural and non-Western societies [were] spontaneous expressions of a collective psyche, emanating from the depths of the national soul,"[9] Lachmann believed that the urgency for creating a musical archive in Palestine was great. Authentic Arab music, he argued, might carry within it "traces of the ancient [biblical] past,"[10] and must be collected as "quickly as possible, so as to secure the invaluable musical tradition before it comes to be transformed or altogether destroyed by the growing European traditions."[11] In comparison with Lachmann's archival drive to preserve and document the original, the pure, and the authentic, Manna's incentive to re-create a present-day musical archive based on Lachmann's recordings is modeled on the idea of the copy, the mimetic, the trace, the impure. Following Lachmann's footsteps, retracing his journey across the country, and recording music in the same communities he originally visited, *A Magical Substance* certainly does not seek cultural purity, Palestinian or otherwise. This very distinction between the pure and the tainted in fact frames Manna's engagement with Lachmann's archive. As she comments, she first learned about Robert Lachmann when reading the memoirs of the renowned Palestinian oud player, Wasif Jawhariyyeh. The latter recounts a dispute he had with Mr. Lachmann, who came to record his playing for a radio show. The two argued about the future of Arab music. While Jawhariyyeh encouraged natural changes and development—including the use of Western-style notation, which he hoped would make the study of Arab music easier and more appealing to new students—Lachmann argued against all Western influences and stressed the importance of maintaining Arab music's purity and authenticity, saying he "would much rather there was in every twenty thousand Arabs just one Wasif Jawhariyyeh who masters music and performance the old fashioned way."[12]

The purity of original authentic oriental Arab music that Lachmann as a classical German Orientalist and ethnomusicologist cherished above all is done away with in Manna's re-created cinematic sound archive of present-day performances of the musical pieces Lachmann initially recorded and archived. The film rejects purity as a qualification and instead highlights the cultural mixture and hybridity of its participants. This is particularly clear in the linguistic flexibility of the director, her parents, and several of her interviewees, who easily switch between Hebrew and Arabic. It is also rendered visible through the familiarity of dishes and cooking techniques shared between the various interviewees and the director. And, of course, there are the musical affinities shared by the different film participants.

The title of the film is taken from a chapter in Michael Taussig's book *What Color Is the Sacred?* entitled "A Beautiful Blue Substance Flows into Me." Manna finds Taussig's use of the color metaphor compelling:

Both color and sound move through time, and are similarly at once authentic and deceitful . . . They are mediums that connect to the vibratory
quality of being, and mediums that encounter us, in a way that doesn't
always give us the possibility to control their entry into our bodies and
our psyche.[13]

Revisiting the musical plurality captured in Lachmann's archive, *A Magical Substance* offers us a glimpse into an alternative geopolitical reality projected across present-day Israel and Palestine. All we have of this alternative reality is Lachmann's failure to bring it about, but it is the articulation
of this failure that nevertheless holds a potential realization in the present,
in the form of an anticipated future.

In one of the film's most poignant moments, Manna visits a young
Israeli-Jewish woman of Moroccan background. She is laboring over a traditional Moroccan dish, recounting her memories as a young girl. She explains how she had to learn to forget her cultural background, but never
failed to notice her grandmother's adamant refusal to obey the Israeli
norms that demanded she stop being Arab and become "only" or primarily
an Israeli Jew. Following this painful account, the young Israeli singer and
musician Neta El-Kayam begins singing in Arabic.[14]

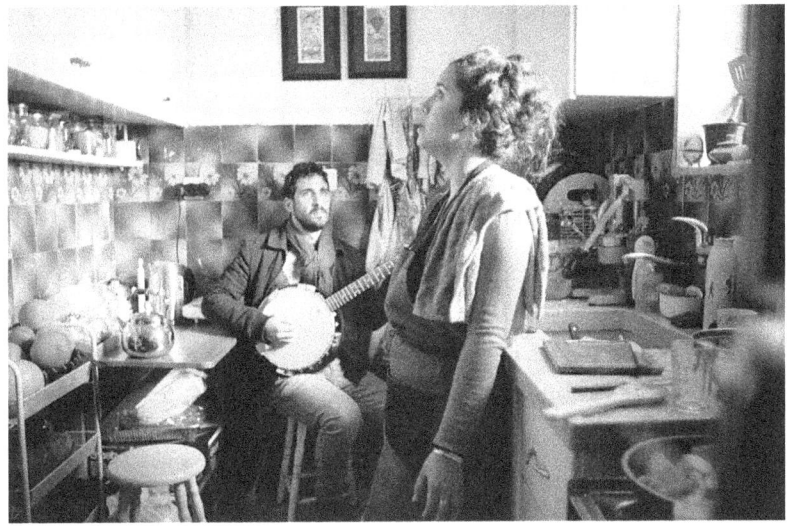

1.2 From Jumana Manna's *A Magical Substance Flows into Me* (2015). Courtesy of
Jumana Manna.

If the oriental (and no doubt also Orientalist) cultural vision Lachmann advanced in the late 1930s failed to impact the evolution of either
Jewish-Israeli or Palestinian cultures in any significant way in the past, this
vision reemerges in Manna's film as a vibrant, if latent, feature of the present, with the potential to thrive in a future yet to come. In this context,
the film refrains from didacticism or prophecy, or the celebratory stance
toward history and the past. Yet, the long musical scene with El-Kayam in
the middle of the film certainly positions the Israeli Moroccan singer who
sings primarily in Arabic as a middle-woman of sorts, and Mizrahi music as
a bridge with the potential to lead to a new shared future between Palestinians and Israelis in Israel/Palestine, even as the "Mizrahi" becomes a new
identity aimed to replace the Arab Jew or the figures Lachmann may have
considered Arab *or* Jew.

And yet, while music certainly functions in the film as a "magical substance" that has the potential to transcend ethnic and national borders, creating a shared cultural framework for Mizrahi Jews and Palestinians, Manna
never fails to contrast this promise with the segregated and partitioned
nature of present-day Israel and Palestine. The scenes in between the film's
main musical parts often include long shots of the Segregation Wall around
nearby Jerusalem, or glimpses of Jewish settlements, both visual reminders of state violence that blocks the present possibility for any meaning-
ful exchange between Israeli Jews and Palestinians. Manna's Mizrahi pro-
tagonists complain about their traditions being censored and cut off from
mainstream Israeli culture, while others take part in building "Judea and
Samaria" (the biblical Hebrew name given to the Occupied West Bank by
Israeli authorities and used by most Israeli settlers), as captured on Manna's
camera when she visits the real estate office of a Kurdish Jewish musician
in Jerusalem. These visual reminders provide a glimpse into the present,
projected back onto the past, as a reflective engagement with Lachmann's
project, rendering it naïve, if not totally obsolete.

Engaging closely with Lachmann's archive, exploring its limitations and
its merits, Manna turns what is otherwise a neglected past—a minor detail
perhaps, a collection of interest to a small and selective group of scholars
who study the history of musicology—into a new mode of remembering, a
celebrated cultural object of the present, and a basis for future imagination.
The film explicitly addresses the question of the archive (Which archive?
Whose archive? What kind of archive? Why archive?) in relation to the
task of remembering and imagining the social life of Palestinians, as well
as the makeup of Palestinian culture and society in Palestine in light of the

forceful erasure of this past by the Zionist conqueror. *A Magical Substance* is not only, I argue, a film about mobilizing the archive in the service of the present and future; it is also, perhaps more so, a reflection on Manna's own abilities and limitations as a young Palestinian artist (who is also an Israeli citizen and daughter of a prominent Palestinian-Israeli historian), to reconstruct certain pre-and post-Nakba historical and cultural moments across the limited conditions of the archive (which separated Jews and Palestinians, Jewish history from Palestinian history, and perhaps also Jewish sounds from Palestinian sounds, as took place in the musical archives). The film is then, in my reading, a metacinematic engagement with the question of historical potentiality, the mobility of the archive, and the ability to capture a futurity that, while dependent on the past, is also unpredictable in its evolution and configurations.

The Orientalist Archive and Its Aftermath

While Manna is grateful for Lachmann, the forgotten antihero and a central figure in her film, she does not shy away from exposing his Orientalist perspective toward the communities he studied as the presumed European specialist. Rather than present Lachmann's recordings and texts as unproblematic sources, Manna highlights Lachmann's patronizing and totalizing Western construction of the Orient (his insistence, for example, on Arab music remaining "pure" and not influenced by foreign elements), while she nevertheless explores his archive as a tremendously valuable source of historical documentation. In her investigation of (Lachmann's) Orientalist ethnographic practices, Manna underlines her own self-ethnographic inquiry, raising uncomfortable questions about the limits of documentation and representation in light of internalized Orientalism. Between sections of reading Lachmann's descriptions of the "magical" sounds of Arab music, Manna films herself at her parents' home, where she takes the role of the ethnographer, posing questions about the past and the present, particularly to her father, the historian Adel Manna, whose mode of researching Palestinian history is more academically traditional than her own.

What might have been a naïve (if well-intended and certainly well-informed) Orientalist fantasy on the part of Lachmann as he sought to document local Palestinian music and use it to promote cultural understanding between Jews and Arabs in Mandate Palestine becomes in Manna's hands a sober commentary on Orientalist representations and a much less hopeful version, if not an altogether rejection, of "coexistence" understood in terms of shared (musical) culture. The film seems to ask: What are the possibilities and limitations of creating a new reality of coexistence in historical Palestine? Whereas in 1936 Lachmann envisioned music as a solution or "glue," in 2015 Manna indicts such a hopeful and naïve perception of music. As Manna travels among musicians across Israel and Palestine, her camera captures a landscape cut apart by walls and fences. Her film makes clear what Lachmann's recordings could not have: Even the greatest manipulation of Orientalist modes of representation cannot overcome or even hide such intense and visible violence.

And yet, by modeling her musical and cinematic journey across present-day Israel and the West Bank on Lachmann's recordings and notes, Manna does more than reflect on the limits of the Orientalist archive. She actively reshapes this archive, relocating it *outside of* the National Library of Israel and the Zionist narrative, and placing it instead in Palestinian hands.[15] In other words, Manna's engagement with the archive and her revitalization of Lachmann's musical recordings defies the very principle of partition by which the collection was made to be part of the Israeli Zionist archive. Yet, Manna defies this principle not by violating the archive or denying it altogether as irrelevant, but by recontextualizing it as part of a new, present-day archive, which, as her film demonstrates, crosses the carefully, sometimes violently maintained boundary between Israeli/Palestinian histories, cultures, narratives, and so forth. This is not a model of coexistence as Lachmann envisioned, one facilitated by a shared musical formation of Jews and Arabs. Rather, it is a mode of being that does away with the national divide and its naturalization.

If the story of Palestine (fragments of which are narrated throughout the film by Adel Manna) may no longer be told except through the mediation of, or in relation to, Jewish, Western, and Orientalist representations and archives, *A Magical Substance* transforms this constraint into an opportunity to rethink questions of mastery and ownership over narratives, history, and archives. The film critically engages with questions concerning ethnographic representation (by both Lachmann and the director herself), archival documentation, Orientalism, and knowledge production, as well as questions about the relationship between Jews and Arabs, and between the history of Jewish expulsion from Europe (which brings Lachmann to Palestine in the first place) and the history of Palestinian displacement by Jews in 1948.

Among other things, I argue that in this film, as in earlier ones (particularly *A Sketch of Manners: Alfred Roch's Last Masquerade*, 2013), Manna chooses to work with what I call "minor archives," that is to say, significantly lesser known, less centered, and oftentimes explicitly marginal and eccentric narratives from/of the past to create a living past that is far removed from the stories of great men, great wars, and the victories that "make history" and headlines. Manna's minor archive invites us to consider less familiar possibilities and configurations of the past and new ways of remembering, thereby opening new possibilities for imagining the future. Manna's cinematic practice advances a conversation about the politics of citation as a way of creating alternative, counterdominant narratives that challenge notions of national coherence and cultural authenticity. What Manna finds in Lachmann's musical archive is an alternative path to the past—not by presenting a glorious pre-1948 Palestine, but by escaping the more rigid historical accounts often found in narratives of victory, loss, war, exile, and so forth.

This musical archive, an archive of sound, invites more fluid and diverse interpretations. Not so much about *what was* as *what could have been and wasn't*, Lachmann's "sound memory"[16] introduces a cultural and social possibility that never became dominant. Lachmann himself reflected on the potential of music to shape a cross-ethnic or cross-national cultural environment and emphasized the important political role of music in the context of Jewish settlement in Palestine: "In no other country, perhaps, the need for a sound understanding of [oriental] music, and the opportunity to study it answer each other so well as in Palestine. For the European here, it is of vital interest to know the mind of his Oriental neighbor. . . . Music will be his surest guide provided he listens to it with sympathy instead of distain."[17]

And "my work necessitates free intercourse with all the different ethnic groups in the country and the Near East generally. It may therefore be made to contribute, however modestly . . . towards a better understanding between Jews and Arabs. . . . Further it might be advisable to try and find a neutral background [outside of the Hebrew University], which would enable both parties to collaborate with each other without being accused of illoyalty by their own people."[18]

Lachmann's call for Europeans (Jewish Europeans in Palestine) to listen to oriental music with sympathy and not disdain aimed at advancing a cultural dialogue between Europe and the Orient. In this vision, the Orient remains an object of inquiry to be professionally studied (by the musicologist) and introduced to the European audience, appealing to its curiosity and liking. *A Magical Substance* highlights these tensions and does not shy away from showing that Lachmann, a refugee seeking shelter in Palestine, also, if unwittingly, took part in an Orientalist outlook and a colonial system of knowledge production that eventually erased Palestine and Palestinian culture even while (literally) recording it.[19]

Still, read outside of the National Library of Israel and the predetermined logic of Zionism (there is no record indicating Lachmann was or was not a Zionist), Lachmann's musical project (his recordings, radio broadcasts, and lectures) appears much more subversive than the sum of its obvious Orientalist undertones. Indeed, Manna finds in Lachmann's archive a radical political vision that sees in music "an alternative form of sovereignty: one that disrupts the constructions of Zionism, and renders visible the complex interdependency of identities that were falsely made discrete from one another."[20] She also finds an alternative subject formation that she uses to advance her own inquiry of future potentialities. Asked what drew her to Lachmann, Manna responded: "He is an odd and interesting person, through which I felt one could reflect on many issues both past and present. He was a Jewish, gay man escaping the Nazis, arriving in Jerusalem with his German partner. He was unable to get funding because his work did not coincide with the political formations that triumphed. [Lachmann] gave me the framework, or the excuse, to explore other things such as notions of heritage and authenticity, the complexities embedded in language as well as the potential and limits of music to overcome political divisions."[21]

Inside and Outside (The Archive)

A Magical Substance simultaneously unfolds two opposing narratives, refusing to choose between them or fix them in a clear hierarchy. It presents us with an aporia and refuses the binary of positivist empiricism. The first narrative emphasizes the power of music to transcend borders and create new libidinal bonds. The second narrative cuts across this hopeful one as a sober counterpoint advanced in between the musical scenes, highlighting a geopolitical reality made of excessive borders, walls, partitions, and divisions. The exchanges between the director and some of her interviewees are also not free of tension. In one of the opening scenes, for example, the director meets a Jewish Kurdish policeman at his home to talk about Kurdish music. While the meeting is civilized, even friendly, the camera captures the subtle underlying awkwardness involved in what seems like a labored effort on the part of the policeman to act naturally with the young Palestinian woman there to interview him: "So, you are making a film about Kurdish music?" the Israeli man asks. "No" Manna answers, "I am making a movie about Robert Lachmann, who was a Jewish German ethnomusicologist who had a radio show dedicated to orientalist music, Mizrahi and Palestinian." The man, still very friendly, seems baffled: "Really? And ah . . . can I ask you a personal question?" "Sure," Manna responds, despite the growing awkwardness of the interaction. "What do your parents think about what you are doing?" When Manna politely answers that her parents fully support her (in making a film about a German Jewish scholar, or in making a film about music shared by Mizrahi Jews and Palestinians), the hospitable Israeli man continues: "And what do your parents do?" At this point the misplaced nature of the exchange becomes quite evident. After all, we know that the director is there to ask questions related to Lachmann's recordings, not to answer questions about her parents' views or occupations. When Manna replies that her father is a historian and her mother a social worker, the Israeli man seems impressed: "Nice, very nice," he comments, leaning back. The silence that accompanies the seemingly friendly exchange highlights the suspicion, hesitation, and subtle, but unmistakably patronizing, undertone. This example, as one among many, underscores how the "magical substance" of music alone cannot undo the colonial setting that governs the present relationship between Israelis and Palestinians. Nor can the archive, or the return to the past, even in its new staging in the present, achieve this alone.

Failing to secure an academic position for himself at the Hebrew University, Lachmann died only four years after arriving in Palestine. His recording and lectures were collected and originally housed in the Hebrew University library on Mount Scopus in 1939. After 1948, the archive, together with the rest of the collection, became part of a demilitarized zone under UN control within the Jordanian-controlled West Bank. It is unknown when, but it is clear that by 1964 the entirety of Lachmann's archive was returned to Israel and placed in the National Sound Music Archive created within the National Library of Israel.[22] While the scholar was rejected by his colleagues at the Hebrew University and remained an outsider, his archive was collected with some zeal and became part of the national collection.[23] The fact that Lachmann's archive is today housed in the Israel State Archives at the Hebrew University in Jerusalem, where Lachmann himself was never able to secure an academic position, is not a minor one. Among other things, it means that the archive, which contains hours of recordings of local Palestinian music, is inaccessible to most Palestinians.[24] *A Magical Substance* directly addresses neither this problem of access nor the broader question of Israeli archiving politics in *A Magical Substance*. And yet, the fact that the film explores, indeed documents and reflects upon, the director's own process of chronicling, archiving, and recording suggests that, like many other Palestinian artists and filmmakers (Elia Suleiman, Emily Jacir, Sharif Waked, Rula Halawani, Larissa Sansour, and Kamal Aljafari, among others), Manna's work highlights *both* the need *and* the inability to chronicle and record Palestinian history independent of Israeli-Jewish history. It similarly highlights the position of the director herself as one situated in between walls and partitions. Given that she is an Israeli citizen, she is not subjected to these borders in the way that Palestinians residing in the West Bank, and even more so in Gaza, are. But, like her archive, she is somewhere in between. This is a position the film explores as carrying potential, rather than loss.

In one of the most poignant moments in the film, Manna holds a folder and reads through its papers. She is, one can safely assume, in the National Library of Israel in Jerusalem. "Invading" the archive, as it were, she unfolds the folder containing Lachmann's writings. The scene captures the temporality and the tactility of the archive as Manna slowly moves the pages and reads Lachmann's notes, which serve as the starting point for her cinematic exploration.

Folding, unfolding, touching, reading, and reciting, Manna's active engagement with Lachmann's folders and recordings as she inserts herself into the Israeli national archive collection can be seen as an act of trespass and subversion. But it is also, and perhaps more importantly so, an act of redemption. She helps Lachmann's collection escape the confining limits of the National Library of Israel, where the recordings and lectures are held captive. She rescues Lachmann from his captivity in the National Library of Israel by emphasizing the ambiguities of his figure and the nonnationalist aspirations that guided his research. Ironically, this act of deliverance requires a Palestinian. *A Magical Substance* indirectly asks: What if Lachmann's vision of Jewish and Palestinian coexistence was taken seriously? What if his radio broadcasts, dedicated to local oriental music traditions across different segments of society had served as the guiding principle for establishing a local oriental culture in Palestine, shared by Jews, Palestinians, and others? And, along similar lines, the film seems to ask: What can we do now, after the fact, in a political reality in which gates and walls radically segregate Israeli Jews and Palestinians? In this reality, the gift of music alone will not do. How can we address history and past failures in the service of promoting a better future? Or, how can we address the past

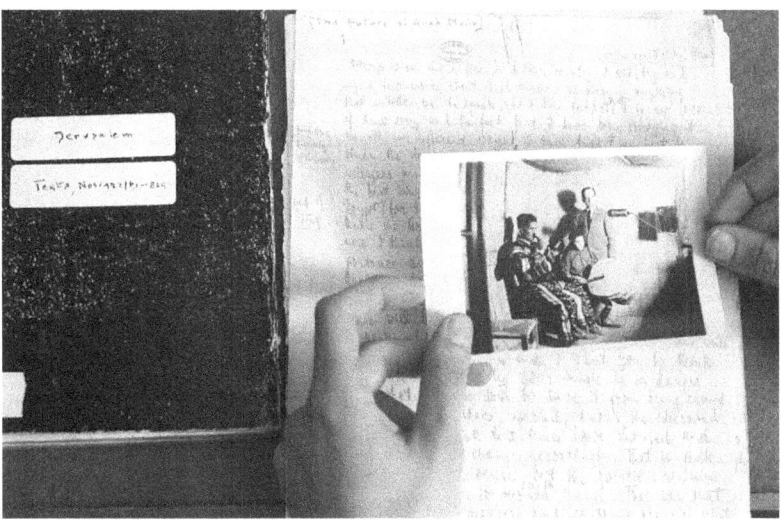

1.3   From Jumana Manna's *A Magical Substance Flows into Me* (2015). Courtesy of
Jumana Manna.

in a more capacious way than as "history"? One answer the film provides
is that we must learn to approach the archive, even when hosted in the
national archive of Israel, as a liminal text that veers away from dominant
national narratives. The archive highlights ambiguity and keeps past failures alive—it can be an inspiration and source for imagining an alternative
future. Indeed, in *A Magical Substance,* Lachmann's archive is not *only* a testimony of a failed historical enterprise. It is also a blueprint for advancing
future political change.

The archival material in the film is presented not as a factual connection
to the past or as an attempt to historicize, but as an invitation to imagine the past as an enticing site of ambiguities. *A Magical Substance* revisits
pre-1948 Palestine by privileging what may appear as the lesser important,
inconsequential moments of history—a failed radio program and the collection of a German Jewish (gay, unemployed) refugee in Palestine that the
film reads as a site of contested memories and unmaterialized potentialities. Lachmann, the shadow protagonist of the film, remains an enigmatic
figure through whom the director tells nuanced and less familiar stories
about the past and present reality of Palestine, replacing the demand to
remember with the right to imagine.

Writing about post-apartheid South Africa, Cheryl McEwan discusses
the importance of building alternative postcolonial archives based on

seemingly marginal materials. These materials, she argues, ensure the pluralism and possible rehabilitation of the national project and offer hopeful
possibilities for the future.[25] If Manna's film draws attention to the mul-
tifaceted social fabric of Israel/Palestine in the past as well as in the present as a source for hope and a recognition of lost opportunities, it does
so not only, as I have so far suggested, by attending to marginal events,
figures, and archival materials, but also by grounding the articulation of
social pluralism (as a historical loss, missed opportunity, and possible path
of becoming) primarily through and in intimate domestic spaces and personal interiorities. In *A Magical Substance*, we meet most of the characters
in their kitchens, over pans and pots, while cooking chicken or pickling
vegetables. Manna's parents are filmed at home as well: they are exercis-
ing along with the TV, watering the plants, making coffee. These domestic
spaces, shot from a close angle, are the intimate views through which she
animates her archival material. Manna frees her archival material from its
static and dogmatic status as "archive" by taking it along with her on an
open-ended journey.

Manna's cinematic fable utilizes archival materials as the basis upon
which the history of Palestine is revisited *not* as a history of "a people" (a
nation or a land), but rather as a history of people: a history more diverse,
more intimate, and more nuanced than that which finds expression in
dominant historical narratives. *A Magical Substance*, as her other films do,
advances nonconformist, even eccentric, accounts of the past, displaying
the backdoor stories of everyday life, decentering the image of "Palestine"
in the past as in the present. Manna opens Palestine—its geography, history,
and culture—to poetic subtleties that undermine the (political) demand
for aesthetic immediacy. Using archival material as an anchor and starting
point for her investigation of the past as well as the present, Manna's film
does not do away with the documentary format, but it certainly rejects
the ethnographic demands often associated with the genre, decentraliz-
ing notions of cultural authenticity, national origins, linguistic purity, and
historical accuracy, and instead offering a narrative format in which *what
was*, *what could have been*, and *what may still become* are brought together and
remain open, possible, inconclusive, and, above all, seductive.

TWO

Lost and Found in
Israeli Footage

KAMAL ALJAFARI'S "JAFFA TRILOGY"
AND THE PRODUCTIVE VIOLATION OF THE
COLONIAL VISUAL ARCHIVE

The city of Jaffa is a media reality whose traces
are embedded in media, in the grains and pixels of
photographs. It is a city mediated by the lenses of
travellers, administrators, amateurs, and filmmakers.
| DECOLONIZING ARCHITECTURE ART
RESIDENCY (DAAR). "A Demolition"

In 1976, three Israeli architects[1] were assigned to find a suitable
location to build the Etzel Museum—a museum honoring the paramilitary group that led the 1948 conquer of Jaffa. On the shores
just south of Tel Aviv, in the area then known as the Manshiyya
neighborhood of Jaffa, the architects came across three Palestinian ruin sites. Describing these ruins as striking for their "'power
of survival"[2] and seemingly oblivious to the violence (once again)
imposed on the people who used to inhabit them, the architects
erected the Zionist memorial museum on top of these sites, keeping them visible *as ruins*. Enforcing a distorted memory of Zionist
survival over the geopolitical space of Jaffa, the museum's construction involved the violent appropriation of the ruins, as well
as of their attending narratives and memories. This is not an exceptional case, as similar acts of appropriation can be witnessed
throughout Israel/Palestine and, for that matter, in many other

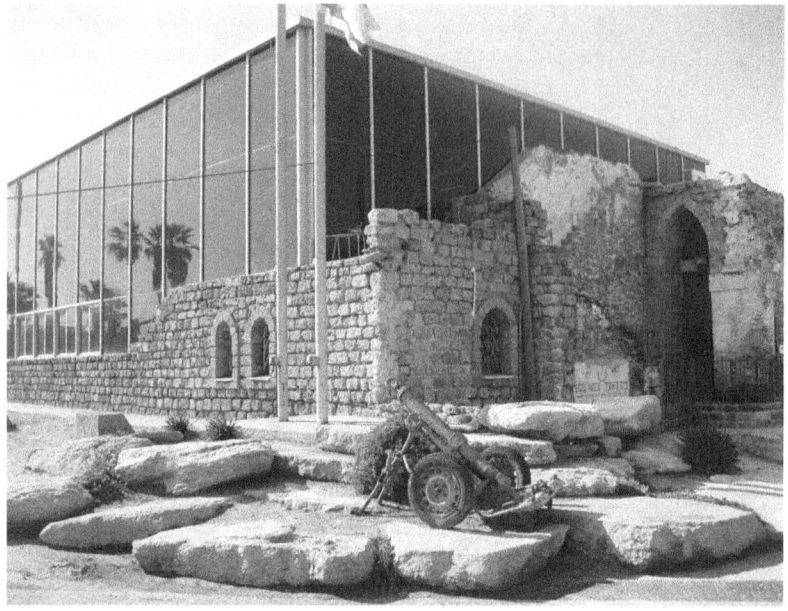

2.1 Etzel Museum in Jaffa, Palestine/Israel. Photograph by the author.

geopolitical locations where native lands and properties are stolen along
with native cultural symbols and memories. Yet, in the case of this museum, this process was particularly visible: the design for the new structure
involved relocating and deliberately exposing the old ruins to make the
museum look like a reconstructed building, despite the fact that no such
building previously existed.

I open with this anecdote because it is telling of the background against
which one should view and appreciate Kamal Aljafari's three mesmerizing
essay-films: *The Roof* (2006, 61 min.), *Port of Memory* (2009, 62 min.), and *Recollection* (2015, 70 min.). I refer to the three films together as the "Jaffa Trilogy," although Aljafari has never grouped them together in this or another
manner.[3] Viewing them as an expanded work enhances our ability to read
Aljafari's cinematic preoccupation with questions of erasure, destruction,
elimination, and gentrification—practices that mark colonial violence
in its urban, architectonic, spatial manifestations. What is perhaps most
noticeable and unique about the trilogy, however, is its ability to convey
loss, damage, and violence while further exploring the role of imagination
and fantasy in facilitating possible subversive reorganization of a massively
violated urban space and a communal memory. While the previous chapter

traced the activization and reworking of a musical Orientalist German Jewish archive from the early twentieth century, this chapter explores the potentiality involved in manipulating the colonial Israeli cinematic archive.

Aljafari's Jaffa Trilogy, while seemingly adhering to documentary practices by cinematically capturing the destruction of the social and spatial-urban condition of Palestinian life in Jaffa, is more accurately a cinematic investigation of the *image archive of Jaffa*. This archive includes Israeli-projected images of mastery and control that visually eliminate Palestinians and impose a fictional reality on the city (what Aljafari has called "cinematic occupation"). It also includes images Aljafari creates from footage taken from Israeli films, citing them as Israeli cinematic fantasies while manipulating them to include "Palestinian ghosts." Aljafari reinserts the Palestinians who were edited out of the frame within the Israeli vision field. In recycling and manipulating the Israeli footage, Aljafari proposes a model of political and aesthetic intervention that exposes the failure of the settler-colonial fantasy to do away with the natives. In Aljafari's films, the Palestinian natives "return" from the place of elimination, from the past, to invade the cinematic frame in the present (what Aljafari calls "cinematic justice").[4]

As noted by David Pendleton, Aljafari's films are not realistic, historical, or documentary depictions of Jaffa; rather, they are poetic expressions of "the fragile rhythms of lives lived in a kind of permanent displacement and the strange limbo of neighborhoods subtly yet inexorably transforming."[5] The "strange limbo" and "fragile rhythms of life" captured by Aljafari's bricolage cinematic style cultivates a patient viewer. Long shots of walls and empty lots are replaced with close-ups of rubble, ruins, and debris. The trilogy is meditative and slow-paced. This slowness marks Aljafari's signature filming style, which visualizes the gradual but ongoing destruction of Jaffa to which the walls and the ruins or, rather, *the images of* the walls and ruins bear witness. The story of Jaffa is not unlike the story of many other Palestinian towns: the native Palestinian population was expelled by prestatehood Jewish paramilitary groups (Haganah, Lehi, Etzel), a great portion of the city was destroyed, and parts of the city were constructed and renovated by and for new Israeli Jewish inhabitants. Yet, Jaffa's story is also unique. Jaffa experienced a great process of modernization and urbanization just before it became a war zone in 1947. The city's population soared from 27,000 in 1922 to 71,000 in 1947 as Jaffa became a central urban center—indeed, *the* urban commercial and cultural center of Palestine—and the home of most local Arabic newspapers prior to 1948.

When the UN Partition Plan (UNGA 181, November 29, 1947) announced that the country would be divided into a Jewish state and a Palestinian state after the end of the British Mandate, Jaffa, located south of Tel Aviv (a city that was central to the Jewish establishment in Palestine from early on),[6] was assigned the status of a Palestinian city. However, the resolution map located it at the heart of the territory designated for the Jewish state. And so, from the moment of the UN declaration, and up to two days before the end of the war and the establishment of the state of Israel on May 14, 1948, "Jaffa [turned into] a combat zone of paramilitary Jewish and Palestinian forces whose fighting [left] its mark on the urban fabric."[7] There are various theories and speculations as to why Jaffa was conquered with greater ease than other Palestinian cities, particularly Jerusalem. Whatever the reasons, the outcome was undeniably devastating for the Palestinian population of the city: the great majority of local Palestinian inhabitants fled, among them almost the entire middle class and intellectual sectors. By the end of the war, fewer than three thousand Palestinians remained in the seized city.

Jaffa was the most important Palestinian city and the economic, social, and cultural center from the late nineteenth century until 1948; yet, after 1948, the city lost its gravity, becoming poor, destroyed, marginalized, and depleted of resources.[8] Jaffa underwent such massive urban destruction and population evacuation, followed by more recent gentrification and repopulation, that what is left of pre-1948 Jaffa, according to Salim Tamari, is nothing but "a figment of the imagination," found nowhere in what is now a "bleached ghost town."[9] From 1948 to the present, Jaffa transformed from a Palestinian urban center into a site of poverty and destruction, and, more recently, a booming Jewish Israeli housing sector with lively tourist centers.[10]

None of these phases are chronologically traced or depicted in Aljafari's Jaffa Trilogy, despite the fact that all three films capture the urban reality of Jaffa as comprising ongoing destruction, reconstruction, gentrification, and loss. The trilogy as a whole maintains a certain poetic distance from the chronological narrative of Jaffa's transformation and, for that matter, from narrative as such. Aljafari, much like Jumana Manna in the previous chapter, tells the story of the past but refuses "history" as an organizing structure. Instead of historical narrative, the trilogy highlights the singularity of images and the aesthetic quality of the filmed devastated urban sites: debris, broken buildings, missing walls, collapsing roof, and ruins.[11] In this sense, there is also a noticeable progression across the three films from narratology to recycling, with the practice of filming being replaced with that of citing and recapturing preexisting footage and images from Israeli sources. Thus, in *The Roof*, a voiceover narrative introduces the political and historical background against which the images (filmed by Aljafari) unfold, and the characters make ironic comments throughout. No such direct verbal or visual intervention is offered in *Port of Memory*, in which dialogue is limited to a bare minimum, and the political commentary—located between the ironic and the melancholic—takes the anachronistic form of a direct incorporation, almost unnoticeable citation, of Israeli cinematic images. Finally, in *Recollection*, both voiceover and narrative structure are completely absent and replaced with a sequence of images, all of which are borrowed from Israeli films, as well as an original soundtrack (recorded by Aljafari) that invites an affect-based viewing experience with little, if any, overt historical reference or analysis.

Rubble, Walls, and a Missing Roof

Kamal Aljafari was born, raised, and educated in Ramle (Al Ramla) and the neighboring, larger, and better-known city of Jaffa. *The Roof* is his most explicitly personal film, centering on the story of his family house:

> It all began in 1948. In May. My grandparents were on a boat on their way to Beirut after their city of Jaffa had been bombed. Over those few days the waves got too big. So they were forced to return. But when they came back, Palestine was already gone. Their homes were gone as well. The people who remained were forced to live in one neighborhood and they were given the houses of other Palestinians. This was the case of my mother's family in Jaffa, and the same happened to my father's family in Ramle. In 1948, the owners of this house were still building the second floor. Today the house is still the same: my parents live on the first floor and above them lives the past.[12]

The melancholia of the first message—"Palestine was already gone. Their homes were gone as well"—is cut through by the irony of the second: "They were given the houses of other Palestinians." Aljafari not only informs us that his parents live in a house where the second floor still lacks a roof; he further complicates the ethos of home by telling us that, while his family lost its house, they took the house of another family who never got any house in return. This Palestinian family that lost a home is nevertheless present, as the ghosts with whom he and his family lived on the second floor. Of course, later in the film we learn that as far as the Israeli officials are concerned, Aljafari's family doesn't actually own the house. They are not allowed to build the missing roof and are told that the house (in which they have lived for decades) is not registered under their name. By state law, they are considered squatters.

Following this personal narrative with irony, the words of the acclaimed Palestinian poet, novelist, and translator Anton Shammas[13] appear on the screen: "And you know perfectly well that we don't ever leave home we simply drag it behind us wherever we go, walls, roof, and all." Shammas's dark irony captures the spirit of the film: while *The Roof* is about the loss of one's home and hometown, Shammas's comment can be taken very literally. "Walls, roof, and all" are never left behind. Indeed, they appear in almost every shot throughout the film: walls, half-built structures, half-built homes, partially constructed rooftops, half-paved roads, and a wall removed (perhaps) by mistake by an Israeli bulldozer make up the visual landscape of the film.

The surface of the unfinished second floor is carefully studied: dust, curves, peeling paint. Nadia Yaqub suggests that, in using "haptic images [*The Roof*] teases the viewer by simultaneously suggesting the auras of the roof and the home beneath it, but refusing to reveal their secrets."[14] I would add that, in all three films, walls and their materiality (rather than people) are at the heart of the cinematic investigation of the past, of memory, of loss, survival, and potential renewal.

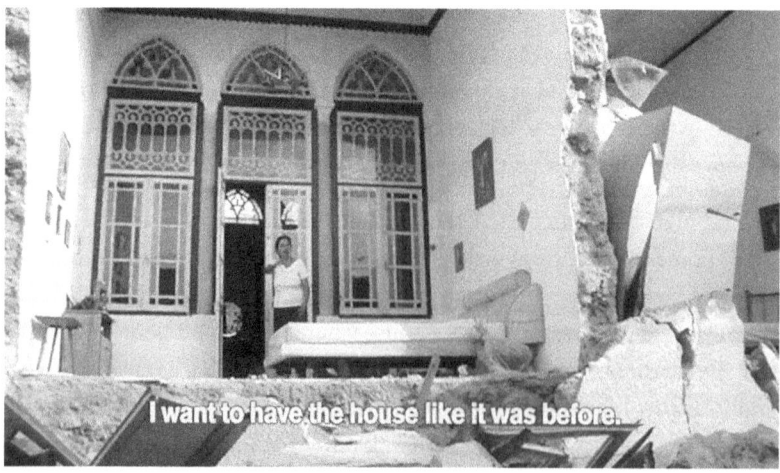

I want to have the house like it was before.

2.2 From *The Roof* (2006), by Kamal Aljafari. Courtesy of Kamal Aljafari.

Asked in relation to his latest film *Recollection* (2015) why his films in-clude so many close-ups of walls, Aljafari replied: "The walls witnessed everything. They were left behind, half destroyed. But even if everyone was gone and the city was empty, the [disappeared] people would still be engraved on the walls."[15] Walls then witness the past, but not historically. They bring us in touch with the past, most explicitly. Their ruination un-folds not a historical narrative but a sensual memory experienced in the present. This haptic dimension of the image is explored to an even greater extent in Aljafari's second film, *Port of Memory*, which relies on walls to tell the story of destruction and reconstruction, but also to investigate the po-etic and political space found in between and across the intersection of reality and fantasy.

Jaffa on Screen

If the investigation of interior spaces, and more specifically of home and family in the context of living without a roof, is at the heart of *The Roof*, Jaf-fa's urban outdoors is at the center of *Port of Memory*. The film captures the spatial reality of a city that is continuously transformed, destroyed, rebuilt, and altered, making the condition of dwelling in it resemble a life caught between reality and fantasy, and more specifically between everyday life and a cinematic set. Aljafari highlights this fantastic element by incorpo-rating two other films into his film: the Israeli-American coproduced action movie *Delta Force* (1986) by Israeli director Menahem Golan and starring Chuck Norris, and the classical Israeli musical *Kazablan* (1974), belonging to a genre of Israeli films about Arab Jewish (Mizrahi) youth attempting (yet facing difficulty) to acclimate into Israel's modern Western mentality. This earlier film was also directed by Golan and starred the (then) celebrated Israeli actor and singer, Yehoram Ga'on. Both films, like many other Is-raeli films, especially from the 1970s, were shot in Jaffa. The first depicts an American commando unit fighting "Palestinian terrorists" in Lebanon during the civil war; in the second, a Mizrahi (Moroccan) young man from a poor neighborhood (staged in Jaffa) falls in love with an Ashke-nazi woman, whose family opposes the relationship. Against the lyrical images of architectural structures and urban landscape of ruins captured by Aljafari's camera, the images incorporated from these two Israeli-American films seem particularly artificial if not altogether grotesque. Jaffa thus emerges in *Port of Memory* not just, or even mainly, as an urban real-ity of destruction and ruination, but also as a cinematic stage upon which

colonial fantasies are imagined and reenacted. Between these two poles—
the reality of destruction and the colonial fantasy of ruins-as-a-film-set to
house all cinematic images of war, poverty, crime, marginality—the film
unfolds a stunning cinematic meditation on destruction and construction:
the destruction of "old" (Palestinian) Jaffa and the construction of "new"
(Israeli-Jewish) gentrified Jaffa, two parallel realities that are nevertheless
codependent and coinhabited. The film simultaneously explores the role of
the archive by collecting and curating many cinematic and photographic
images of Jaffa, a city that has long served as a movie set: a cinematic canvas
upon which Orientalist and colonial fantasies and desires are repeatedly
projected.

Opening with a close-up of ruins, the first shot soon exposes a wider
image of a structure, probably a house: a structure in a state of becoming
ruins. The walls are peeling, electric wires poke out from all directions, and
several stones are broken.

As in *The Roof*, cinematic intimacy is reserved for the walls. The camera studies them closely, revealing their texture, colors, and shapes: torn-
down walls, falling walls, missing walls, damaged walls. If Aljafari's poetic
rendition of destruction references the spatial reality of the city, it is further informed by the colonial fantasy of destruction the Israeli-American
cinematic productions elaborate. *Delta Force*, like similar war movies that
were filmed in Jaffa, used the city as a set because it already looked like a
destroyed Mediterranean city under fire. In *Delta Force*, Jaffa was chosen as

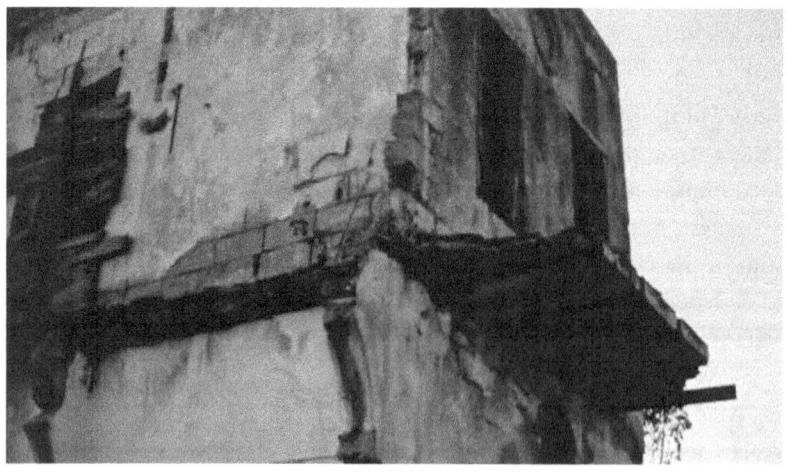

2.3 From *Port of Memory* (2009), by Kamal Aljafari. Courtesy of Kamal Aljafari.

a stand-in for Beirut after the civil war, despite the fact that the two cities look nothing alike. It was of course a much easier choice for the studio than to film in Lebanon. Furthermore, the film was shot in Jaffa not just because the city was thought to resemble Beirut (under destruction), but because it was only in Jaffa that the director and the studio could obtain a permit to literally bomb an entire building for the purpose of filming it, and to shoot at many others. In other words, Jaffa wasn't only a film set that was supposed to resemble Beirut; it was also a city that was easily turned into a simulated quasi-war zone for the purpose of filming. To cinematically capture the destruction of war using real bombs and live ammunition seems costly, insanely dangerous, and altogether completely fantasmatic, and yet this is precisely how *Delta Force* was made. Buildings and neighborhoods in Jaffa were bombed, shot at, and destroyed, as the camera rolled: "Action!"

Given that many crime and war movies and television shows have been shot in Jaffa since the 1960s, our image of Jaffa is inevitably also impacted by these images of destruction, violence, and crime.[16] *Port of Memory* does not try to do away with these images or recover an authentic and untainted Jaffa. On the contrary, many of the characters in the film are watching and appear to even enjoy some of these violent films and images, which Aljafari himself confesses to have enjoyed as a child. The visual archive of Jaffa is the only account one has, Aljafari seems to insist. Beyond the borders of these colonial, Orientalist, and capitalist archives lies no "authentic" image, only variations of visual manipulations. Aljafari begins in this film a practice of decolonializing the image, which he further develops and elaborates in his most recent film yet, *Recollection*. This practice comprises *working through* the colonial image and the colonial archive, not unlike Jumana Manna's critical engagement with Lachmann's Orientalist musical archive discussed in the previous chapter. But Aljafari's engagement with the Israeli cinematic archive is even more direct and explicit: borrowing and digitally manipulating the images, Aljafari creates a new cinematic language *with* and *through* them, resulting not in corrective authenticity or a rehabilitated native space, but a subversive imitation and mimicry that expands the archive beyond its initial set borders.[17] Thus, for example, in one of the most powerful scenes in the film, we follow Salim, Aljafari's uncle, as he walks through narrow alleys of his neighborhood toward the beach. Suddenly, and for the first time in the film, a song erupts and breaks the silence. We are introduced to a new figure whom we have not previously seen. To most Israeli viewers of an older generation, he is immediately recognizable as Kazablan, the iconic character of a Moroccan young man who belongs to a street group of other poor Mizrahi men and falls in love with a middle-class Ashkenazi woman. The Israeli musical film by the same name, *Kazablan* (released in 1974) offers a localized version of Romeo and Juliet—an impossible love that prevails. The film was shot in Ajami, the same neighborhood at the center of Aljafari's film. In Golan's film, Ajami is home to Mizrahi Jews who protest the intention of the predominantly Ashkenazi authorities to tear down their old homes. The bitter irony is that the staging of this inter-Jewish ethnic and class drama in Jaffa involved the complete erasure of the actual inhabitants of Jaffa at the time—the majority of whom were Palestinian facing the very real threat of their homes being torn down. In other words, one narrative of oppression (Mizrahi oppression) is narrated, staged, and filmed over another (Palestinian oppression). Indeed, the conditions for articulating the first are based on the elimination of the second, with Jaffa transforming once again from an actual city into a fantastic film set. But what Aljafari does with this cinematic violence is more than simply denounce it. *Port of Memory* incorporates the most famous scene from *Kazablan*, in which the main character (played by famous Israeli actor and singer Yehoram Ga'on) walks down the very same narrow streets as the director's uncle did in the previous scene. In the Israeli film he sings a song about longing for the home of his childhood in Morocco:

> *There is a place, far away, beyond the sea*
> *Where the sand is white and the house warm*
> *Where the sun lights over the market, the street and the port*
> *Home is there, beyond the sea.*

The melody is moving and catchy. Aljafari retained the original Hebrew soundtrack, thus allowing the pain of Kazablan (the character) to be heard (in his own language), while also reminding us that for Kazablan, Jaffa is a film set: a mere fictitious frame onto which the character projects narratives from other places and times. It is then to the sound of Hebrew and the original score of *Kazablan* that Aljafari reintroduces his uncle Salim. When Salim reemerges on the screen and begins to walk, seemingly in Kazablan's space just a few steps behind him, the two films overlap two temporalities and two narratives that otherwise appear mutually exclusive: Aljafari's footage is projected over Golan's film. Salim and Kazablan now walk side by side: inhabitant and actor, Palestinian and Israeli. One speaks in Arabic; the other sings his pain and longing (for Morocco) in Hebrew. Who is shadowing whom? Who leads in whose footsteps? Who is the ghost? This double walk, one footage over the other, I suggest, unfolds the current story of Jaffa as a narrative about colonial annexation of both geographical space and the space of imagination. It also, not unlike Manna's film, projects a cinematic poetic of aporia, calling not for clear resolutions as much as pointing to their impossibilities and the need to think and imagine Palestine differently by revisiting, not denying or rejecting, the colonial archive.

With the figure of Salim appearing and disappearing in and out of narrow alleys, and in and out of the Israeli film frame, the question of the spatial politics of Jaffa becomes also, if not more so, a question of visibility, invisibility, and haunting in the archive. In Golan's film, Palestinians remain invisible, while emptied Jaffa serves as a canvas, a film set, and a stage; Aljafari's reuse of Golan's film, and his uncle's invasion into it, highlights this emptied-out reality as a myth. Aljafari's filmed images, reinserted into Golan's film (the latter from the early 1970s, and the former from three decades later), are marked by the slightly different color and quality of the footage. This visible difference, immediately noted by most viewers, highlights the temporal gap of this hybrid image. The Palestinian who is eliminated in the Israeli film returns into the frame as a belated ghost. He has by now (already) become part of the very frame that tried yet failed to keep him out of sight.

When Kazablan walks around the streets of Jaffa singing about his lost hometown in Morocco, he is in fact already—at least for contemporary Israeli viewers—a walking cliché. The film was a big hit when it came out in 1974, and among the first of its kind (a Bourekas film fashioned on the

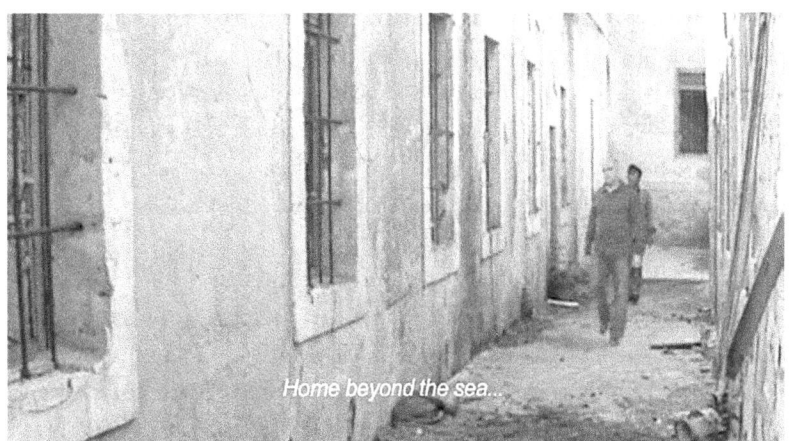

Home beyond the sea...

2.4 From *Port of Memory* (2009), by Kamal Aljafari. Courtesy of Kamal Aljafari.

style of American musicals, as Ella Shohat notes),[18] but today it seems anachronistic, if not altogether absurd. If anything, the film today functions as a quasi-cult film enjoyed by a few Israeli film buffs. Incorporating the iconic nostalgic singing scene in *Port of Memory* is therefore also an ironic nod, at least toward Israeli viewers. It is in a paradoxical manner an act of intimacy for the viewers familiar with the scene, the film, the lyrics, and the actor. It is through the audience that misses the irony that the power of this incorporation is perhaps best brought to light. Thus, Aljafari reports that before screening his film to an Arab audience (in Lebanon, Qatar, and Palestine) he was nervous about the reaction to his inclusion of a Hebrew song and an Israeli actor/singer in the film. To his surprise and great relief, the audience didn't seem to mind the Hebrew song at all. On the contrary, "They found the song beautiful and moving and identified with its lyrics about exile and longing for home."[19] It is precisely here, between the ironic quotation and the melancholic translation, that Aljafari's citational cinematic practice finds its greatest political potential. For, on the one hand, the film refuses to give in to the seductive powers of melancholia (Aljafari was surprised that his Arab audience found refuge in the melancholic song), but it also rejects the modus operandi of the ironic mimetic gesture associated with most practices of (mis)quoting.[20] The incorporation of *Kazablan* in *Port of Memory* is thus *both* sincere and ironic. It is a critical nod that does not evacuate sincere identification. In this case the identification takes place between the unthinkable: colonizer and colonized, Israeli and Palestinian, Israeli actor and Arab audience, Hebrew and Arabic, Golan's macho popular cinema and Aljafari's poetics of marginality. It is also in this ambiguous and contentious space that Aljafari inserts the figure of the ghost: the screened image of his uncle Salim, who joins Kazablan but whose presence on the screen supplants the latter. While the shared walk begins with the original *Kazablan* movie soundtrack, it is slowly replaced with the sound of Salim's footsteps alone; and as the ghost materializes and becomes more visible on the screen, Kazablan drifts away until he is no longer visible.

What, then, are the politics of cultural memory advanced here? Clearly, this is no simple replacement of one narrative (of Kazablan, the Israeli film, the pain of the Mizrahi) with another (of Salim, the Palestinian projection, Palestinian loss). Rather, in projecting the latter onto and into the first, Aljafari creates a cinematic poetics of shadowing, layering, and cross-temporality that is far removed from the simple economy of replacement (one instead of the other). Relying on the evocative song of

Kazablan (in Hebrew), Aljafari generates an unexpected mode of intimacy that "allows the Hebrew language to serve as the narration for a Palestinian experience."[21] The image of his uncle walking through the ruins of Jaffa overlies that of Kazablan, but the voice of the latter, his lament song, remains to accompany Salim's steps. If this intimate possibility is momentary and fleeting (once Kazablan is gone, Salim walks down the narrow alleys alone), the slightly lingering sound of lament nevertheless connects the two figures, the two images, the two narratives of loss—a potentiality lost, and found, in the Israeli footage. This poetic moment at the center of the film is soon replaced by images of destruction. The camera lingers on a construction site: stones, metal, plastic containers, a mixture of trash and debris. As we continue to watch Salim, a sudden unexpected sight of a white jeep bursts onto the screen. From the minor key of lament we make a full 180-degree turn from the slow pace of Aljafari's camera to the manic images of American Hollywood production at its best. Yells in English are followed by sounds of explosion as the driver propels the jeep onto the sidewalk. Gunshots come from all directions, windows, and doors. It takes a minute or so for us to realize that we are, once again, in the space of yet another movie, and another cinematic fantasy—this time the popular Israeli-American production of *Delta Force* (the first, as sequels two and three followed). As the jeep drives off the screen, we are faced with the quiet images of the present: a construction site by the ocean, pamphlets calling upon the local Palestinian population to evacuate their houses, and in the background a bulldozer arm moving up and down as it rhythmically digs into the ground, reminding us that the slow business of destruction continues. Is it part of yet another film set? Another shooting? An ever-growing visual archive? Perhaps. But, even if so, this setting is prone to manipulation and change as Aljafari's third film installment demonstrates beyond doubt.

Re-collecting Images

Recollection, Aljafari's third film, completes the Jaffa Trilogy. Unlike the two earlier films, *Recollection* is entirely composed of footage taken from other films, that is, Israeli films that Aljafari collected, edited, and manipulated to create a visual portrayal of Jaffa without recording a single shot of the city himself. In other words, *Recollection* gathers images that the director found in over sixty Israeli films shot in Jaffa between the late 1960s and the mid-1990s. It is a film made in its entirety out of the Israeli cinematic archive and its images of Jaffa.

Although he worked with digital renditions, Aljafari's film has the visual quality of an 8 mm home movie. This seems fitting, since Aljafari made *Recollection* on his laptop at his desk in his apartment in Berlin. This intimate and solitary process of editing—citing, cutting, erasing, duplicating, framing, photographing, and arresting the original (Israeli) cinematic images— resulted in a layered imagery that is both homey and eerie, both close and remote. This uncanny bricolage[22] of images is made even more uncanny by the fact that the great majority of the Israeli films Aljafari builds upon are popular 1970s B-movies, known in Hebrew as Bourekas, and 1980s Israeli-American Hollywood war films.[23] The personal and sincere home movie Aljafari created at his desk comprises re-collected images and cinematic citations of tacky pop culture originals—a popular archive indeed.

By cutting, photographing, and digitally manipulating the Israeli cinematic images (some black and white, and others in color), Aljafari was able to bring back to life images of a city that no longer exists, and perhaps never existed: a city that was first destroyed, and then renovated and gentrified to a degree that it no longer resembled the Jaffa where he grew up. *Recollection*, then, is first and foremost about collecting images of a city that has become a memory. As such, the film is also about memory *as* collection. The re-collection of city images functions as a sort of resurrection practice, by which the archive is treated like a patient in the hospital: the wounds cleaned and bandages applied. Aljafari achieves a form of cinematic justice through the act of cutting and pasting.

In the many Israeli films from the 1960s to the 1990s that he watched, Aljafari found visual testimony of an architectural and spatial reality that is long gone: walls, cars, building, stores, towers, paths, and alleys; some of which he remembered from his childhood, and others that his older relatives, neighbors, and friends recognized. The cinematic colonial archive, like the musical Orientalist archive of the German ethnomusicologist Robert Lachmann discussed in the previous chapter, provides the otherwise missing traces of a past long altered. Looking closely at the images, to try to reconstruct the image of the city and rebuild its past on the screen, Aljafari began to identify some hidden figures behind the structures—a kid peeking from behind a side wall, likely curious about the film crew shooting in his neighborhood; another boy watching from behind a car; a woman looking out of the window; two men standing on the balcony; and even his own uncle, emerging from behind a wall and quickly crossing the street. Barely visible at first, these characters, shot from a distance and out of focus, are all located at the margins of the frame. They were likely

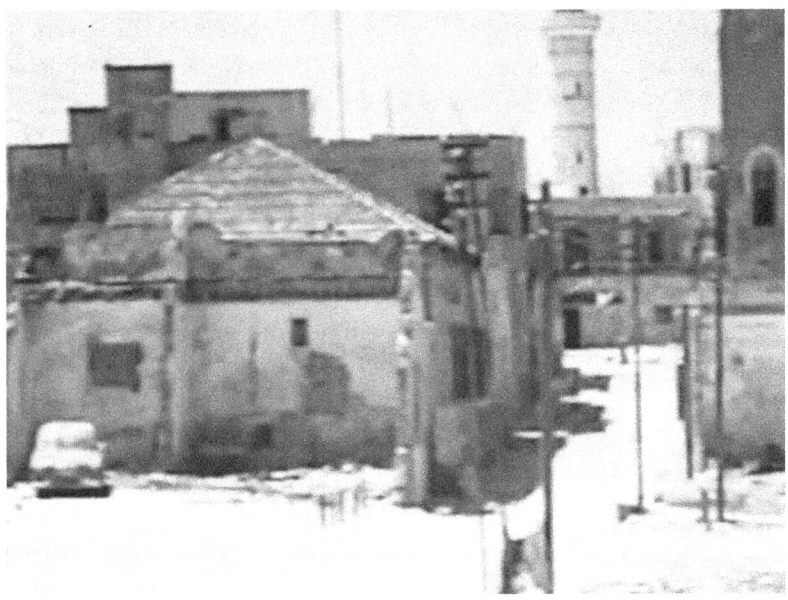

2.5 From *Recollection* (2015), by Kamal Aljafari. Courtesy of Kamal Aljafari.

unintentionally filmed. They appear *despite* what we may safely guess was the Israeli film crew's intention to do away with the Palestinian residents and make room for filming their Israeli actors. As Aljafari began to spot these barely visible characters on the margins, recognizing some of them as his own relatives and friends, he decided to digitally remove the Israeli actors who blocked the view. Gradually, more hidden images of residents of Jaffa, mostly Palestinian, but also some Iraqi Jews, began to emerge on the screen—ghostly figures that have always already been there and have never left—on the sides, behind walls, looking through curtains, gathering in the corners.

Recollection also brings together a marvel of architectural shots— the background and setting for the Israeli films—along with an original soundtrack recorded in part in Jaffa (sounds of the ocean, sounds of foot-steps), and in part in the director's apartment in Berlin (Aljafari recorded the sounds of his apartment at night so that he would be able to hear all the sounds he normally misses when he is asleep). Placing special microphones inside the interior walls, Aljafari sought to "listen to the sound of the walls." He repeated the act with the sea, placing microphones under water.[24] At times, the filmed images are arrested, and a photographic image, a still photograph taken from one of the films, is projected onto the screen: "I wanted to dig into the films by emphasizing the materiality of the photographs."[25] Digging into the films, as it were, Aljafari lingers on tiles, blocks, walls, creating in turn a unique slowed-down temporality of the urban space: "The image and sound of a place after a catastrophe."[26] Filmed to resemble a dream, with sudden cuts and multiple image repetitions (certain images repeat throughout the film: a blue car, a man crossing the street, bulldozers by the ocean), *Recollection* unfolds like flashbacks of stubborn images that refuse to let go: Is this a fantasy of a time yet to come? Or a recurring nightmare?

This dream-like reality opens with the familiar stocky figure of David Ben Gurion, who is walking through an orchard before he suddenly disappears. We are then introduced to a colorful group of Israeli actors from the musical *Kazablan* before they disappear as well. The rest of the film no longer documents this seemingly magical disappearance of Israeli figures. Rather, it simply renders visible the Palestinian characters found in the margins of the frame after their removal—figures Aljafari found, cut from, and pasted into the reworked Israeli cinematic archive. Relying on digital technology, but imitating the mechanics of photography, Aljafari mined the entire collage of images collected from Israeli films, eliminating all the Israeli actors, and then cut and pasted some of the Palestinian characters to create, toward the end of the film, a new and redeeming image of gathering: "These phantoms are [now] walking together, hand in hand singing. It is a song where they are declaring themselves. They decide to walk and sing and talk to the world. It's a final march where these ghosts are no longer ghosts."[27]

In some ways, then, Aljafari developed, expanded, and enriched his practice of cinematic montage from *Port of Memory* to create *Recollection*. But, the difference between the two films is also profound. To begin with, *Port of Memory* only includes two short scenes from Israeli films, into which the director inserts Palestinian characters he himself filmed, creating a double-layered cinematic image. In *Recollection*, the Israeli cinematic archive provides the only source for all the images. Furthermore, as I have mentioned above, instead of inserting Palestinian characters into the Israeli frame (*Port of Memory*), *Recollection* finds and exposes Palestinian characters who are *already* present in the original Israeli films. He renders them visible by removing the Israeli characters that otherwise block them from view. The violation of the archive then (the erasure of the film characters) is one that exposes the violence inscribed in the creation of the original

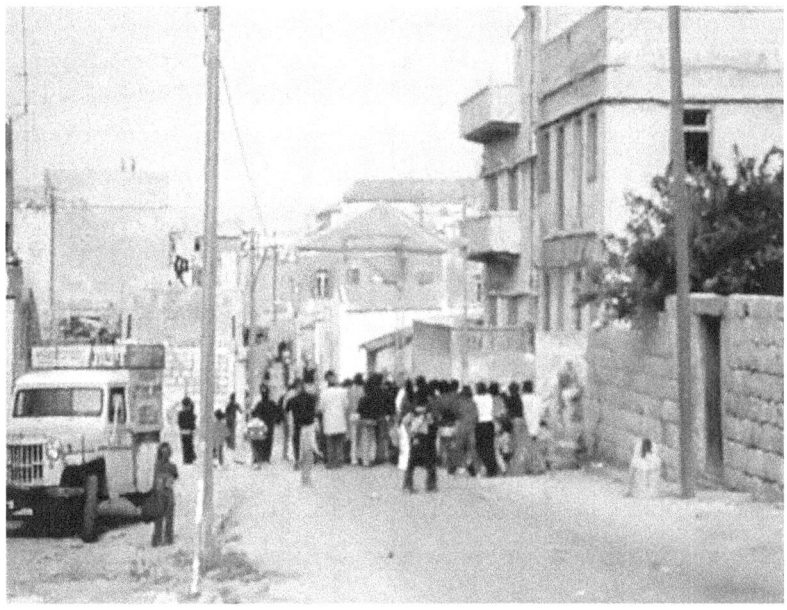

2.6 From *Recollection* (2015), by Kamal Aljafari. Courtesy of Kamal Aljafari.

archive: the conditions of documentation that enabled the creation of the body of these Israeli films to begin with. If the Israeli films erased or hid the Palestinian presence behind Israeli actors, Aljafari simply removes these actors to reveal the hidden layers of the image.

Recollection highlights the bitter irony in the colonial fantasy that seeks to master the visual field. While desiring to do away with the colonized inhabitants, to render them invisible and eliminate their history, colonial modes of representation nevertheless often unwittingly document the colonized, thus including them—even if only as the "excluded"—within the colonial archive. In the case of Israel, this is particularly poignant. As noted by Saree Makdisi, despite Israel's ongoing and persistent attempts to cover up, remove, hide, and eliminate "anything Palestinian," the "stubbornly persistent Palestinian presence" nevertheless manages to invade almost every aspect of everyday Israeli life.[28] In *Recollection*, the persistent presence of the native stands at the heart of the investigation of the conditions of visibility and invisibility in Jaffa. The film reconstructs a visual documentation of a long-gone reality through, and in reliance on, Israeli films. According to the director, over 80 percent of the images capture a city that is today eliminated or exists only in ruins—as destroyed buildings, structures, parks, homes, and walls. Un-ghosting the ghosts by making their presence in the colonial cinematic archive visible, *Recollection* is the most optimistic of the trilogy films. Its narrative of redemption is certainly more victorious than that of *The Roof* or *Port of Memory*, both of which conclude on a much more melancholic note. The director's use of citations progresses across the three films: from *The Roof*, which is primarily filmed by the director and included only a few scenes that introduce other images (primarily TV images viewed by Aljafari's family), to *Port of Memory*, in which the director edits a few scenes from Israeli films into his own, to *Recollection*, which is entirely a work of editing and manipulating Israeli footage. In other words, the redemption staged by Aljafari is one not of creating a new reality or new images, but of putting back together what was always already there in the colonial archive: finding the Palestinians, the memories, the walls, the buildings, and the city that may have appeared lost, but can be found in the Israeli footage.

The ominous and powerful gathering of Palestinians toward the end of the film—this mass of figures, characters, and bodies lost, unseen, and invisible under the colonizers' gaze—is re-collected into a new image. It exposes the failure of the colonial fantasy to do away with the colonized, who not only continue to invade the cinematic frame but also move further from its margins to its center. The move from documenting and filming (*The Roof*) to hybridizing and mixing (*Port of Memory*), and then to collaging, editing, cutting, erasing, and reframing (*Recollection*), is not a simple methodological or technical change, but one that has great political and poetic implication. In advancing a vision of Palestinian redemption as a process of un-erasing and re-inserting, Aljafari adopts a practice of recycling (Israeli) film footage from within the colonial archive, that very apparatus of erasure, to re-generate the re-appearance of his Palestinian character through and on top of the recycled film material. This act of cutting, pasting, and editing should not be confused with a simple replacement of the archive, given that the characters are in fact *already* found in the original footage. It is therefore more of an act of remembering and re-centering the margins than an act of archival imagination. The image of redemption and gathering does not take place in a nostalgic past, clean of the violation of colonialism, occupation, erasure. Nor does it take place in a mystical future projected into a temporal and spatial frame that is pure and clean of signs of the colonizers. On the contrary, the Palestinian crowd gathers *within the Israeli film frame*. Through this footage, against its background, and in relation to its spatial configuration, this image of regathering takes place not as a simple return or a forgetful departure, but as a creation of a new collective emerging out of conditions of colonial erasure and violence. Inserted back into the Israeli footage—the very archive that sought to ensure the erasure of Palestinians—the final image of this collective gathering functions as a reminder that every archive has its secrets and its ghosts. And while every archive exposes and hides, aiming to convince us that what we see/find/read is "all there is," the archive is always haunted, and the day may always come when its ghosts decide to gather and make their appearance no longer possible to deny or hide.

THREE

"Suspended between Past and Future"

LARISSA SANSOUR'S SCI-FI ARCHAEOLOGICAL ARCHIVE IN THE PAST-FUTURE TENSE

All archaeology ends in archives. | **AARHUS UNIVERSITY**, "Archive Archaeology: Archiving and Collecting the Past"

The significance of Palestine since prehistoric times in the development of civilization cannot be overestimated. . . . The maintenance of conditions under which [archaeology] can be pursued [here] is a genuine concern of civilization. | **NADIA ABU EL-HAJ**, *Facts on the Ground: Archaeology Practice and Territorial Self-Fashioning in Israeli Society*

Chapters 1 and 2 dealt with a poetics of archival mimicry and citationality. Raising questions about ownership and mastery over the archive, both chapters stressed the potentiality of activating and manipulating the Orientalist and colonial archives to advance a radically different vision of the future, from which Palestine may become. This chapter and the following one focus on a specific archive and specific modality for thinking about archives: namely, archaeology. Both chapters suggest a close relationship between the archive (as an idea, a figure, a concept) and archaeology, while further approaching archaeology as a significant, indeed fundamental national archive.

....

Archaeology, like anthropology, history, and other social sciences, is a modern discipline. That is to say, it has only recently become a standalone discipline and gained its status as "a science." Established in the late eighteenth century, archaeology's scientific status grew substantially throughout the nineteenth century, with the development of indexing methods (excavation, recording, and cataloging) that complemented the evolutionary theories of the times.[1] Archaeology peaked to become the ultimate archive of the nation and of the human: the method and means through which modernity has framed its relation to past civilizations, to antiquity, and to itself in terms of cultural heritage, national origins, and even racial DNA.[2] "This has become the archaeologist's grandiose task," C. W. Ceram writes: "To make dried-up wellsprings bubble forth again, to make the forgotten known again, the dead alive, and to cause to flow once more that historic stream in which we are all encompassed."[3]

Presented as excavation, unearthing, categorizing, and cataloging, the findings of archaeology "are presumed to embody cultural roots."[4] To *embody* rather than re-present. Archaeology claims to disclose *reality*, instead of re-present or re-create the past, which would be the work of, for example, a historical novel. Considered as enabling a direct encounter with, and a material link to, the long-lost past, archaeology finds its importance there. It understands the present and future in relation to a lost (now found) past that justifies and explains certain national, ethnic, or racial affiliations *historically* and in terms of "roots," "sources," and "heritage." As a discipline and a method, archaeology has created some of modernity's most important and influential archives. Indeed, archaeological archives are unlike any other archives in the sense that they claim to "expose" findings—to unveil a certain material reality, which is the reappearance of the past in the present and the past given back to the present: "The secrets of the past lay buried beneath the surface of the present, waiting for him [*sic*] who should be able to pluck them from their hiding place and give them back to the world."[5]

Archaeological findings pierce the more or less coherent temporality by reimplanting the past within the present as a direct corporeal experience with antiquity. In this sense, archaeological ruins are not like written texts or images collected in an archive. Archaeology fancies itself the archive of all archives, as ruins promise immediate contact with the past. It generates a present pregnant with the past, collapsing the temporal gap between the archival material (the ruins) and the present encounter.[6] Archaeology, then, produces a magical archive, a nonarchive that is more importantly an "epistemological strategy" and "a mode of knowing."[7]

Psychoanalysis, too, is a modern science, an epistemological strategy, and a mode of knowing that magically locates radically new ways of healing the psyche. Like archaeology, it promises to expose the past long buried out of sight and finds answers that explain (and heal) present suffering and enigmas. More specifically, it is a modern science that borrows the metaphoric language of archaeology to talk about the inner psyche of both the individual and the collective ("civilization"), and to analyze them in terms of layers of experience and memories. The most painful experiences are said to be repressed (buried away) in the unconscious, and in need of exposure, revelation, and reinscription into the present to ensure healing: "Pulling them from their hiding space" and "giving them back to the world."[8] Freud notoriously made an explicit analogy between psychoanalysis and archaeology: "[The analyst's] work of construction, or, if it is preferred, of reconstruction, resembles to a great extent an archaeologist's excavation of some dwelling-place that has been destroyed and buried or of some ancient edifice. The two processes are in fact identical, except that the analyst works under better conditions and has more material at his [sic] command to assist him."[9]

To Freud, psychoanalysis, like archaeology, was, to use Joanna Montgomery Byles's words, "A heroic investigation of legendary reality." Both sciences "uncover a lost reality: ancient worlds that have become legendary with time," and both also "deal with the unexpected presence and power of the past," giving us "access to ourselves through our past cultural and personal histories." Similarly, both sciences use the concepts of "surface and depth, manifest and latent, adult and infantile, civilized and uncivilized, historic and prehistoric, fact and fantasy."[10]

Shared by both archaeology and psychoanalysis, then, is the commitment to collect information from/about the past—to "dig out" parts of the past that are otherwise in danger of escaping memory (collective and personal) and hence of disappearing altogether. The archaeologist looks for "proof" of past existing civilizations, while the psychoanalyst, at least as Freud imagined her, looks for ways into the invisible and suppressed layers of the psychic, where memories are hidden and holding within them one's most important narratives: one's repressed forgotten past.[11]

The analogy between psychoanalysis and archaeology, advanced by "the father of psychoanalysis," who was also a well-known avid lover of antiquity and "antique things," was further meant to reassure skeptics that psychoanalysis was a science, modeled on a methodology of excavation. The analyst was an archaeologist of the mind, who digs, finds, exposes, and reveals repressed memories—not one who invents or creates fantasy.[12]

I bring up this old bond, this mirroring relationship between archaeology and psychoanalysis, as a pretext for my discussion of Larissa Sansour's *In the Future They Ate from the Finest Porcelain* (2016, 29 min.), because the film advances two competing narratives, which are also two competing logics: the first, promoted by the narrator, is that of the archaeologist, and the second is promoted by her therapist, that of the psychoanalyst. These two narratives at times merge together, but for the most part offer different explanations, follow a different temporality, and promote a radically different mode of "archival repair."

Narrative Terrorist on the Sofa and in the Field

In the Future is cowritten and codirected by Sansour and Søren Lind.[13] This twenty-nine-minute film is a visual feast not only for lovers of the postcolonial alternative sci-fi genre,[14] but also for fans of uncanny dystopic aesthetics. The film brings together nineteenth-century Orientalist depictions of "biblical scenes" (vast empty desert, men in white robes, and gloom and doom images of a looming judgment day and apocalypse),[15] with more familiar sci-fi imagery (spaceships, metal, weaponry, bombs). As such, *In the Future* is a mesmerizing sci-fi dystopia presenting biblical imagery and futuristic sci-fi iconography in an essay-film format and breathtaking cinematic experience. The hypnotic quality of the images is coupled with a poetic text (voiceover) that takes the form of a dialogue: an exchange between a psychoanalyst and her patient delivered in elegiac and coded language, like the words of a secret, mystical poem.

Some of the imagery clearly correlates to the spoken text, but for the most part it does not. This double mode of expression—one textual, the other visual—is to a great degree responsible for the film's enigmatic, even bewildering nature.[16] It is also the format by which Sansour positions two narratives and two worldviews together and against each other: a psychoanalytic narrative that focuses on the narrator's personal trauma and is advanced through terminology borrowed from a therapeutic setting (memory, dreams,

pain, loss, trauma, and "working through"), and a narrative of archaeological plotting, advanced by the narrator who refuses to engage in a therapeutic exchange with her analyst, and instead talks about her guerilla plans to
embark on a massive burial of materials intended as future archaeological
findings.

....

The screen is dark. Light comes in slowly, gradually revealing eight spaceships, four stationed on each of two opposite sides. The flying machines
look like huge bugs with angry orange eyes. One by one these futuristic
creatures leave the ground and begin to float toward us. The opening
sequence of *In the Future* is alluring. The sci-fi imagery is coupled with a
metallic sound that draws us into an unknown reality that is nevertheless
based on a familiar sci-fi dystopic visual grammar: grayish sky, heavy metal
machinery, the absence of living beings.

The frame remains gray for a short while before a single figure appears.
She is barely visible, but as soon as she begins to move toward us, we recognize a slim silhouette. Her face remains invisible for a while, hidden behind
a large cape. We will soon realize that she is a self-identified "narrative-
terrorist." After a few more seconds of silence, the voiceover begins. We
awaken from a mesmerizing visual feast, and from this moment on, the visual and the audio (the image and the text) compete for our attention.

"Sometimes I dream of porcelain falling from the sky, like ceramic rain. At
first it's only a few pieces, falling slowly like autumn leaves. I am in it, silently
enjoying it. But then the volume increases; it's a porcelain monsoon, like a
biblical plague."

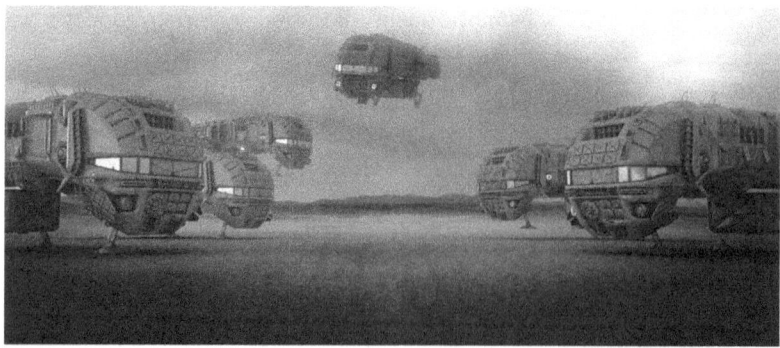

3.1 From *In the Future They Ate from the Finest Porcelain* (2016), by Larissa Sansour.
Courtesy of Larissa Sansour.

This voice, a female voice, is soft and gentle. The narrator speaks slowly in Arabic while her words are translated into English on the screen.[17] She is addressing another woman, asking her to help her understand this recurring dream. As the conversation between the two women progresses, we realize that we are eavesdropping on a therapy session—a conversation in which the analyst will try, and fail, to bring the "narrative terrorist" to discuss the meaning of her recurrent dream in relation to her personal trauma: the death of her young sister, who was mistakenly shot. The narrator has an altogether different interpretation, one which the analyst has no desire to engage *but* as a pretext or a stand-in for unrecognized loss and traumatic denial. "What do you think it means?" the narrator asks about the images in her dreams: the porcelain plates raining over her. The analyst loses patience. She wants to go back to discuss the death of the young girl, the sister, her patient's trauma. "I don't think it means anything. It's just an image," the analyst responds. The irony of this answer is obvious. After all, it is uttered in a context in which a great number of images of porcelain plates are displayed scattered on the ground, falling from the sky, hitting the narrator. Are we, as viewers, really supposed to believe that these images "mean nothing"? That they are "just images"?

While the dream is left impenetrable, the analyst tries to bring her patient to talk about her dead sister—the source of her trauma and loss. On the screen, meanwhile, the imagery changes drastically from the opening sequences of the spaceships. The new images are still grayish and uncanny, but they now include picturesque images of a vast desert with an almost hand-drawn quality to them. They are overlaid with a collage of old black and white (or rather sepia) photographs of various people. There is something overtly naïve about the setting, which makes the frame look like a school poster presentation. An ensemble of nineteenth-century Orientalist photographs float in front of the desert as if glued to the surface. At the center of the screen are two young girls (perhaps the narrator and her dead sister?). They are dressed in long heavy fabric dresses and head coverings standing with their eyes shut. It is hard to tell if this is a photo, a painting, a digital reproduction, or a video clip of a performance. On the right side of the frame, two older bearded men are seated, also dressed in the type of traditional oriental garments seen in nineteenth-century European paintings of the Orient. On the left, three other figures are dressed in European travel or exploration outfits: one in khaki shorts and shirts, the other two in raincoats and dress suits. They seem to belong to a different era, but they certainly do not seem to share the temporal frame with the old bearded

men. Why are these images brought together in this frame?[18] Suddenly, the
girls' eyes open and the figures begin to breathe. The accumulating tension
in this slow-moving frame relies on a delicate mix of animation and lifeless-
ness, stillness and mobility, object and human: the pairings Freud initially
associated with the uncanny.[19]

At this point, both the visual and the audio are enigmatic and compete
over our attention, calling back to a rivalry between two epistemic modes
of organizing knowledge and temporality: the archaeological and the psychoanalytic. While the therapist encourages the self-proclaimed narrative-
terrorist (her patient) to talk about the past and her dead sister ("the reason
for us having this conversation"), the narrator insists on talking about archaeology and its ability to generate an alternative future. The "narrative
terrorist," then, refuses to become the patient of psychoanalysis; instead,
she fashions herself as an archaeologist.

For the great majority of the film, this pull between the psychoanalyst and the terrorist-archaeologist—who is above all, as we shall see, an
archivist—continues. The analyst tries to pull her patient back to the present
therapy session ("You are no longer in the desert do you remember? You were
talking about being buried, [you are] buried in your own fiction"), while the
narrative-terrorist insists on the power of fiction, especially the fiction of
archaeology, to move her forward rather than backward, drawing on a logic
quite different from that of "working through."[20]

Both archaeology and psychoanalysis are presented in *In the Future* as
a means of coping with loss and trauma by means of "digging." But, if the
latter centers on digging with the hope of recovering a repressed trauma
to work through this loss and free the present; the first, as advanced by
the narrator, seeks to undo the temporal relationship between past, present, and future by simultaneously digging and burying. The digging in this
case is less about recovery and more about imagination and re-creation.
As this narrative rivalry continues between therapist and patient, psychoanalyst and archaeologist, the screen continues to unfold images mostly
comprising filmed archival photographs that Sansour collected from
various sources (the Library of Congress, the United Nations Relief and
Works Agency for Palestine Refugees, and several private Palestinian collections).[21] Commenting on her use of archival material, Sansour notes: "I
am intrigued by how our gaze intervenes in the meaning of archives. It was
important for me to tap into this idea of *archival intervention* by turning still
archival imagery into live motion [film]."[22]

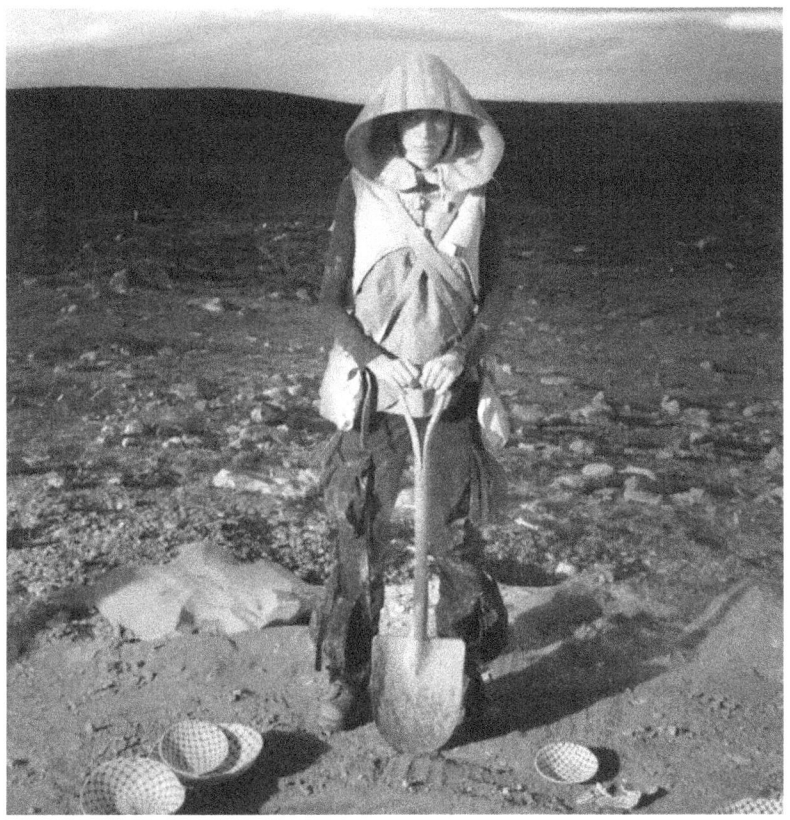

3.2 From *In the Future They Ate from the Finest Porcelain* (2016), by Larissa Sansour. Courtesy of Larissa Sansour.

The visual impact of such "archival interventions" is both stunning and uncanny—a perfect combination for a dystopic outlook: a vast desert covered with pieces of broken porcelain, a futuristic city looming in the distance, elderly men with long beards and white robes sitting on the ground, mid-century-looking (British?) soldiers, women in long traditional dresses, and futuristic space travel vessels all make for a less familiar archive of *either* Palestinian history *or* sci-fi cinema, instead offering a dazzling, enigmatic, uncanny, and seductive cinematic archival intervention.

There is also an obvious visual anachronism to the film, which imprints "the archive" (as a concept, an idea, and "an aura") on every frame.[23] The deliberate anachronism, coupled with the futuristic aesthetics of sci-fi, is responsible for the sense of temporal and spatial disorientation the film generates. Whereas some of Sansour's earlier works, particularly *Nation Estate* (2012, 9 min.), engage directly with familiar visual icons of Palestinian national symbols and investigate the political power of nostalgia, *In the Future* offers few if any such iconic references and turns away from nostalgia in favor of a dystopian outlook. At the same time, the temporality captured by the film is not simply "futuristic." More accurately, it is a highly confusing temporality in which the past gains its meaning and significance *only* in the future, and only in between text and image: between the times in the film where text and image overlap, and the times where their coexistence marks a schism. The past also gains meaning between the efforts of the psychoanalyst to redirect her patient to the "origin" (to the trauma) and those of the "narrative terrorist," who is more interested in re-creating a past rather than in coming to terms with it.

"We are depositing facts in the ground for future archaeologists to excavate," our narrator announces. When future archaeologists find these pieces, she continues, it will support "decades' claims to the land, de facto creating a nation." At this point, the psychoanalytic frame that the therapist tries to enforce loses its hold. The narrative-terrorist engages in an ever more extravagant plan for building a nation, making grand declarations about archaeology, fiction, digging, and burying.

....

How does one read a film that both begs for interpretation (the setting of the narrative is a psychoanalytic session after all!) and yet refuses the very mode of interpretation it hosts, since the narrator denies the therapist

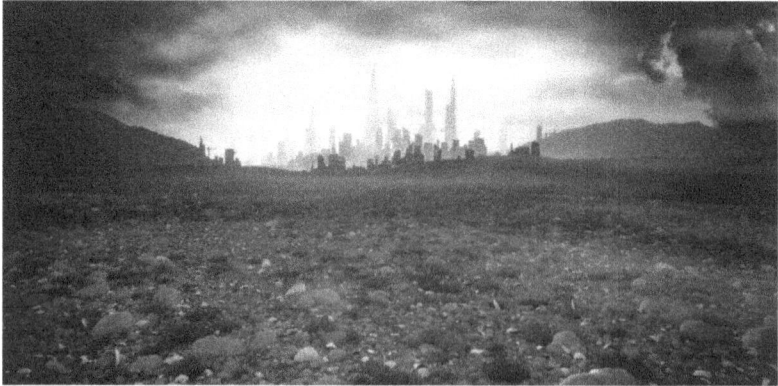

3.3 From *In the Future They Ate from the Finest Porcelain* (2016), by Larissa Sansour. Courtesy of Larissa Sansour.

access to her inner psyche, advancing instead a narrative and a mode of action that in psychoanalytic terms would be called "resistance to analysis"? Unlike Sansour's earlier films, *In the Future* offers few overtly recognizable political, historical, or geographical demarcations. Although we see a desert and recognize the nineteenth-century Orientalist framework of most of the integrated archival photographic imagery, none of these images is fully identifiable. Familiarity with the iconography of modern Palestine and the history of political Zionism is surely helpful in deciphering some of the visual cues, but one must be careful when following the cues of the narrative-terrorist not to fully surrender to the allure of interpretation. After all, while Palestine, modern Palestinian history, and its encounter with Zionism are unquestionably central, one must recall that "Palestine" as a figure, a place, a memory, history, a political entity, or even a metaphor is present in the film *only* as absence, *only* as "already lost" or not yet found. That is to say, if it "appears" on the screen, it appears *only* as a radical disappearance: without a trace of archaeological evidence. This is a disappearance so total that it can only be redeemed by means of fictive intervention, which itself amounts to the creation of an otherwise missing archive: the burial of objects in the ground, to be found (as an archaeological past) in the future. This is a solution the psychoanalyst rejects, doubting it can have any impact on (political) reality; she half mocks her dreamy patient, "You are suggesting that fiction has a constitutive effect on history and political reality?" But the narrator, the terrorist, considers this fiction as the only way to create a future out of nothing: "Archaeology is epistemology . . . it not only creates facts; it generates identification. . . . They will claim the land on our behalf." The narrator, in other words, uses the logic of archaeology to build an archive. *In the Future They Ate from the Finest Porcelain*—what might at first appear in the title as a grammatical mistake comes to be understood as a future discovered past. "They" will become known through the discovery of their archaeological traces, when "in hundreds of years someone will dig out the porcelain."

To "read" Sansour's film, which refuses to be fully read, we are better off letting go of the psychoanalytic attempt to trace the narrative back to an original site/time of trauma. Sansour's film more or less directs us to do so. It invites us into a therapeutic setting, where we become witnesses of a therapy session only to observe the psychoanalyst's failure to draw her patient in. The outcome of this rejection on the part of the "narrative terrorist" might be a state of a total mental breakdown, as the therapist seems to think. "Who are these people you hope would be discovered in the future?"

she asks, but the narrator has a confident answer, even if it remains obscure to analysis: "They will exist [and] they are us and we are them!"

In an interview published after the release of the film, Sansour addressed the question of adopting fiction versus reality and fabulation versus historical facts. "My film" she says, "revolves around the very notion of the post-factual."[24] Sansour engages this notion of the "post-factual," which for many of us has become a familiar everyday hazard, living under conditions of "fake news" and experiencing the inability to produce, circulate, or believe "facts." Sansour's narrator, however, decides to transform this hazard into an empowering instrument. She has not invented the postfactual condition, but given that she is already subjected to it—as she explains, "Our life is already determined by a fiction imposed upon us"—she decides to borrow and manipulate the tactic.

Archaeology is inevitably anachronistic and circular. Its findings are identified and historicized from the vantage of the present to reflect back the stories the present already knows about the past, but are proclaimed to have originated in the past. The past thus projects into the present the evidence of "findings" that prove those stories right. Since the nineteenth century, archaeology has functioned as an important nation-building tool, with modern nations worldwide claiming connections to ancient roots, heritage, and land.[25] In Israel, perhaps more so than anywhere else, the popularity of archaeology and its centrality to the project of nation-building has made it a full-fledged "national hobby."[26] Political Zionism's investment in archaeology serves to make vast-reaching claims about the historical rights of Jews (seen as modern Israelites) to the land of Palestine and their role as indigenous natives, rather than colonial-settlers, who have returned to their long-lost land. Archaeology as a national hobby serves to bring together an earlier (primarily Christian) *theological* practice of excavation in the holy land, which was itself motivated by, and in the service of, a narrative of origins and (Christian) redemption—the revival of biblical times and the projected future return of the Jews to the holy land.[27] The more recent practice of "Jewish digging" in the service of Jewish *national* revival also takes the form of return: to history, to the land, and to a national existence.[28]

The narrative-terrorist, then, did not invent the idea of building a future society based on archaeological findings that prove the long-lost civilization has returned to its rightful nation. As she mentions: "This fiction is already imposed on us." What to the psychoanalyst seems a fictional sublimation and discredited escapist narrative fleeing the pain of trauma, is to the narrator an already existing historical-political precedence, indeed quite a successful one, which she is eager to mimic.

Masquerading as a science of discovery, archaeology is deployed to generate (national) narratives of origins, belonging, and rights. "Since our lives are already determined by a fiction imposed on us," the narrator comments, "it is possible [for us] to stage a resistance through a counter-narrative: an alternative fiction. You just replace one myth with another." The remaining portion of the film alternates between this utopic vision, including the narrator's fantasy of victory ("replace one myth with another"), and the dystopic conditions that render it impossible. "Isn't what you are envisioning just a polemic utopia?" the psychoanalyst intervenes. "It is too late for that," the narrator answers, "this place was always a barely functioning dystopia."

As observed by Nadia Abu El-Haj, Israeli archaeology is not just about looking for evidence of an ancient Jewish past in Palestine; it is about determining the very criteria of what is considered an authentic historical account. The archaeological record is thus advanced as holding "remnants of nations and ethnic groups," and what is found is already classified as evidence for "distinctly demarcated cultures that could be identified and plotted across the landscape."[29] Above all, then, the role of archaeology in early twentieth-century Palestine was to make "Palestine" disappear: "By the turn of the twentieth century, Palestine no longer existed 'on the fringe or beneath the surface of [European] scientific collective consciousness.' It had 'coalesced into' (Daston 2000: 6) a specific, historic domain of scientific inquiry, one that was to have political consequences that progressively exceeded the Palestine Exploration Fund's initial religio-cultural and imperial convictions and their immediate archaeological and scientific goals."[30]

The "ongoing work of archaeology [in Israel] was constitutive of the territorial self-fashioning of Jewish nativeness out of which a settler colonial community emerged as a national, original and native one," El-Haj argues. To fight this narrative of indigeneity, backed by biblical archaeology, our narrator, the self-identified terrorist, must become an archivist of the most effective kind: planting evidence for archaeologists of the future to "dig out the past."

Sansour's use of an archaeological temporality—through which the past is found in the future that projects a dystopic utopia—not only allows her to escape the visual register of the settler colonial present and project an image of the future; it also allows her to highlight the circumstances in the present that make contemplating such a future difficult if not impossible. The "no place"/"good place" (the double meaning of utopia)[31] in Sansour's film provides an uncanny return of the repressed, a projection of the past into the future mediated and weighed down by the impact of continual trauma: "They are us and we are them." Even more significantly, the Zionist utopia, indirectly alluded to by the narrator's speech about the power of archaeology in cultivating national sentiments, is modeled on science fiction—the very genre In the Future adopts. The very distinction, then, between fiction and history, and between science fiction and politics, is dissolved as the film simultaneously creates and negates the possibility of an archaeological archive of/for the future.

In revisiting archaeology as a fantastic science and a science of fiction, Sansour further destabilizes any clear distinction between utopia and dystopia. Hence, archaeology functions in the film at once as a model for the narrative-terrorist to imitate ("replacing one myth with another") and as a recipe for failure. If, as Frederic Jameson convincingly argues, "the condition for utopia is exclusion,"[32] Sansour's dystopia is best understood as an expression of a forceful return of the excluded—a return that comes after the fact and breaks apart the utopia/dystopia dichotomy. This return of the excluded (from the utopian vision) brings the logic of nationalist utopia (Zionism) to its natural and unavoidable dystopian end—not simply by replacing one myth with another, but by highlighting the fictionality of both.

The film closes with a visual citation: a long table that seats an eclectic crowd including a soldier, perhaps Ottoman or even British; a couple of young women in long dresses; one man in a formal suit; a nun; a couple of young girls in school uniforms; and the narrative-terrorist-archivist seated in the center and wearing her expedition outfit. The table is covered with plenty of porcelain plates, wine glasses, and food. The iconography of "The Last Supper" is unmistakable, and there are many biblical references: the shroud of Turin, the plague, frogs falling from the sky. But questions remain: Does this iconic staged image refer to the lost civilization that will be found in the future? Is this a staged memory of a fictional past? Part of the narrator's dream? Are we looking at the people who ate from porcelain plates? Or is this an image of the future, capturing the postdiscovery moment of the hidden porcelain plates, following the successful plot of the narrative-terrorist-archivist? Is it an image of hope in the biblical sense—of resurrection? Or is it an apocalyptic image, with biblical Christian references to the end of the world and total apocalypse?

Augmented by Iraqi electronic musician Aida Nadeem's haunting soundtrack, the film leaves these interpretive possibilities open. It ends with the voice of the narrator, repeating the same words with which the film begins. Recalling her dream, she describes "a porcelain monsoon drop-ping over her like a biblical plague." What do we make of this dream, these words, and the image of the dining table?

It is tempting to map these closing words and images onto the present reality, but Sansour's film refuses to provide such closure. Indeed, it is only by maintaining the tension between (our) desire to read the film referen-tially, mapping the images and the narrative back onto a preexisting and familiar political setting, and the film's resistance to allow for such a coherent reading that we can arrive at the intricacy of the political intervention. This intervention is itself modeled on various degrees of suspension, including the inability to fully distinguish utopia from dystopia, fantasy from his-tory, and past from future. The narrator resists her analyst's attempts to decipher her behavior and render it a legible narrative of loss and trauma. In a parallel way, the film at once flirts with and resists the possibility of generating a coherent narrative of resistance.

In the Future's postfactual narrative and indecisiveness advances a post-national engagement with the question of Palestine, including an overt mockery of archaeology as a national archive. The film gives shape and form to the "hopeless hope" of the excluded—those excluded from the win-ning national (Zionist) utopian project, itself modeled on and advanced through ongoing archaeological efforts to turn the landscape of Palestine into the most cherished Jewish national archive. Given that utopia, by na-ture, always excludes,[33] *In the Future* mobilizes distinctive *dystopic utopian* aesthetics to convey something more: to articulate the possibility of a dif-ferent kind of hope. This nonutopian, nonnationalist, nonnostalgic hope may seem like nothing more than "science fiction," but it is just as reason-able and plausible as the fictive national utopians we accept as our political reality.

Writing about the use of sci-fi in African American literature, art, and pop culture in his groundbreaking essay from 1993, "Black to the Future," Mark Dery notes that the future becomes an opportunity through which African Americans can assert themselves artistically. These artists may have been robbed of their past and present, but they nevertheless "intend to stake their claim in the future."[34] More recent scholarship on African American speculative literature highlights the radical political potential of black feminist sci-fi writers such as Octavia Butler and Phyllis Alesia Perry. Sami Schalk suggests that for marginalized people, sci-fi can mean imagining a future without racial, gender, and sexual oppression. But this imagination is not always utopian. More often it advances what Justin Louis Mann has called a "pessimistic futurism," which maintains a pessimistic view of the present while leaving room to imagine a radically different future.[35] In a similar way, *In the Future*'s investment in fiction and the future offers ways to move beyond the present and the past, nostalgia, oppression, and the state, so as to enable a vision of a radically different future.

In the Future introduces a temporal dimension to the present impossibility of Palestine (as a nation-state at least) and the lack of archival "evidence" to its past existence. It introduces the future as the time of Palestine, the time of imagining Palestine, the time of becoming, which is shamelessly fictive: a counter utopia, which is not simply a dystopia. The future Sansour envisions takes us into an uncertain terrain where the question of Palestine is posed in a futuristic posthistorical and postnational time of becoming.[36] This futuristic Palestine in-becoming is a montage of excessive images that both find and lose "Palestine" as they replace the monopoly and authority of the historical and archaeological archive with a more self-critical act of digging and burying; burying and digging. And perhaps this too is part of the film's reflections on the working of the archive, which as Derrida reminds us, "buries just as much as it digs up."[37] The future that emerges out of this act of digging and burying, of imagination and negation, is the film's point of departure, and its embrace of the time of "not-yet-ness."[38]

This future not-yet-ness time of becoming depends on the ability to cultivate a dystopian-utopian imagination unbound to the historical archive or archaeological myths about origins and nativity. Confronting these myths, Sansour avoids presenting possible political solutions or desirable outcomes. Rather, by liberating Palestine from common debates over ownership and from its prosaic status as a political entity and geographic territory, she allows it to be imagined and reimagined; allows it to become. This is certainly a futuristic project, but not a messianic or utopic one. Nor should this dystopic not-yet-ness imagination be conflated with despair. Rather, it is a critical rethinking of political hope in a time of hopelessness and stagnation.

FOUR

"Face to Face with the Ancestors of Civilization"

RUANNE ABOU-RAHME AND BASEL ABBAS'S ARCHIVE OF THE COPY

The [Palestinian] villages that no longer exist were pushed out of the public sphere. They carry new names of Hebrew settlements (*yeshuvim ivri'im*). But these villages left some traces in these new settlements . . . a stone fence, bricks of ruined houses.
| AZMI BISHARA, "Between Place and Space"

The destroyed site of a Palestinian village becomes the place from which to think about the incomplete nature of the colonial project . . . it activates a potentiality to become unbound from colonial time. | "Ruanne Abou-Rahme and Basel Abbas in Conversation with Fawz Kabra"

Revisiting many of the inquiries followed in the previous chapters—the incomplete nature of the colonial project, the ability to manipulate the colonial archive, the view of the present as an archive for the future, and the impetus to imagine a radically different future—this chapter continues exploring the interplay between archaeology and national archives, by, among other

things, thinking through the nature of the archive and its political potentiality in digital times.

Ruins

Between 2016 and 2019, Palestinian artists and collaborators Ruanne
Abou-Rahme and Basel Abbas created their latest work, *And Yet My Mask
Is Powerful*. Like most of their earlier works, *And Yet My Mask* is a complex,
multilayered, and elastic installation that involves fieldwork, activism, documentation, and exhibition, moving in and out of the gallery space. The
project began in 2016 when the two artists led several tours with Palestinian youth to the ruins of some of the over four hundred Palestinian villages
within Israel uprooted and ruined during the Nakba (1948). The impetus
behind these tours was not only to locate and mark these hard-to-find and
often well-hidden sites of Palestinian ruins, but also to further render them
as part of a living archive of the present. Filming and audio-recording the
tours and later exhibiting the recordings in the gallery along with flora and
other organic material collected at the sites, the two artists highlight the
archival aspect of their performative-activist tours, creating what they call
"an archive that lives and breathes."[1]

At the heart of *And Yet My Mask* are these guided tours, which foreground
the performative acts of return of Palestinian youth to the ruins of villages
destroyed in 1948; but, the performative returns function in this context not
as an expression of nostalgic longing for a past long gone, nor as a symbolic
act of memorializing, but rather as an invitation to rethink the temporality of the ruins.[2] By relocating the ruins to the present, as sites of social
gatherings, Abou-Rahme and Abbas's performative tours challenge the
common framing of the remains of destroyed Palestinian villages as part
of the (lost) past, whether as symbolic signs of victory (within the Israeli
national imagination) or as loss (within the Palestinian collective imagination). While similar tours to destroyed villages exist, their main rationale is
witnessing: participants in the tours are invited to the site of destruction to
listen to testimony from elder refugees about pre-1948 life in the village and
the events of 1948. This is true for tours led by the Israeli organization Zochrot (Hebrew female plural form for "we remember") as well as for tours
led by the Haifa-based Palestinian youth organization Baladna (Arabic
for "our homeland").[3] By contrast, Abou-Rahme and Abbas's tours invite
participants to "experience" the site, not to witness—they do not include
testimonies or accounts of the past. Instead, participants are encouraged to

interact with their surroundings: touch, collect dry leaves, and sense their own bodies in the space of the ruins. The artists' rejection of the ruins as *lieux de mémoire* (sites of memory) aims to emphasize the status of the ruins as part of the landscape of the present. For this purpose, the tours to the destroyed villages mainly emphasize interaction with the organic surroundings of the sites: identifying and collecting vegetation and flora to include in the gallery exhibit. The collected flora, pine branches, and burnt wood all become part of what Abou-Rahme and Abbas describe as "an archive that resists colonial erasure. The very tissue of the place that refuses to turn into 'ruins.' A swarm of non-human life forces, from insects to wild thorns and pomegranate trees . . . and the living archive that [still] lives and breathes."[4]

....

The sight of ruins of destroyed Palestinian structures is not uncommon in the contemporary Israeli landscape—an arch, a gate, a half-standing house, a broken water tank. They remain even if they often become visible only thanks to a warning sign: "Area closed due to renovations," indicating the area is not to be approached or entered. While a great number of the more than four hundred Palestinian villages Israel destroyed during the 1948 war were completely demolished, leaving behind no trace, these remaining structures are often hidden by newly planted trees and parks: archaeological sites controlled and carefully preserved by the Israeli state.[5] In most cases, ruins that remain visible and preserved are sealed off ("under renovation"), and go through a process of *re-signification*. Some eventually become sites of Israeli culture and tourism, as in the case of the old Jaffa train station, now functioning as a vitalized outdoor shopping mall. Many of these ruins go through a process of de-Palestinian-ization, becoming "symbolic markers of primitive and ancient features of the landscape" or "a-historical natural entities, like rivers or water pools."[6]

Within this process of hide-and-seek, destruction and renovation, inscription and resignification, Israeli archaeology plays a specific and significant role in camouflaging Palestinian ruins. Israeli archaeological efforts keep the ruins' Palestinian-ness visible enough to satisfy Orientalist imagination, but sufficiently hidden so as to incorporate them into the Zionist national imagination of the landscape as always already Jewish.[7] But even *when* the ruins are explicitly and openly presented and recognized as *Palestinian*, the role of archaeology is to situate them as archaeological findings— that is to say, as remains of a lost past, cut off ("closed for renovation") from the present. As a kind of cemetery or memorial site—empty, nameless, destroyed, or "preserved"—these ruins mark the border between the past and present, the dead and the living, the Palestine that *was* and the Israel that *is*. Israel's avid attempts to obscure the ruins or maintain their status *as ruins*—a passive body signifying a past but no present or future—are part of a broader vision to render the potentiality of Palestine as an impossible and visually *unimaginable* future.

This chapter engages closely with *And Yet My Mask Is Powerful* to rethink the figure of the Palestinian ruins as an archaeological *myth*: an ideological ploy on the part of Israel to keep "Palestine" in the past and block its vision as a viable future. My reading of the work centers on ruins, but also expands the critique of Israeli archaeology to include a discussion of the "artifact" and the role of archaeology in generating a powerful (Zionist) national archive based on narratives of origins, material findings, and a mission of civilization articulated in both ethno-national and religious terms.

Archive

And Yet My Mask, like several of the duo's earlier works, engages with archives, the idea of the archive, and above all the impetus to archive (to store, frame, put in place, catalog, collect, save, preserve). The work similarly deals with the question of temporality and highlights the political limitations of linear time, which rigidly divides, separates, and organizes the relationship between the past, the present, and the future. My engagement with this work suggests that the most significant aspect of Abou-Rahme and Abbas's practice, which runs throughout their artistic oeuvre, is their commitment to replacing common archival practices of *recording, cataloging,* and *documenting* with practices of *enacting, performing,* and *copying.* The latter all target the temporality of the archive, insisting it is, or *ought to be understood as,* the present, and not, as is more common, the past.

If these ruins today function within the Israeli archaeological archive as marks of the (forever) gone past, *And Yet My Mask* invites us to literally revisit the ruins (go on tours) as part of a new archive of the present and an archive of *becoming.* The ruins become a site from which to "think about the incomplete nature of the colonial project," and discover a "potentiality to become unbound from colonial time."[8] This potentiality is best understood in relation to Walter Benjamin's concept of the "time of the now" or the "now-time" (*jetztzeit*): a prefiguration of temporality for which Benjamin mobilizes a mystic-materialistic imagery to propose a countermodel to the dominant perception of linear temporality and causal progressive history.

For Benjamin, this "now-time" is a time *felt* (an affect) as a certain density of experience and immediacy, which blasts moments of the present and past out of a linear sequence of events:

> The past can be seized only as an image, which flashes up at the instant when it can be recognized and is never seen again. . . . To articulate the past historically does not mean to recognize it "the way it really was" (Ranke). It means to seize hold of a memory as it flashes up at a moment of danger. . . . Historicism contents itself with establishing a causal connection between various moments in history. But no fact that is a cause is for that very reason historical. . . . A historian who takes this as his point of departure stops telling the sequence of events like the beads of a rosary. Instead, he grasps the constellation, which his own era has formed with a definite earlier one. Thus he establishes a conception of the present as the "time of the now," which is shot through with chips of Messianic time.[9]

Understanding Benjamin's concept of the "now-time" as an *affective experience* of immediacy may help us better comprehend Abou-Rahme and Abbas's suggestion that the organic and concrete material, along with the actual experience of being present at the site of ruins, opens up a temporality that is "unbound from colonial time." Indeed, the artists are unambiguous and unapologetic in using (like Benjamin) a mystical and sensual language to describe this very experience: "For us the site itself, the *physicality* of it, has an effect on the body. This feeling in and on the body is not a discursive project. It is a feeling of potentiality that one senses though the organic elements that escape all attempts to arrest them. The plants are so alive. They don't follow this or that national order or colonial timeframe. Ecology has its own system, its own temporality [one in which] we are not the center."[10]

And Yet My Mask returns to the site of the ruin, and then to unbind it from history's chronological narrative. This critique of colonial temporality is part of a larger critique of historical thinking, in which archaeology and the archaeological archive are in charge, as it were, of exposing the past and keeping it *in the past*. Against the archaeological archive and its temporal logic, the two artists proposed an alternative archive, which they describe is better situated for the purpose of interrogating the present and its relationship to the potentiality of the past and the future. In this work, as in the duo's previous and most known work, *Incidental Insurgents* (2012), this alternative archive is modeled on the principle of "chance" or "chance meetings." The two highlight chance in their work in order, I propose, to critique dominant theoretical approaches to the archive and to indirectly, yet scathingly, critique the archive understood in terms of an inner logic (rather than simply "chance"). Emphasizing the central role of "chance" in their own archival practices, Abou-Rahme and Abbas draw attention to the conditions under which archives in general are created and circulated in present day through chance encounters, rather than through an imposed so-called intrinsic logic that is commonly historical and national. In an interview held a few years after the uprising in Egypt in 2011, Abou-Rahme and Abbas expressed their frustration with how scholars and artists continue to theorize archives and archival practices in relation to obsolete principles, ignoring the fact that archives and archival research have changed dramatically in digital times. In a reality controlled by massive globally distributed online archives (Google, Facebook, YouTube, etc.), they argue, the temporality of the archive has also profoundly shifted. Nowadays, the event and (its) archive can no longer be fully separated, nor can we continue to talk about the archive as if it is still centralized by the nation-state:

> Critically for us, a fundamental change in our understanding of the archive solidified when the revolutions began to take place in the Arab world. We experienced and engaged with these movements through the real time material that was being uploaded on such sites as YouTube and Twitter. . . . This sudden ability to be connected at any moment to a continual stream coming from people involved in the revolution was phenomenal. . . . Suddenly the potential of the people to subvert the representations of the state was palpable. We came face to face with a *living archive*. . . . Increasingly in the last few years we have been engaged with archives to the extent that they can be a way for us to read the *potential of the moment*, to navigate the unsettling sense of being simultaneously in the midst of *not-yet-material and the already determined*; a temporal tension between what seems "permanent"—a repetition of capitalist–colonial present—and what could be "impermanent" both believing and dis-believing in the present possibility of a future of our own making, though not in a retrograde sense but as a way of finding a new imaginary and language.[11]

While Abou-Rahme and Abbas highlight the technological changes and the effect of digital archives on the nature of archival research and practice, their own artistic intervention goes beyond an argument about technological determinism. Their emphasis on "chance," and on the organic aspect of the "living archive," highlights not only the potentiality of digital archives as such, but a potentiality associated with the question of *reading* the archive as such. We are invited to take the case of digital archives as a way to reflect more generally on the possibility of mobilizing the archive as *both* and *at once* a mode of documentation and of political intervention: "For us the vitality that turns the archive into something living is fundamentally connected to a moment of political becoming, when the individual through a subjective gesture or act becomes part of a common moment and articulates the potential of the multitude . . . in the sense that we feel that the possibility for everyone to be an archivist is actively reshaping the archives to come."[12]

Both the democratization of the archive ("everyone can be an archivist") and the role of chance in archival reasoning, which need not hide behind a "deeper" (historical) logic, suggest that it may be time to rethink the politics of the archive in relation to not only documentation but also political intervention. Highlighting the generative power of the archive, Abou-Rahme and Abbas, not unlike Arjun Appadurai, argue that archiving is a practice of everyday life and a tool open to imagination, manipulation, and future creation of "new solidarities" and "new memories."[13] Archiving can be a practice "fundamentally connected to a moment of political becoming."[14]

In *Incidental Insurgents* (2012), just as in *And Yet My Mask*, the artists explicitly highlight the associative connections they make in creating their archive, using it to produce a new decentered collective across times, geographies, languages, and histories. Describing their work, the artists tell us that they have had a chance meeting with Victor Serge's novel *Unforgiving Years*, which then led them to another chance meeting with the mostly unknown Palestinian bandit Abou Jideh, who becomes a central figure in their project. Several other "chance meetings" with various texts and films (a novel by the Brazilian writer Roberto Bolaño, films by Jean Luc Godard, early pamphlets of the Palestinian Communist Party) resulted in the creation of an "open archive" of "figures who seem *almost incidental* to moments of insurgency."[15] These "almost incidental figures," brought together by "chance meetings" (or so we are told) across time, geographic locations, languages, and histories, take the shape of an archive in the gallery. This is an example of what Hal Foster calls "archival art,"[16] but it is also an archive that draws attention to its own status as an archive and places its authority under scrutiny. While we are certainly made to appreciate the archive's aesthetic and affective value (the work is very aesthetically pleasing), we are also explicitly invited to question the archive's historical validity and au-

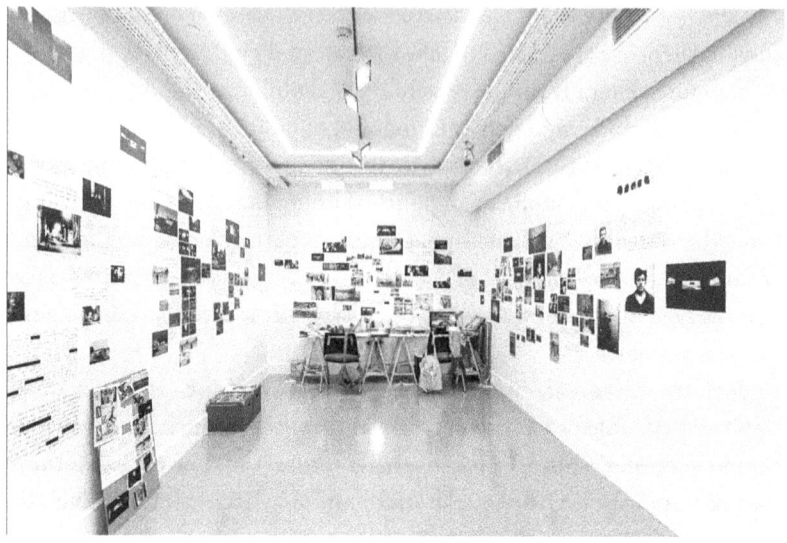

4.1 From the exhibition *Incidental Insurgents* (2012), by Ruanne Abou-Rahme and Basel Abbas. Courtesy of Ruanne Abou-Rahme and Basel Abbas.

thority. Or rather, we are asked to question it *through* the very claim of the archive to serve as a reliable and objective source of historical knowledge. Archival knowledge, the work highlights, is always *created* and *curated*. It is always generative, beyond its documentary value.

Incidental presents the artist's studio as the scene of a detective investigation, cluttered with notes, photos, films playing on a loop, open books, maps, posters, sketches, and vinyl records. The work calls attention to its own status as an (artistic) archive and questions its own historical authority. It thus manages to simultaneously archive (create an archive) and de-archive (question the validity of the very archive it builds).[17] *And Yet My Mask* returns to a similar critical preoccupation with the archive, only this time it is more specifically the archaeological archive that is placed under scrutiny. The work exhibits the artistic and research process involved in generating information about archaeology, ruins, artifacts, and Israeli museums, primarily through the Google search engine—the de facto archive of our time.

Along with the film and audio documentations of the tours the artists lead to the ruins of Palestinian villages, and side by side the organic material collected during these tours, the artists present many photo-images of their computer screens, which display Google textual and image searches.

The exhibit once again underlines "chance" and again highlights it as a key factor in today's archive and archival research, suggesting "chance" can no longer be considered external to the archive, but must rather be theorized as a key component of archival knowledge production.

Commenting on this aspect of their work, Abou-Rahme and Abbas note: "Our frustration with many archival practices used and theorized today is that they continue to imagine the archive as a dusty basement only open to specialists. In reality, archives today are much more open and accessible. They are also to begin with less coherent, less centralized, perhaps less 'Archivable.'"[18] This concept of the "less Archivable" is key, I argue, to understanding *And Yet My Mask*. Accordingly, I read the work as a project primarily dedicated to the un-archiving of the archaeological archive—to rendering it less archivable. Mobilizing several key conceptual features of modern archaeology ("ruins," but also "the artifact" and the idea of "ancient civilizations"), the work revisits the Israeli national archaeological archive, questioning the state's monopoly over archaeological findings. Pulling out archaeological findings (the ruins, the artifacts) from the museum and from behind the enclosed fence ("closed for renovation"), the work weaves them into the fabric of the present; the fabric of everyday life.

Archaeological Findings: Between "the West Bank" and "the Judea Desert"

And Yet My Mask, as the title of the work suggests, is not only about ruins but also about a mask. This is not the Fanonian "White Mask" that is imposed on the self and scars with profound alienation (*Black Skin, White Masks*), but rather a protective and empowering mask, a powerful mask. The title of the work is borrowed from Adrienne Rich's poem "Diving into the Wreck" (1973).[19] Verses of the poem appear throughout the video installation and in the book published after the exhibit. In the poem, the mask refers to a scuba diving mask that allows the narrator to breathe under water as she dives into the ocean in search of a wreck:

> First having read the book of myths,
> and loaded the camera,
> and checked the edge of the knife-blade,
> I put on
> the body-armor of black rubber
> the absurd flippers

the grave and awkward mask

. . .

I go down.
Rung after rung and still
the oxygen immerses me
the blue light
the clear atoms
of our human air.
I go down.

. . .

First the air is blue and then
it is bluer and then green and then
black I am blacking out and yet
my mask is powerful

. . .

Inspired by the idea of an empowering mask, and reflecting on the similar role of masks in the context of Palestinian resistance, Abou-Rahme and Abbas embarked on an online Google Image search, similar to the one they conducted about "ruins."[20] In this case, two key words, "Palestine" and "mask," result in many predictable online images: Palestinian youth in black ski masks, faces covered with keffiyehs, *anonymous* masks,[21] and masks made of the Palestinian flag, all of which are commonly used to ensure the anonymity of protestors. But, among these familiar images, one less common image appears: an image of a nine thousand-year-old Neolithic mask described online as a mask "found in the West Bank." Intrigued, Abou-Rahme and Abbas trace the image from one Google search to another, until they eventually find themselves in a "Google Virtual Tour" operated by the Israel Museum in Jerusalem.[22] Following this online tour, Abou-Rahme and Abbas soon learn that the mask they encountered belongs to a larger group of twelve Neolithic masks collected and exhibited in the museum in 2014 under the exhibition title "Face to Face: The Oldest Masks in the World." But while their own Google Image search indicated that the mask was found in the West Bank, the language used by the Israel Museum suggested that most of the exhibited masks were found in "the area between Jerusalem, the Dead Sea and the Judea Desert."[23] The online presentation, led by the Israel Museum's principal archaeological curator, Dr. Debby Hershman, describes the masks as material evidence of "the first permanent settlers, the ancestors of civilization." Visitors of the virtual tour are invited to "discover *here*, in the Judea Mountains and the Judea Desert [an ancient civilization that] laid the foundation of life as we know it today."[24] The deviation in name (from "the West Bank" to "the area between Jerusalem, the Dead Sea and the Judea Desert") is part of a common Israeli practice of renaming that resignifies not only a territorial imagination but also a temporal one. It effectively replaces the present reality of the West Bank, where Palestinians live under indirect Israeli military occupation, with a projected geopolitical imaginary located in a far-removed biblical time.

The printed catalog that accompanies the exhibit of the Israel Museum, a copy of which is also included in Abou-Rahme and Abbas's show, further underlines the rhetoric of discovery and possession involved in the Israeli archaeological project. We thus read that "*our* masks" can be found in "*our* encyclopedic holdings" and that thanks to the most advanced technology of "*our* time," one may enjoy "*our* findings" by surfing the web and without even visiting "*our* museum." This rhetoric, used to frame the story of the nine thousand-year-old masks—their discovery, preservation, collection, and presentation—carefully and systematically promotes an ideological agenda that balances universalism and particularism, with "our ancient ancestors" standing for *both* ancient civilization (the origins of mankind as such) *and* the more specific ancient inhabitants of the Judea Mountains ("the creators of the land of Israel"). This rhetoric reveals that the centrality of the archaeological project as a national archive in Israel is not limited to the restoration of a biblical landscape and the solidification of the narrative of Jewish indigeneity, as many scholars have previously noted.[25] It is also, and no less so, about the image of Israel as a modern nation that contributes to the (modern project) of archaeological salvation as such (using the "most advanced technology of our time").[26]

But what is most striking about this rhetoric is not what it says, but what it does not say, or what it hides and renders invisible. First is the fact that the masks "found" in the West Bank were actually taken under conditions more akin to looting, given that they were "found" in a territory under military occupation. Second is the fact that the West Bank in its present formation is inhabited by Palestinians who become fully invisible under the biblical idiom that creates a seamless bridge between the "founders of life as we know it today" and the "creators of the land of Israel," as well as between the "Judea Mountains," the "here" of the Israel Museum, and the "there" of the ancient ancestors.

In an attempt to bring the present *back to the present* and confront the force of oblivion advanced by the Israeli archaeological archive and its idiom, Abou-Rahme and Abbas embarked on a guerilla hacking project. Gathering computerized information from the Israel Museum's Google Tour, the two created several 3-D print copies of the Neolithic masks, using black plastic material and stone. This guerilla aspect of the work soon became central as the artists began to bring the masks along with them to some of the tours they led, encouraging participants to use them in whatever fashion they wished. Then, in the summer of 2018, the Israeli public interest in the Neolithic masks was renewed when a new mask was also reported to have been discovered in the West Bank, this time by a settler "taking a walk in the hills south of Hebron."[27] This "miraculous" discovery, like many similar other cases, was followed by an intensive Israeli archaeological dig in the area, which once again brought public attention to the illegal archaeological activities Israel regularly conducts in the West Bank. It is of course not a secret that Israeli archaeologists, both professional and amateur, often operate in the occupied Palestinian territories against the rules of international law.[28] Nor is it a secret that Israel makes extensive use of archaeology to establish the historical right of Jews over the West Bank.[29] The authoritative idea of a divine promise (a land promised to a people) makes clear the immanent theological and political power of the Zionist archaeological project. The modern, semisecular Jewish state may have been established in 1948, but its *actual* time is biblical. Within this expanded mythical-biblical temporality, Palestinian history, while not necessarily or overtly denied, is considered but a small and late incarnation—an episode in a much *greater celestial* narrative of (Jewish) destruction and revival.

In her groundbreaking book, *Facts on the Ground: Archaeological Practice and Territorial Self-Fashioning in Israeli Society,* Nadia Abu El-Haj shows how archaeology in Israel functions as a fundamental national archive that all citizens are encouraged to take part in, either as professional archaeologists or curious amateur diggers. Given that the West Bank is identified as the "biblical heartland," Israel finds no need to explain or apologize for conducting extensive archaeological research in this occupied territory since 1967, with both official and unofficial projects. The outcome of this *archaeological fever* is profound, as it solidified both the argument about Israel's historical rights to the land and Israel's important role as the protector of history. By this logic, the very "right" that justifies Israeli archaeological digging in the Occupied Territories is said to be "proven" by the material the digging unearths. This is a circular mechanism by which archaeological findings affirm an *already existing* textual archive, "render[ing] visible what is 'already known.'"[30]

This circular logic may operate in all archaeological archives, given that the search and the findings are always already *read into* and *through* a pregiven historical narrative, but it is particularly potent for archaeology in the Promised Land, given the theological implications. Many have recognized the flawed nature of (most) biblical archaeological arguments: "The use of Scripture to date [archaeological findings] is simply a case of circular reasoning," notes a leading Israeli archaeologist.[31] Others, like archaeologist Yonatan Mizrachi, have demystified the ethnocentric and theological-ideological frameworks that ascribe such archaeological endeavors as ill fit for modern scientific research or political decisions: "An archaeological find should not and cannot be used to prove ownership by any one nation, ethnic group, or religion over a given place."[32] Yet, whether the findings of biblical archaeology are fiction or fact, and whether they prove anything of historical substance, the *affective impact* they have as concrete materialization of an otherwise textually based cultural imagination (the Old and New Testament) cannot be overestimated or overstated. These archaeological findings supply an enticing substantiation in the form of visible and tangible matter that promises to put civilization and justice "back into order."[33]

Israeli archaeology, while certainly not a single coherent project, nevertheless continues to serve as the nation's most important archive that de facto makes "Palestine" an entity of the past absorbed into the archaeological archive of Jewish history, locality, and belonging. If Israel is *"the home of the spiritual heritage of the great monotheistic religions,"* Israeli archaeology is primarily dedicated to highlighting the "historical link between the Jewish people, the Bible and the Land of Israel, uncovering the remains of the *cultural heritage of the Jewish people in its homeland*."[34]

The story of the Neolithic masks, while not proving Jewish ties to the land, is an example of how a general archaeological zeal (to recover the "oldest settler community and the origins of civilization") also and forcefully becomes articulated in terms of national triumph. Thus, for example, the catalog of the 2014 exhibit reveals that the Israeli archaeological authorities first became aware of the Neolithic masks back in the early 1970s when the legendary Israeli defense minister Moshe Dayan bought a mask from a local Palestinian dealer in Hebron. It is well known that Dayan, who victoriously led the 1967 Israeli war and the project of unifying Jerusalem, established a vast collection of antiquities, which he acquired through illicit excavations during three decades between 1951 and 1981. These activities, far from being secret, have often been justified by Israeli scholars and politicians by presenting them as necessary acts of preservation—as saving antiquities from neglect in the hands of Palestinians, who do not appreciate their archaeological merits. Thus, for example, Dayan's biographer writes that the latter "saved antiquities from destruction" and was "a sort of Robin Hood who fought stupid bureaucracy."[35] Dayan, the Robin Hood of Israeli Archaeology, military general, and government minister, thus appears in this context as a key national hero, not unlike the strolling Jewish settler who is said to have "stumbled across" a mask on his leisurely walk in 2018 in the hills of Hebron. In a direct response to this national rhetoric and bravado, Abou-Rahme and Abbas advance an alternative model for thinking through the archaeological archive, replacing the aura of "salvation," the original, and the authentic with what they call "an archive of the copy."

Archive of the Copy

Armed with 3-D–printed plastic copies of the Neolithic masks, Abou-Rahme and Abbas added a new performative aspect to their tours and the following exhibition. Not only did the masks become part of the tours, but also the two simultaneously circulated a fictive narrative about a secretive Palestinian youth movement that performs rituals with "awkward masks" (to borrow Rich's words) in various sites of Palestinian ruins. The following text, widely circulated online during the exhibition, is part of their released statement:

> Neolithic masks taken from the West Bank and surrounding areas, and stored in private collections are hacked and 3D-printed. The oldest known masks, dating 9,000 years, mutate from dead fossil to living matter. Copies circulate in Palestine, eerily akin to a black ski mask. A group of youth wear them at the site of a destroyed Palestinian village. *Becoming other, becoming anonymous*, in this accidental moment of ritual and myth. Initiating a series of trips to possess and almost be possessed by these strangely living sites of erasure and wreckage.[36]

This dramatic account of hacked masks, transformed from dead fossil into living matter, circulated among Palestinian youth, possessing and being possessed, can be described as a parodic repetition of otherwise common paranoid Orientalist accounts of dangerous Arabs/Muslims and their mysterious and alarming rituals. Palestinians in particular have a solid record of being "othered" by such Orientalist depictions. Hence, the alleged ceremonies of "becoming other, becoming anonymous," functions as *both* a direct reference to Gilles Deleuze's concept of becoming *and* a nod to pervasive Orientalist imagination.[37] This textual, performative cyber act of spreading "fake news" joins the logic of the printed copy mask in celebrating the fake, the copy, and the fabulated as a radical alternative to the economy of archaeology and its investment in the original, the authentic, the real. As the two artists state, somewhat ironically: "At the end of the day, we conclude that our masks are better. Our copy, made of black plastic is flexible, bendable, and much easier to carry than the original masks. And since these masks are ritual masks after all, we reckon that ours is more user-friendly."[38]

Abou-Rahme and Abbas's investment in the copy is also an attempt to critically reshape our understanding of the archive's political potentiality: "The power of the archive is for us *all about the copy:* the possibility of duplicating, reproducing, and opening the 'original' ajar to an infinite realm of mutation and a vast web of circulation."[39] The copy, then, becomes an avatar for rethinking the archaeological artifact, the fetish of the original, and the museified object, just as the ruin is rethought as a site of potential rehabitation and livelihood.[40]

As an archive of the copy, *And Yet My Mask* is in a direct critical dialogue with the mysticism of archaeology as a science that provides the illusion of direct contact with the past and past civilizations. More specifically, the work targets the explicit colonial implications of archaeological endeavors and archiving in the Israeli context. If the Neolithic masks (the masks of "the very first civilization") are displayed as "Israeli findings" (from the Judea Mountains) and exhibited in the Israel Museum, the hacked copies of these masks are a reminder that these artifacts, which were "found" under circumstances that render such "finding" more akin to looting, are now "stolen back."

The guerilla practice of hacking, copying, mutating, and broadly circulating both the copy masks and the "fake news" about them breaks open the Israeli archaeological archive and the protective borders of the Israeli national museum, functioning in turn as the haunting of the "other" and the "anonymous."

The investment in the copy in this case is also a way of working with and thinking through plenitude versus scarcity. When there are enough copies for everyone, there is no need to cling to this or that original. The value of the copy is that it can be shared rather than owned by a few (as in the private collections of wealthy collectors). In this sense, the value of the copy is intrinsically democratic. It also offers a radically new way for thinking about archaeology in this context, since earlier Palestinian responses for the most part were committed to tracing ancient roots to the land to rival with the Zionist archaeological mission to claim it for Jewish ownership.[41]

In a later reincarnation of the work, these copy masks were exhibited as part of a group show in the Palestinian Museum in Ramallah ("Jerusalem Life," curated by Reem Faada in 2017), making the copy (perhaps a direct reversal of what Homi Bhabha calls "an act of colonial mimicry")[42] even more explicitly a haunting colonial residue. While the Israel Museum presents the original artifacts found/looted in the West Bank, the Palestinian Museum exhibits the hacked copies as a reminder that such acts of colonial violence leave behind traces, and that these traces—the copy, the hacked— always come back to bite.

Excavating for the Future

Like earlier projects by Abou-Rahme and Abbas, *And Yet My Mask* culminated in an exhibition and later a book publication.[43] The exhibition brought together the various aspects of the work: the tours to the ruins, the production of the copy mask, and the engagement with Adrian Rich's lyrics. It took the appearance of an archive, with the artists documenting and exhibiting their research and creative process. In the gallery space, filmed and audio-recorded footage from the expeditions to the destroyed villages (a five-channel video projection and a two-channel sound and subwoofer) was projected through a thick green filter.[44] In addition, the gallery displayed a vast documentation of the artists' research process, including video stills, photography, drawings, poetry, journalistic notes the two took before and during the visits to the destroyed villages, computer desktop screenshots of their various Google searches, and a hand-noted catalog from the Israel Museum along with various other texts about Neolithic masks. In addition to these images and texts, the artists presented a vast collection of flora and dried vegetation collected during their tours.[45]

Writing about an artistic trend, which he calls "digging," the curator Dieter Roelstraete recently warned us about the "the archeological imaginary in art":

> A steadily growing number of contemporary art practices engage not only in storytelling, but more specifically in history-telling. . . . With the quasi-romantic idea of history's presumed remoteness . . . these artists delve into

archives (this is where the magical formula of "artistic research" makes its appearance) and plunge into the abysmal darkness of history's most remote corners. They reenact . . . reconstruct, and recover. . . . One of the [most privileged] ways in which this historiographic "turn" has manifested itself lately is through a literalized amateur archeology of the recent past: digging.[46]

The main problem with "digging," Roelstraete tells us, is that the aura of the past becomes so great that the artists are no longer able "to grasp or even look at the present, much less to excavate the future." *And Yet My Mask*, which documents acts of return to destroyed Palestinian villages, and situates the artists in the position of "researchers, as they display their research process," may seem at first to fall into the "digging" trap described by Roelstraete. Quite the contrary, though, I argue the work is a deliberate attempt to *"excavate the future."*

Indeed, the work mobilizes the figure of archaeology to explicitly critique the discipline's politics of excavation and reassert the potentiality of replacing the desire for digging out the past with a politics of digging out the future. It is in this regard that we must also understand the performance of "return" to the destroyed villages not as an act of "returning to a specific village [or] reclaiming any specific sites," but as an act of returning to the possibility of imagining otherwise.[47] Speaking of the tours, Abou-Rahme and Abbas note that by "return" they mean "a performative intervention into a reality and a time of a still unrealized future."[48] This is not to be confused or conflated with fetishizing the site of origins, the locus of trauma or historical loss. On the contrary, the idea of return here focuses on the productive possibility of revisiting colonial violence in order to move forward *despite it*. In this sense it is a matter of "rewinding," to use Ariella Azoulay's words, and not simply "returning": "To rewind is not to return to an idyllic moment in the past, but rather to refuse to recognize in the violent outcomes of imperialism . . . the archival acceptability of its violence or to validate the separation of people from their objects and the material environment in which their place is carved."[49]

This performance of return (the actual visits to the destroyed villages) is not a display of nostalgia or an act of mourning. Rather, it is framed and takes place in a temporality of becoming ("becoming other, becoming anonymous"). To paraphrase Nasrin Himada, who writes about the work, it is above all a "return to a position of non-belonging . . . a return to a Palestine in all its possibilities—always in futurity."[50]

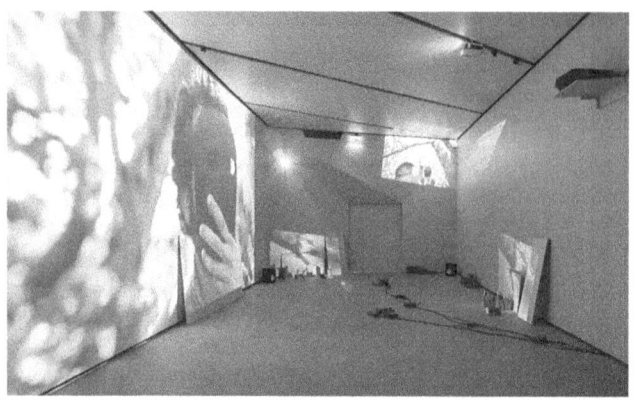

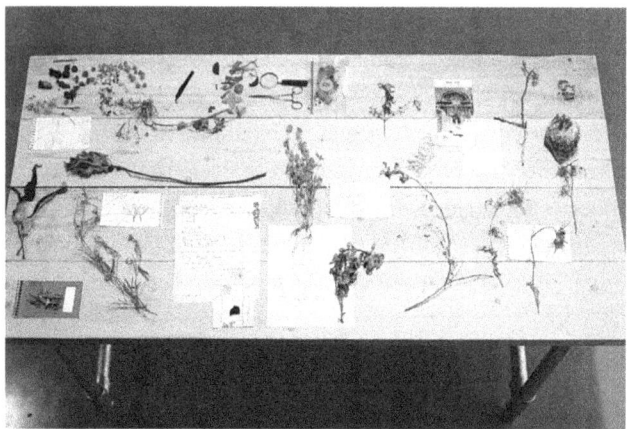

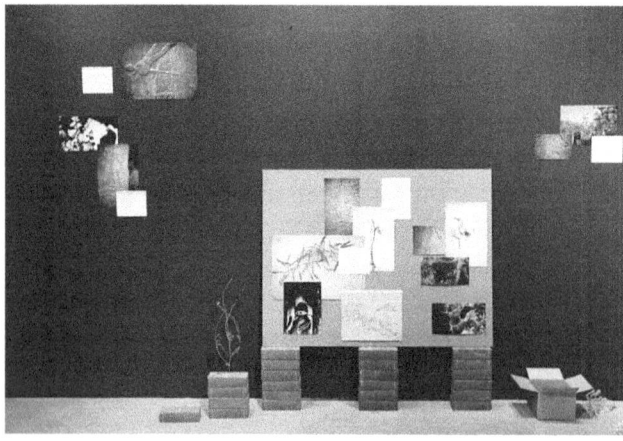

4.2-4.7 From Ruanne Abou-Rahme and Basel Abbas's exhibition, *And Yet My Mask Is Powerful* (2017). Courtesy of Ruanne Abou-Rahme and Basel Abbas.

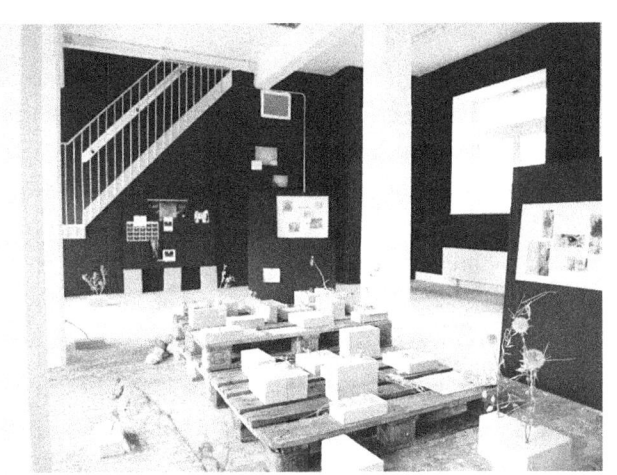

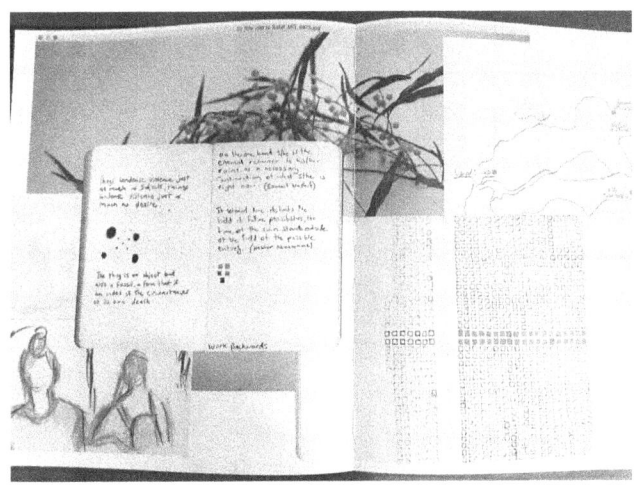

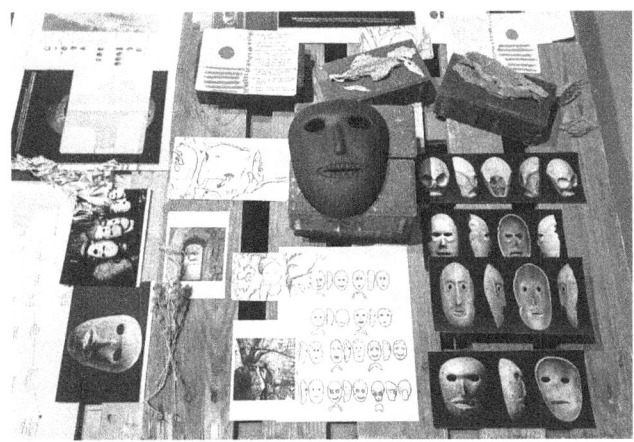

Returning to the site of the wreck, armed with the protective copy masks, Abou-Rahme and Abbas repudiate the status of the ruins as archaeological "dead matter" that index a lost, gone, destroyed past (and are preserved *as* a site of such destruction). *And Yet My Mask*, like Rich's poem, places a great weight on "and yet." Yes, the ruins are a sign of destruction— *and yet* they may also become the site from where to rethink destruction and reimagine the possibility of revival.[51] In Rich's poem, the poet comes to explore the wreck and to assess the damage and the potentiality of the treasures that prevail:

> I came to explore the wreck.
> The words are purposes.
> The words are maps.
> I came to see the damage that was done
> and the treasures that prevail.

And Yet My Mask follows a similar movement. Empowered by the (copy) mask, the journey to the wreck, to the ruins, is one that does not stay with the damage. It is a gathering, a renewal, and even a humorous opportunity for fabulating alarming "fake news" about returning natives and mysterious rituals. *Return* in this context means *returning to the present*, which has one primary goal: to excavate the future.

FIVE

Gesturing toward Resistance

FARAH SALEH'S ARCHIVE OF GESTURES

We have arrived in a situation where we do not
know—at least not yet—how to move politically.
| HANNAH ARENDT, QUOTED IN ANDRÉ LEPECKI,
"Choreopolice and Choreopolitics: Or, the Task
of the Dancer"

How can the body become a medium through which one
can grasp and question the political situation in Israel/
Palestine? | ARKADI ZAIDES, IN RENAN BENYAMINA,
"Archive: Interview with Arkadi Zaides"

To navigate the tension between art and activism
[I needed] to develop alternative knowledge using
the body as archive. | FARAH SALEH, "Archiving
Gestures of Disobedience"

This chapter explores in further depth the potential of bodily experiences and performative gestures as a model for creating affective archives. Abou-Rahme and Abbas's work, *And Yet My Mask
Is Powerful*, discussed in chapter 4, engages with rituals and performative acts of return. This chapter, engaged with a different
medium—dance—expands the discussion of the role of performativity and embodiment to suggest that the transformation of
archival material through the inscription of text (written, visual)

onto body alters the traditional role of the archive from a system of recording and documentation directed at the past. With the body functioning
as a new archive, we are faced with the prospect of an ever-changing and
evolving archive—one somatic and far less predictable or documentable.

....

Distinguishing between the archive and the repertoire, Diana Taylor suggests that whereas archives tend to preserve collective memories by cataloging, ordering, and keeping events recorded and "pinned down" (like the
printed words captured in a book), the repertoire is attuned to memory's
more malleable, dynamic, and expansive forms, as articulated in the movement of the body: "'Archival' memory exists as documents, maps, literary
texts, letters, archaeological remains, bones, videos, films . . . all those
items supposedly resistant to change. . . . The repertoire, on the other
hand, enacts embodied memory: performances, gestures, orality, movement,
dance, singing—in short, all those acts usually thought of as ephemeral, non
reproducible knowledge. . . . The repertoire both keeps and transforms
choreographies of meaning."[1]

Yet, could it be that these two—the archive and the repertoire—do not
necessarily differ from each other so much after all? Could the archive itself
be mobilized, animated, and activated through the performative lenses of
the repertoire? Could the archive, when performed and embodied, become
an alternative archive: a somatic archive, arranged through choreography?
Could there be an archive that not only does not resist change, but in fact
encourages it and is structured on the basis of ongoing performativity,
transformation, de-formation, and disorientation?

This chapter engages with the work of Palestinian dancer, choreographer, performer, and self-identified "archivist-activist" Farah Saleh to suggest that rather than a split between repertoire and archive (a split that
unambiguously favors the ephemeral and the performative over the documented and the textual), we ought to think about different modalities of
archiving and different archival imaginations—some significantly more
dynamic, fluid, and changeable than others.[2] As earlier chapters of the book
suggest, it may not be particularly productive, politically or otherwise, to
reject the archive or the principle of archiving *as such*, or to embrace the
repertoire as an alternative to archival acts. This is mainly because it is
hardly possible to identify a unifying definition of the archive (or the act
of archiving), which today, perhaps more than ever before, appears

to us in its multitude.[3] If it is true that the structure of the archive tends to invite historical research and that it is inclined to identify, enclose, and situate events in their past context and hence to resist change and reorientation, it is also true that this aspect of the archive can, and indeed *is*, repeatedly challenged and manipulated, particularly by artists whose critical engagement with various archives (and the concept of the archive) produces *actual* changes in the ontological and affective status of what we continue to call, perhaps for lack of a better term, "the archive."

Farah Saleh, whose dance practice often bridges between the dance studio, the stage, and the street as well as between art and activism, *and* between preexisting visual and textual historical documents and embodied performances, is an artist whose interest in the archive and the concept of the archiving precisely centers on the possibility of altering, manipulating, and transforming historical archival material by reengaging the archive through a transformation of artistic mediums and the inscription of text onto body and body language. Her dance often involves the translation of textual and visual documentations into embodied performance, and hence a reconfiguration of visual and textual archives into somatic expressions or deposits.

Saleh's dance performances often center on creating what the artist calls "archives of gestures." She models her choreography on the logic of the archive by cataloging and exhibiting gestures based on a close study of historical documentation. At the same time, her performed gesture archives resist the overarching historical narrative that sets the archival findings in order and gives them the interpretive status. Instead, the newly created archives—performed, danced, inscribed onto the body, delivered as somatic expression—constitute an *affective experience* that refuses or cannot be "fully read." The outcome is a dance that resists any overarching narrative, and hence resists functioning as static, stable, or reconfigured archive. This is true for Saleh's latest works *What My Body Can/t Remember* (2019) and *Gesturing Refugees* (2018), as well as older works such as *A Fidayee Son in Moscow* (2014). Many of these works directly engage with visual and textual archival materials as well as oral testimonies, converting these as it were to a new medium (dance) and a new language (gestures). "Considering my body as an archive," Saleh comments in one of her many interviews, "I can teach, demonstrate, and construct new gestures with viewers. [My body remembers] and their bodies remember. It's not only a matter of muscles but also of mental memory."[4]

In the dance world, the technique of movement most closely associated with this understanding of dance's functionality—as a transmission
of mental memory—is known as Gaga Movement. It was developed in the
mid 1990s by Israeli dancer, choreographer, and student of Martha Graham, Ohad Naharin, and has since become globally popular. Described
as a modality of choreography, a method of healing, and "a transmission
of somatic knowledge," Gaga is a movement that highlights the ability of
"retrieving gestures from the past or borrowing gestures from others [so as
to] produce new innervations. . . . Gestures migrate and in migrating they
create unexpected combinations, new valences, alternative cultural meanings and experiences."[5] In this sense, the body in its somatic expression
is thought of in terms of an archive that migrates across bodies, times,
and different psychic experiences. But if Saleh's choreography is to be discussed in relation to Gaga, it also must be distinguished from the popular
modality of Gaga as primarily an expression of freedom, pleasure, and joy:
"Gaga is a philosophy that works to take you back to a time when the mind,
eager to lord over an uptight body, wasn't such a tense, superficial pilot. To
practice Gaga you can't be too far removed from your sense of humor. . . .
Come on, enjoy making a fool out of you."[6]

Although Saleh's dance often appears playful, and her own movements
as well as those of her dancers highlight freedom and a certain degree
of embraced "foolishness," Saleh's dance practice is overtly political and
explicitly committed to modes of political intervention in the public space.
If anything, I would suggest her work presents a politicized version of Gaga,
with "gesture" taken as not just an expression of "pleasure," as Naharin and
his followers often suggest, but also a transmission of symptoms and somatic recording of distress across bodies, time, and place.[7] Remarking on
her process of performing gestures, Saleh notes:

> Considering my body as an archive, I feel I can create an access door for
> viewers by deconstructing movements. From this perspective, I can teach,
> demonstrate, and construct new gestures with viewers. This process rep-
> resents the exposure of my archive, namely my body, to them. . . . Even if
> they don't try them physically, their bodies remember, since it's not only a
> matter of muscles but also of mental memory. . . . Thanks to this process,
> [body memory] grows and changes from one person to another. . . . The pur-
> pose of all of my pieces is to open up discussion about social and political
> issues.[8]

With the body serving as the new medium or platform for creating a new archive, based on other archives, but not pinned down to any actual document, Saleh's newly formed "archives of gestures" spring forth and depart from historical indexicality. Saleh approaches archival documents (photographs, texts, oral testimonies) neither as sources of authoritative knowledge about the past (how things *really* were back then) nor as sacred containers of memories to be delicately approached. On the contrary, the archival material she uses serves as an inspiration in the sense that it provides a porous and elastic starting point from which the dancer departs; creating in turn her own gestural archive by means of somatic coding and decoding, embodied imagination and exchange.

If the archive is seductive by nature, as Derrida and many others have suggested, Saleh's work highlights the fact that the archive's seductive nature emanates not from the allure of the original, but rather from the archive's ability to spark and elicit an *affective* reaction or interpretation and fabulation across bodies and generations. While Saleh's work often springs from her initial meeting with archival material (primarily photographs), her choreography centers less on the object itself than on the impact of the exchange: the meeting between the past and the present, the photographed and the viewer, the archival document and her own body as well as the exchanges between one's own body and the bodies of others: other dances and, during live performances, also the audience. Indeed, her work foregrounds the archive's seductive propulsion but turns it from a quest for historical truth and origins into an adventure of collaborative exchange and imaginative elaboration—or *critical fabulation*, to borrow Saidiya Hartman's term, inscribed *on* and *through* the body.

The rest of this chapter focuses on one work by Saleh: her video-dance installation and film *C.I.E.* (2016). Three photographs, one painting, and several texts and oral testimonies serve as the historical archive that Saleh uses to create a four-part filmed dance performance, which she describes as "an archive of gestures of resistance" that escapes "the dominant Palestinian nationalist and non-Palestinian narratives."[9] An archive of gestures, then, that remains invisible or unrecognizable in the dominant collective memory, and not so much because it is absent from the historical (textual, visual) archive itself, but because it goes unnoticed, remaining unheard, insignificant, or marginal—made forgotten.

This work returns me to the book's main concerns—the mobilization of archival imagination for a future framework of speaking about, envisioning, and advancing the becoming of Palestine not as a resurrection of the past, but as a reality that never ceased to be and that must be imagined in the future tense. In line with what Ariella Azoulay calls "potential history," I read Saleh's work as a "a commitment to attend to the potentialities that the institutional forms of imperial violence—nation-states, museums, archives and laws—try to make obsolete or turn into ruins."[10] And more specifically, as a work that highlights the role of body as a somatic system through which to "unlearn the archive"[11] as an institution and a guardian of the past, turning it instead into a "different genre of narrative than that known as history":[12] a narrative of potentiality that blurs the distinction between the imaginable and that which is not. Within this alternative narrative of potentiality, *gestures* function as the means of bridging the past and the future, the imaginable and unimaginable, the archivable and unarchivable, making connections across time and space and between different bodies: those seen in the photographs, Saleh's own body, the bodies of other dancers, and the bodies of the audience.

C.I.E.: Gestures of Resistance

> Power can begin as a secret kept or as a gesture glimpsed in a hallway.
> | KATHLEEN STEWART, *Ordinary Affects*

The acronym C.I.E. stands for "Cells of Illegal Education."[13] The phrase sounds like it comes from the genre of science fiction, but it has a rather prosaic origin in the Israeli occupation. It was coined by the Israeli Army during the First Intifada (1987–91) to refer to groups of Palestinian youth who were suspected of breaking the military closure on all education systems. Gathering for the purpose of education was equated with gathering for the purpose of menace. All such gatherings of students, young and old, were thus deemed "illegal." Throughout the many years of the Intifada, the Israeli military took this notion of "illegal education" to great lengths: military orders closed all Palestinian schools and universities, effectively criminalizing education. Students and academics risked arrest for holding classes in defiance of the military orders, and carrying textbooks was sufficient grounds for interrogation and detention. Birzeit University, the main university in the West Bank, was closed for four and a half years (1988–92) during the First Intifada. Accounting for this closure, Gabi Baramki, who was the president of Birzeit University from 1974 to 1993, explained the establishment of the "illegal cells" as follows:

News would be circulated about the locations in which secret classes would be held. Science students . . . would be smuggled into the campus at night to do their lab work. . . . We held classes in private homes, fields, company offices, mosques, and churches. The whole community pulled together to lend premises and support our continuing efforts to keep the university functioning. . . . Meanwhile, soldiers would scour the town for such classes. What this often meant was that they would look inside buildings for young people with books sitting around a table. Having identified them as students engaged in the illegal act of furthering their education the soldiers would storm in and try to arrest all those present.[14]

The video-dance installation C.I.E., created and choreographed by Saleh and performed by Saleh and several other dancers (Salma Ataya, Fayez Kawamleh, Ibrahim Feno, Maali Khaled, and Hiba Harhash), is composed of four short dances, each opening with and responding to a visual image introduced beforehand (photograph, painting). The images, archival photographs, and painting depict the actual "illegal education gatherings" from the years of the First Intifada and serve as the opening framework of each of the short dance performances. C.I.E. "returns" to the visual archive to reenact these "cells of illegal education" first by mimicking the images (staging the dancers in similar positions to those of the people captured in the photographs), and then by elaborating, altering, and fabulating: "I use the archives in order to imagine what happened before, during and after each frame."[15] While the images serve as the historical index grounding the events in time and space, the reenactment gradually breaks free into a life of its own, with "gestures" functioning as the glue that makes *new connections* between bodies: the bodies in the photographs, the bodies of the dancers, the bodies of the audience. C.I.E. unfolds a gestural archive that travels from body to body over time and space, producing a living, embodied archive that expands and changes in unpredictable ways.

The C.I.E. video-dance installation translates and converts, transforms, and deconstructs still images, turning them into performed movement. This change in medium is a key feature of the work and, as such, it is highlighted and pronounced *within* the work itself. Each of the four dances opens with the visual references (three photographs and one painting) followed by the dance performance. If the thematic and formal (arrangement of bodies) similarities between the image and the performance are clear, the clash between the static frame and the moving bodies is emphasized by their juxtaposition. Indeed, the embodiment of the images draws attention to the deviant nature of the performance.

"Performing the archive," as Simone Osthoff writes, produces "an ontological change—from the archive as a repository of documents to the archive as a dynamic and generative production tool."[16] *C.I.E.* assembles and creates an archive of gestures by engaging photographs and paintings from the First Palestinian Intifada. This archive is generative not only because it enacts, embodies, and brings to life the gestures otherwise frozen and static in the images, but also because it functions as a platform from which to critically question "what gestures count," and what gestures are archived and remembered as "gestures of resistance."

For Saleh, "archive fever" is not about finding and documenting historical truth. Rather, it is about the ability to use archival material (historical documentation) as a launching point for articulating a political intervention of fabulation and repair. The fever, in other words, is less about the desire to archive (again), and more about the desire to un-archive the archive: to elaborate, subvert, and imagine otherwise. Enter gestures.

In the Shadow of the Intifada

An oil painting by the renowned Palestinian artist Tamam Al Akhal depicting students gathered in a kitchen, "In the Shadow of the Intifada" (1989), is the first image on the screen and the first visual document to be rendered into dance in *C.I.E.* The painting depicts a large group of young students gathered around a small wooden table. An older man faces them, probably their teacher. Nearby, a couple of younger children are planting a tree. The scene seems calm, even dreamy. But a closer look reveals that the top of the building is about to collapse and that there is fire and smoke on the far-left edge of the frame. It thus appears that the peaceful gathering of students will not last for long. A caption soon appears on the screen: "We used to enter the kitchen secretly one by one and tried studying architecture." After a short break, marked by a black screen, the first performance begins. It is the longest in the four-part sequence (approximately five minutes): the setting is a small kitchen with a dining table in the middle and a few white plastic chairs. The first performer makes her way into the kitchen. Hesitantly, she turns to make sure no one is following her. She approaches a chair and sits down at once. A second dancer squeezes his way through the door after momentarily hiding behind the entrance wall. Each of the six dancers enters the room separately in a different way: some walking determinedly, some nervously waving their arms before entering, and some visibly agitated and jittery. When they are finally gathered around the table, they begin to communicate mainly by tapping and banging on the table, pulling each other's arms, and walking around the table. Their movements are calculated, precise, and well synchronized: at once, they all take out their plan papers, and together they collapse in their seats. Sounds of drafting papers and rubber bands join the squeaks of the chairs and the banging on the table. For the next five minutes or so, we are invited to see an "illegal cell of education" in action. But far from straightforwardly depicting a realistic scene of a classroom, even one meeting in secrecy, the performed architecture class seems overtly theatrical and over-the-top performative: every movement seems calculated, choreographed, rehearsed, and synchronized to perfection. Swinging, shuffling, puffing, banging, standing, sitting—the dancers move around the table, around each other, and around the papers, in both an extravagant and a remarkably precise and measured manner.

Their gestures are exaggerated and melodramatic, but similarly harmonized and calculated. The overt theatricality captures our attention, directing it less to the scene of the class than to the gestures themselves—to the gestures *as gestures*. If the initial impetus of the class setting is, presumably, to mimic the visual image, the excessiveness of the gestures departs from this. Indeed, the visual archival document appears to quickly lose its historical grip on the performance. If anything, the exaggerated gestures can

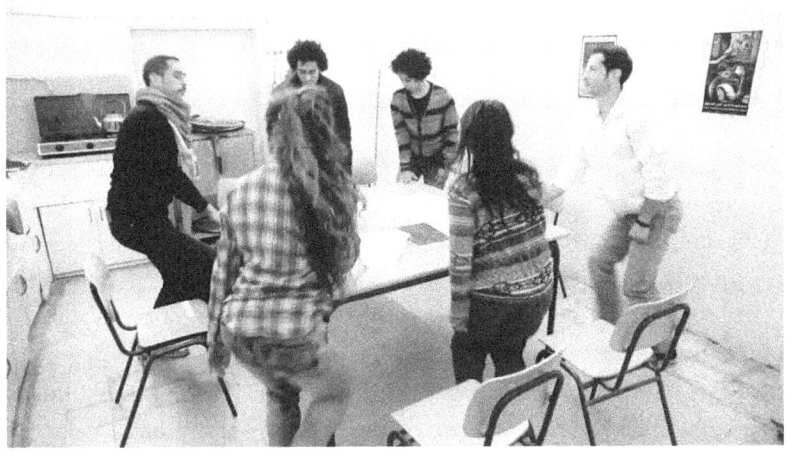

5.1 From Farah Saleh's video-dance installation, *Cells of Illegal Education* (C.I.E.) (2016). Courtesy of Farah Saleh.

be read as the *afterlife* of the historical moment captured in the painting—an afterlife that has a life of its own, that moves and vibrates between bodies across time and space. Archival memory is not just a result of documentation and preservation, but also a force that escapes the circumscription of memory. It is a force that works *on the body*, and hence the gestures enacted in *C.I.E.* are not only calculated gestures mimicking the afterlife of the image, but also symptomatic outbursts of the workings of a collective past experience on the present bodily constitution. This is how the body *now* speaks the *then*—not through mimicry or remembering, but through a more direct embodied experience of holding and acting out transgenerational gestural memory.

The Forbidden Area and a Historical Moment

The second piece in *C.I.E.* is a very short dance that primarily serves as a connecting sequence between the first piece (the classrooms setting) and the third, which takes place outdoors. The six dancers, who just finished the class, make their way through the empty hallway of a school. The scene is uplifting and resembles a typical Hollywood-style high school musical. But the full impact of this staged freedom, this youthful hallway dance, is best achieved in the transition to the third, static installation that follows. The screen turns black again. After the "click" sound of a camera shutter, a photograph appears. It is black and white and dated 1987. Six young men are gathered, some seated, some standing or kneeling. They grin with expressions of joy and triumph. Some are holding their hands up in the air, and some cling to their notebooks. The text on the side of the screen reads: "A historical moment. After we managed to enter illegally into the university and had a class in the lab." Soon after, another "click" introduces a new photograph with the same composition of bodies, only this time in color. It takes a few seconds to realize that this is actually *not* another photograph, but a staged video clip featuring the same six dancers posing like the original photograph: some are seated, others stand, making the same hand gestures and facial expressions. It is a perfect mimetic copy of the archival photograph—almost, but not quite.

   The juxtaposition between the photograph and its reenactment highlights a significant difference: the gender makeup of the group. While the original image includes six young men, the mimetic enactment includes three men and three women. Replacing the image of all-male students with three men and three women, Saleh does not simply mimic, but also

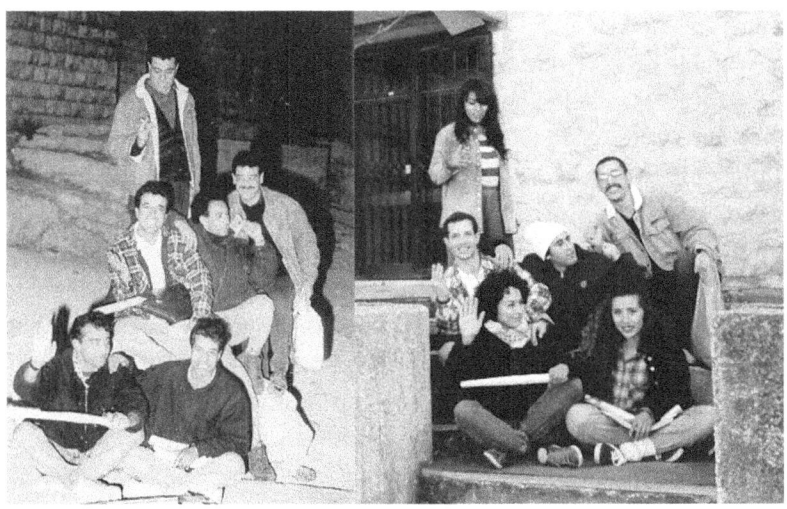

5.2 From Farah Saleh's video-dance installation, *Cells of Illegal Education* (C.I.E.) (2016). Courtesy of Farah Saleh.

"corrects" the image, as it were, drawing attention to the absence of women in the historical record of student resistance. While the absence of women may be overlooked in the encounter with the original archival image alone, it cannot *but be* noticed once the image is placed side by side with its restaging. We are faced with a difference that makes a difference. Reflecting on this intervention, Saleh comments: "My artistic practice attempts to collect fragments of a gestural collective identity, and reconstruct a genre and [a] new archive that [has so far been] ignored or obscured."[17] Saleh's archive of gestures, then, is a *corrective archive*: less committed to how things "really were" than to the editing process of how things are remembered, archived, and passed on from one generation to another. If the reenacted photograph is only partly loyal to historical truth, its importance as a political intervention lies not in loyalty to the original or to historical accuracy, but to the potential activization of present-day affective reactions to historical documents and archives, including the desire to "correct" and "improve" them so as to make them worth remembering.

This is a crucial point. *C.I.E.*'s intervention as a work engaged with archives and archival imagination is not limited to the common practice of reviving and recentralizing "forgotten" or less dominant historical memories by drawing attention to lesser-known, minor, or neglected archives. Surely, this is part of what Saleh does in *C.I.E.* by centering the work on a much less familiar visual archive of the First Palestinian Intifada and one that highlights lesser-known "acts of resistance." Calling attention to mundane small acts (such as gathering for an illegal class) as acts of resistance, *C.I.E.* intervenes in an economy of representation and archivization that commonly glorifies more spectacular acts of resistance through iconic images of teens throwing stones, young men burning tires, arms lifted and fingers in the "V" for victory sign, etc. Describing her process of selecting archival images, Saleh thus notes that her first goal was to capture "a whole array of gestures that are left outside the mainstream Palestinian narrative of revolt."[18] But this is only part of what *C.I.E.* achieves. The work stages and advances a critical encounter with the historical archive as such. This critical encounter takes the form of maneuvering between mimicry (staying loyal to the historical indexicality of the visual archive) and explicitly manipulating the archive by staging an unreliable and unfaithful performance that alters and subverts the original. In many ways, *C.I.E.* raises the question: why loyally archive or document the past when you can improve it by generating an alternative re-membering?

In this sense, *C.I.E.* is not just a newly created archive of lesser-known gestures, but also an "illegal gathering" itself. Staging and reenacting acts of illegal education, *C.I.E.* not only revives or glorifies past bravery and resistance, but also highlights the need to rethink the appeal of commemoration. Drawing attention to the image's insufficient allure, *C.I.E.* indirectly asks: Who benefits from archival representations? What is the meaning of revisiting the past through archival documents? And how can we do more than duplicate memories: How can we generate *better,* more inclusive memories for the future? The work seems to suggest that the political potentiality of archives is not found in the historical act of learning about the past and how things were back then, but in actively engaging with archival material to generate new memories *over and above* the preexisting ones. In other words: for the past to be cherished or indeed worth remembering, it must be *re-remembered* and made relevant to the current political moment. Only such a corrective and imaginary approach to the archive can advance what is otherwise a source of historical memory toward a living memory significant to the present and future. In the particular case of the group photo revisited and enacted by the dancers, the point of the performance is not simply to imprint the image yet again on the body of the dancers, but to further revisit and draw attention to past inadequacies. The change in the gender makeup of the photograph highlights not what the archive already captures, but the reality that escapes the visual document and that thus must be re-remembered by divesting from the historical impetus to stay loyal to representations of the past as they really were and instead embracing the poetic capacity to imagine otherwise: the historical event as it could have been and could still become.[19]

Mock Lectures

The final dance installation in *C.I.E.* begins once more with the "click" sound of the camera shutter. Two photographs appear on the screen, followed by a short text: "We organized a mock lecture in front of the sealed university entrance and produced propaganda postcards." The photographs show a small group of students sitting on chairs in front of the closed gates of Birzeit University in Ramallah, facing a professor who is standing behind a podium. The students are seated; a couple of them are visibly raising their hands to indicate they have a question or an answer to share with the rest of the class. The shut gate is also visible, reminding the viewers this class is being held by a university that is under siege.

The text informs us that these images are staged. No such class actually took place, and the photograph, dated 1987, is a photograph of a "performed class": an image created for the purpose of making "propaganda postcards."

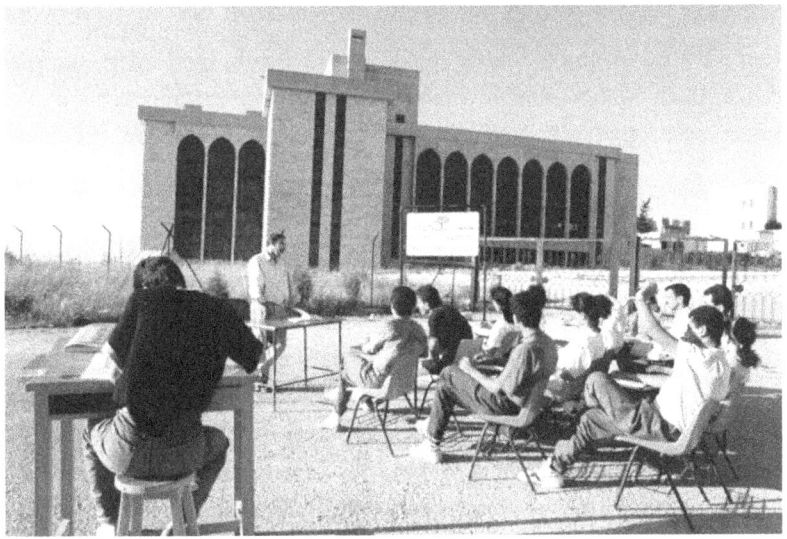

5.3 From Farah Saleh's video-dance installation, *Cells of Illegal Education* (C.I.E.) (2016). Courtesy of Farah Saleh.

Such postcards were indeed made during the First Intifada and broadly circulated, aiming to draw international attention to the sanctions the Israeli occupation placed on Palestinian education. While the first image we see is such a postcard, the second image is not an actual photograph, but again a performative video recording that imitates the original. Our six dancers are reenacting the (performed) propaganda image. Momentarily static, and then mobile. By duplicating the staged lecture and highlighting the fact that the "original" image is itself an *image of a performance* ("a mock lecture"), this last piece of C.I.E. further blurs the distinction between the "authentic" historical or archival document and the *staged* or performed repertoire; between, more broadly speaking, the documentary and the performative.

If the original document is performative (a "mock lecture"), the relationship between the first performance and the second performance can no longer be thought of in terms of authentic versus replica or document versus performance. If Illegal Cells of Education were already performed *during* the First Intifada—that is to say, they were already *both* a reality and a performance—C.I.E. reenacts this potential performativity as a mode of *staging resistance* and by keeping the centrality of the performative aspect alive throughout the process of evaluating the archive's political value.

An archive of gestures that focuses on performances of disobedience, C.I.E. invites us to think about the need to experience the archive itself as a performative reenactment, not of the past per se but of historical potentiality. Returning to images of classrooms as sites (and sights) of resistance, Saleh's dances render this less iconic site of resistance memorable, but do so by gradually breaking away from the visual archive: becoming significantly less mimetic and visibly more erratic, quirky, and idiosyncratic. Getting up from their seats at the "mock lecture," the dancers in the final piece begin to gather as they jerk and shudder, making chicken-like movements with their necks, and uttering strange sounds. It's hard to tell if the gestures are meant to convey excitement, nervousness, fear, or all of the above. Once together, the dancers begin to whistle, swinging their bodies around from side to side, shaking their hands, pulling their heads backward, and, finally, standing close together with their arms locked as they begin to walk backward, looking back and forth from the camera to behind their shoulders. More than the earlier pieces, this closing dance (approximately four minutes in length) is enigmatic and playful, as the dancers emit strange sounds and perform mysterious convolutions.

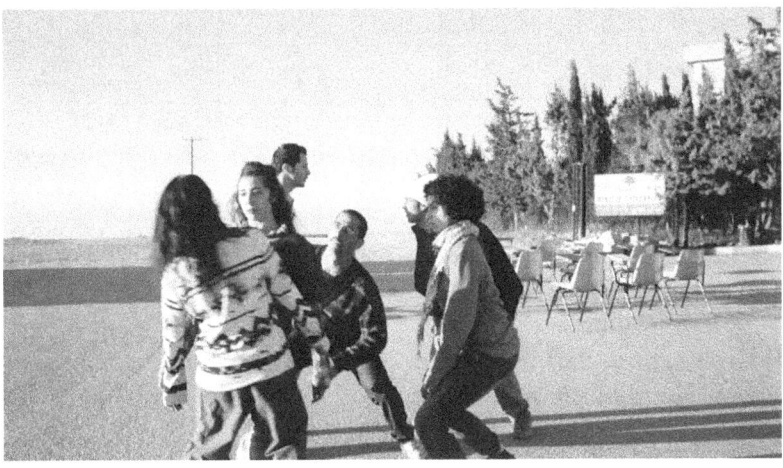

5.4 From Farah Saleh's video-dance installation, *Cells of Illegal Education* (C.I.E.) (2016). Courtesy of Farah Saleh.

Within the logic of the work as a whole, these are all "illegal gestures" of "secret cells": bodily configurations and movements that are "left outside the mainstream Palestinian narrative of revolt," to borrow Saleh's words. "Excluded from the national narrative," outside of collective memory, irrelevant to the story of resistance, these gestures mark the margins of the official story of resistance. The jittery movements, fragmentation of the body, and animalistic and overtly bizarre repetitive convolutions all animate the otherwise innate, frozen, archival images and texts. But, more than that, they introduce us to unfamiliar gestures that rupture our otherwise straightforward reading of the archival images. The docility of the historical archive is replaced with a performative reiteration that refuses to be confined or restricted to history and the historical borders of the archive. The archive of gestures created in *C.I.E.* is eventually one that *actively* undoes its status *as* an archive—becoming less and less decodable, less recognizable, and less classifiable. The principle of (reliable) documentation is gradually replaced as we progress from one dance to the other with a principle of innovation. Describing her process of working with the photographs and translating the still images into embodied movement, Saleh notes that her commitment to the archive is never one of mimetic reenactment, but always one of deformation: "I do not aim at merely reenacting gestures. I also aim at de-forming them."[20]

Choreopolitics: Gestures as Resistance

> Choreopolitics requires redistribution and reinvention of bodies, affects, and senses through which one may learn how to move politically. | ANDRÉ LEP-ECKI, "Choreopolice and Choreopolitics: Or, the Task of the Dancer"

> Gesturing may very well remain a resource for resistance to homogenization, a way to place pressure on the routines demanded by technical and techno-logical standardization. | CARRIE NOLAND, *Migrations of Gesture*

Etymologies and dictionary definitions make clear that gestures are not simply movements or motoric gags, but rather a "way of" or "mode of" carrying or bearing the body, even an approach to how one organizes the "attitudes of movements."[21] Gestures are expressive and performative in the sense that they convey a message. Carrie Noland writes, "Gestures give shape to affects that might not have precise, codified or translatable meanings."[22] Partly enabled by the gap between the sociopolitical regimes of (trained and repeatable) movements and their varied iterations, "gestures," Noland concludes, "cannot be reduced to a purely semiotic (meaning-making) activity but realize instead—both temporally and spatially—a cathexis deprived of semantic content." That is, "Gesture can indeed transmit a predetermined, codified meaning, but it can also—and simultaneously—convey an energetic charge or 'vitality affect' that overflows the meaning transmitted."[23] This operative doubling explains why there is a long tradition of studying gestures as *both* a form of language (linguistics, semiotics) *and* a nonverbal mode of communication (phenomenology, dance theory, New Materialism). Different disciplines understand the relationship that gestures establish between the body and the linguistic sign in distinct ways, but most scholars seem to agree that a gesture is a sign of sorts, and that it ought not to be thought of as a mere movement or corporal pulse.

For my own purposes of reading Saleh's work, I advance an understanding of gestures as primarily performative and theatrical. When Saleh creates what she calls "an archive of gestures," then, it is an archive not of various random bodily positions and movements, but of measured and staged configurations of bodies and signs that must be "done right" to be recorded as gestures. In other words, there is nothing natural or immediate about this archive.[24] Indeed, it would be wrong to simply read Saleh's archive of gestures as an archived habitus that attempts to capture and classify a range of Palestinian movements. Marcel Mauss uses the term *habitus* to describe *techniques du corps* (techniques of the body): the ways the body moves at the level of the individual, restricted and guided within a pregiven collective.[25] Pierre Bourdieu adds that habitus is an individual's predisposition to act and move in certain ways in relation to the predispositions and traditions of the group to which one belongs. Bourdieu has famously noted that the mimetic is at work in reproducing the habitus: "The body believes in what it plays at: it weeps if it mimes grief. It does not represent what it performs, it does not memorize the past, it enacts the past, bringing it back to life. What is 'learned by the body' is not something that one has, like knowledge that can be brandished, but something that one *is*."[26] If Saleh's work were about producing an archive of the Palestinian habitus, it would have created something like a close study of "the techniques of the body" in resistance. But *C.I.E.* instead opts to stage, study, and perform "gestures" that explicitly break away from the mimetic principle (whether it is the familiar setting of a classroom or a bodily arrangement captured in a historical photograph).[27] With an array of gestures made of spasms, bodily jerks, animalistic movements, and sounds, *C.I.E.* hardly archives anything akin to a (Palestinian) habitus. I suggest the way to read the archive is to reverse the temporal frame: the gestures are not mimicking and representing the past (imitating gestures captured in the visual archive); they are, rather, present expressions of a past actively *working on the present*.

Reading Saleh's "archive of gestures" as, above all, an *acting out*—a reaction *to* rather than a representation *of* the past in its continual living in the present—I suggest we take seriously the work's refusal to "represent" and hence its refusal or failure to *cohere into an archive*, or at least not a historical archive that one would approach to learn about what things were "really" like back then. Salah's "archive of gestures" is an archive of the present. If it captures the impact of the past on the present, it does so not only symptomatically, by suggesting the past lives on in the present or that traumas of the past are marked in bodies transgenerationally. As an archive of the present, *C.I.E.* invites us to consider the present as a time from which the past can be not only revisited, remembered, and archived, but also improved and altered.

Hannah Arendt tells us that we do not yet know "how to move politically." I suggest that Saleh's "archive of gestures" is built around this very question: how do we move politically? My reading of *C.I.E.* highlights the importance of learning to move *away* from the overtly readable and toward the less identifiable, less recognizable, less achievable. Bound up in a history of repeated performances, "gestures" function as bodily citations that signal repetition and diversion. So much so that even "a well-disciplined body" (which Foucault notes "forms the operational context of the slightest gesture")[28] may indeed enact, perform, or better yet *fail* to perform gestures as expected. My reading of *C.I.E.* proposes precisely this: that the work uses and archives "gestures" as performative signs that gain their political meaning from the relationship they articulate *between* mimicry (repetition) and failure; between, that is, the ability to rearchive the past and the refusal or inability to do so, without violation.

....

In her lecture "When Gesture Becomes Event," Judith Butler revisits Benjamin's writings on Franz Kafka to ask, "What is the role of gesture as a mediation between language and performance?"[29] Like Benjamin, she suggests that gesture conveys something the linguistic register fails to account for, while at the same time, like the linguistic sign, gesture holds meaning in repetition, performativity, and citationality. This understanding of gesture as performative and citational is key for discussing Saleh's work and dance performances. Saleh's focus on the gesture—on "collecting" gestures and "archiving" gestures—involves, I suggest, less an act of preservation than an act of translation, mediation, and reformation, which *as such* refuses to become fully readable.

My reading of *C.I.E.* as an "archive of gestures" suggests that this archive both invites interpretation (historical contextualization, deciphering of bodily codes and movements, identification of the mimetic relationship between image/performance) but also exceeds and deflates interpretation, as it invites interpretation to fail. What I mean by this is that the work engages in historical restoration while at the same time it refuses to be fully historically read. Butler writes that a gesture, "as a citation," becomes "its own event."[30] This becoming of an event is precisely what takes place in *C.I.E.* through the work's display of, and engagement with, the relationship between the visual archive and the dance performance. Bringing the visual reference and dance reenactment together, *C.I.E.* highlights the citationality of the gesture as an event in and of itself: an "acting out" that is both the mark of a symptomatic citational inscription of trauma and resistance (passing transgenerationally across bodies), *and* an act of resistance to the predictability of the citation.

Writing about dance's political potentiality in a general theoretical manner, André Lepecki has argued that "danced techniques of freedom suggest choreography as technology for *inventing movements of freedom*,"[31] and that "moving politically is predicated on the need to be constantly reminded, daily, that whatever this moving accomplishes and brings into the world at any given moment, will be always provisional and incomplete. Thus the necessity to start again, to insist, no matter what, on the urgent challenge posed by that endless *not yet*. Not yet, not yet. Again and again. Anything else would be conformity."[32]

Saleh's archive of gesture may seem at first to offer something quite different. An archive based on and created in relation to preexisting archival materials may seem held down by history and the force of repetition. It may even be seen as homage to the past and a mapping or recording of past movements—an inscription of the past on the body. But *C.I.E.* is anything but a record, or a simple record of the past. The work is marked by excess that draws attention to itself as such: unarchivable, undocumentable surplus of idiosyncratic gestures that gradually increases. This is the inscription of the "endless *not yet*. Not yet, not yet. Again and again." The dance releases the movement from its historical citational role as it begins to replace the mimetic draw with an inscription of a new gestural language.

"Archive of gestures," then, is not an archive of documented gestures from the past. Far from it, Saleh's dances bring to the forefront undecipherable gestures that refuse and refute full readability. Within the context of a hypervisible militarized "Israeli-Palestinian conflict," recognizable gestures are often limited to a few familiar body movements and postures: stone-throwing, kneeling, shooting, crowds escaping tear gas, crowds waiting at checkpoints, and the like. In this militarized theater, aiming, hitting, shouting, shooting, escaping, throwing, pulling, burning, waiting, and running are the familiar ways bodies are configured. Saleh's "archives of gestures" seem to come from an entirely other reality. Chicken movements, spasms, robotic banging, head twists are all part of a new archive Saleh creates *in relation* to preexisting archives and historical documents but always *in departure*: returning to these historical sources and moments to unplug a potentiality lost to them; lost *in* them and reviving them not as a glorification of the past or a commitment to (national?) memory but as a promise of yet-to-come, unknown, "not yet."

In many ways, *C.I.E.*, like earlier works of Saleh, is a meditation on the role of historical documentation, the archive, and the repertoire in the building and preservation of collective memory. As a dancer, Saleh highlights the role of the body not simply or mainly as a vessel upon which the past is inscribed but as an active agent in propelling otherwise lost potentiality, lost visions, and lost opportunities into the future. Drawing attention to the productive space opened between the archive (as a source of documentation of the past) and the body that interacts with the archive, Saleh's work underlines the importance of speculative performativity in opening the otherwise sealed archive to make it an immanent (and relevant) part of the present—not as an archive *per se* but as a promise. . . . "Not yet, not yet."

"O my body, make of me always a man who questions!" are the words with which Franz Fanon closes his masterpiece *Black Skin, White Masks* (1952). Saleh's work, I suggest, advances a similar quest, directed *to* and *from* the body. The body is the site from where questions are asked and from where no past (alone) can provide an answer. In Fanon's case, the various critical engagements he conducts throughout the book—first with existentialism, then with psychoanalysis, then with Hegel's phenomenology, and finally (and most passionately) with Negritude—all provide partial, often contradicting and frustrating answers to his humanist quest for a future unburdened by racial and colonial injustice. *Black Skin, White Masks* returns to these various philosophical schools to find some useful tools in each of them, but for Fanon to articulate his deep skepticism in the power of the past to provide a political agenda for the future. Engaging respectfully with the writings of his teacher and friend Aimé Césaire, throughout the book, Fanon ends up in a position quite removed from that advanced by the poetic and political promise of the Negritude movement. Not that the traumatic past of slavery, the more recent violence of colonialism, or the overlooked great achievements of the colonized do not inform Fanon's aspirations, but those alone do not guarantee the task with which he chooses to close his book: "O my body, make of me always a man who questions!" To read *C.I.E.* as an inscription of a similar political move and a similar call for the body to serve as the site of an ongoing quest for a future yet to come is to suggest that the work engages in an archival imagination *for* the future. The past here is obviously important, as it is for Fanon, but it is primarily so in guiding us away from repetition and toward an ongoing search for the not yet. This search is invested in questions and in the promise of a body that *always questions* above and beyond providing any answer.

Walking Backward

The final image of *C.I.E.* is of the six dancers holding each other, hesitantly walking backward, nervously looking around as they walk away from and down the hill of Birzeit University. They form a tight cluster, perhaps preparing for a confrontation at the bottom of the hill. Will they fall? Will they arrive? Will they be confronted? How far backward will they walk? I read this open-ended "end" as a call for poetic freedom granted by the speculative, the potential, the "still not"—all of which require a critical return to, and distance from, the past. Walking backward in this case is a performative gesture that stages the question: How far back should we walk? And how can walking backward help us move forward? In other words, I read the ending scene as a metacommentary on the question of the archive, staged and revisited throughout the performance as a whole. Opening with a painting as the first archival reference, Saleh's dance functions as the added layers of paint to the canvas. This canvas is not idealized as the "original" or the archival source, but is rather elaborated upon, and painted over with body movements. The dance performance in the kitchen/classroom features the dancers as architecture students. They hold blueprints, dancing around and with them. Perhaps blueprints, like the canvas, are not "good enough." Blueprints can't simply be remembered, revisited, as the archival past, but must in fact be activated to become relevant to the present. The archive in Saleh's work is a blueprint and a canvas. It is a starting point to which the dancer pays homage, but certainly also a platform through which she elaborates her astute critique of the very limits of walking backward. Walk carefully, look to the sides, and always remember that the archive is but a canvas and a blueprint that can be changed, improved, and made to serve the future.

Afterword

When it comes to archives and Palestine, most critical accounts focus on loss, silencing, and destruction. The loss of the PLO archives in 1982 and the disappearance of many Palestinian films, photographs, and footage after the Israeli invasion of Beirut serve as a central example of the violent archival conditions Palestinians are subjected to, with Israel systematically rendering the Palestinian historical narrative invisible, traceless.[1] Given, however, that it still remains unclear whether the vast amount of Palestinian archival materials have been lost, looted, or destroyed by Israeli forces, there are also a fair number of efforts invested in continuing to search for, salvage, and restore whatever archival material can be saved.[2] Loss and recovery; melancholia and redemption: these have been the main pulls of engagement with Palestinian archives. As noted by Nadia Yaqub: "The idea of a lost archive is laden with romance; the state of being lost suggests that it can be found again, prompting questions, speculations, and treasure hunting. It also resonates with the conceptions of Palestinians as a people defined by loss . . . since the early 2000s there have been numerous efforts to re-create the [Palestinian film] archive by gathering and digitalizing scattered copies of films."[3] Romanticization of the lost archive is met with an understandable restorative fever—to find, save, and rescue the traces of history. But in the space opened between nostalgia and the desire to recover, other, more ambiguous and less redemptive archival imagination sprouts.

Important cinematic projects by Palestinian directors such as Azza El-Hassan (*Three Centimeters Less* [2002], *Kings and Extras: Digging for a Palestinian Image* [2004], *Always Look Them in the Eyes* [2009]), Ghada Terawi (*The Way Back Home* [2006]), and Basma

Alsharif (*O, Persecuted* [2014]), among others, have complicated this binary pool by working with Palestinian archival footage in a more overtly
critical way. Azza El-Hassan's documentary film *Kings and Extras* (2004),
for example, centers on a search for the missing PLO film archive, and yet
the value and meaning of this search and the price paid for the ongoing
investment in such archival recovery is just as much part of the film. Including a section about Hiba Jawhariyah, the daughter of PLO filmmaker
Hani Jawhariyah, who lost her father as a young child, El-Hassan asserts,
"The real quest in the film is for an understanding of the cost and value of
Palestinian images. Who has paid what price to produce Palestinian films
and photographs in the past and in the present."[4] While El-Hassan does not
question the importance of image-making and archive-digging, her film
certainly implies that no archival recovery project should be subjected to a
nostalgic image of the past or a victorious perception of recovery "without
cost." *Kings and Extras* ends with the director walking through the Palestinian cemetery in the Shatila camp in Beirut, accompanied by former PLO
filmmaker Kais al-Zubaidi. Death of the archive? That would be too strong
a reading, but I do think the film invites a critical engagement with the idea
that fighting dispossession must rely primarily on recovery of past loss. Or
with the idea that such recovery does indeed promise to lead us out of the
graveyard. While forming a collective (national) identity around a shared
experience of loss is natural, common, and powerful, as is the desire to fight
this loss by means of recovery, such recovery must also include a critique
of the past and an active engagement with the archive toward a different
future. This is how I read the final scene of the film, which begins with the
search for a lost archive and ends in a graveyard of Palestinian martyrs.

Another example of a critical engagement with the promise of archival recovery, one even more explicit, is found in Basma Alsharif's short film
from 2014, *O, Persecuted* (12 minutes). This is a film about a film, but also a film
filmed over a film: as Kassem Hawal's PLO militant film *Our Small Houses*
from 1974 plays, we see Alsharif painting over it and over the screen—an
act she films forty years after *Our Small Houses* was made.[5] But *O, Persecuted*
is not simply a film of revisitation, or of covering up. While Alsharif does
indeed paint over Hawal's film, gradually blocking it from view, we see this
action in reverse (the opening screen is black, while the images from Hawal's film increasingly appear) and also at 2.5 times the speed. The outcome
of this manipulation is a purposely distorted and contrasted set of images
and sounds: a black screen is replaced with partly recognizable figures,
guns, dropped bombs, and partly visible English subtitles: "Die or Kill, Kill

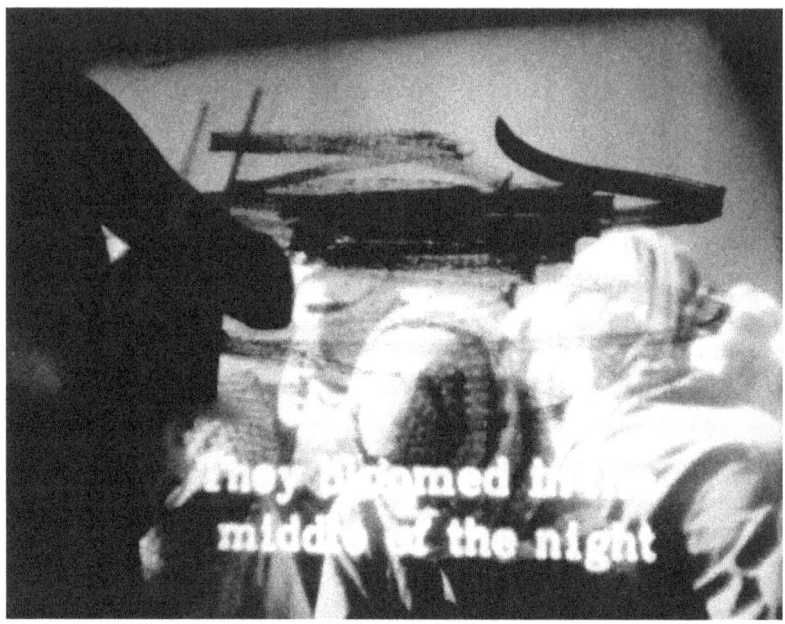

A.1 From Basma Alsharif's *O, Persecuted* (2014). Courtesy of Basma Alsharif.

or Die," "Everyone must join the struggle," "Homeland." The audio is partly from Hawal's movie and partly an added metallic soundtrack. Only much later in the film do we begin to see the director coloring the screen: first we see only her arm, then her whole figure. At that point we realize that what we thought was an exposition of the archival film—perhaps its restoration—is nothing but an illusion: the exact opposite played in reverse. In reality, what we are seeing, albeit backward, is Alsharif covering up the film, using Hawal's film as her canvas, painting over it, and thus erasing it and blocking it from view.

Commenting on her choice of showing the film backward, Alsharif notes:

> Initially, the film was based only on this act of uncovering, but as soon as I made the first cut, there was something sort of placid and banal about this act alone, something limited to a past, and my feeling about conjuring this history in the present was anything but passive. I was asked to engage with this material, through a commission by the Palestine Film Foundation in London. I saw it as an incredibly generous opportunity to speak to the current political climate.[6]

To present the engagement with the archival material as simply an "act of uncovering" would be to limit one's engagement with the archive to the past. To "speak to the current political climate," Alsharif chose to *cover* the archival film and document this violation in reverse so that it initially appears as a process of revelation, restoring, exposure, and rehabilitation. This illusion of discovery and restoration is thus presented as precisely that: "An illusion." It is one that Alsharif wishes to challenge: "There's this huge effort to restore these films, but a lot of those films are propaganda and for me, the way they speak is problematic. . . . Sometimes I think these things should be buried. I wanted it to seem like I'm taking a corpse out of the ground. We're digging up this thing that says, 'Look, we were so great! But we weren't . . . if we were, we'd be free.'"[7]

Far from being a simple scrutiny of the PLO's tactics or cinematic aesthetics, Alsharif's filming choices and commentary are best understood as a broader critique of a certain archival fever that is mobilized by bravado and a national utopian or nostalgic vision. "Digging a corpse of the ground," to borrow Alsharif's metaphor, cannot become the end goal of any significant political engagement with the present. The engagement with the past and with archival recovery gains its political meaning only when this act of "Recovery" is itself scrutinized and critically examined for what it seeks to carry as a promise of recovery. Rejecting the use of the archive as a corpse (or in the case of El-Hassan, a graveyard) is by no means a rejection of the archive as such. Far from it, *O, Persecuted* is about the incentive to engage the archive, but for the sake of the future.

In the final segments of the film, black-and-white images of a belly dancer are projected over images of weapons from Hawal's film. A gun is aiming directly at the dancer's genitals, or so the conflation of the images suggests. From this disturbing set of images, a sudden transition takes place: color film of dancing young women in small bikinis appears on the screen accompanied by loud dance music. This is Israeli footage taken from parties in Eilat, the most southern city of Israel, bordering the Sinai Peninsula: the gate to heaven for young tourists and a city known for its hotels, beaches, and nightlife. Why this sudden transition? If momentarily we are invited to consider the colorful Israeli footage in contradiction to the PLO's solemn black-and-white militant images, this reading quickly becomes invalid, as the black-and-white figure of the almost naked belly dancer is screened over the young Israeli women dancing in bikinis. The images are slowed down: a nearly naked woman dancing in black in white to Arab music is merged with the half-nude Israeli women dancing to techno music. Alsharif posits the figure of the sexualized woman as the crossover between the past and the present; the black-and-white images and the colorful ones; the Palestinian archival images and the Israeli footage. Alsharif's film speeds up the past, but it literally slows down the present. I read these cinematic manipulations within the theoretical framework developed in this book and along its lines. I consider them as a commentary on the prospect of engaging the archive primarily as a way of critically evaluating the present and reading it as an archive carrying future potentiality.

Remarking on her conflation of the women's images and her choice for slowing them down, Alsharif notes that the Israeli imagery of the beaches and nightclubs "is still superimposed by Orientalist imagery of the belly-dancer." Noticing this connection of exploitation across archives of radically different natures, time, nationality, she adds, "starts to unravel the present."[8] But in conflating the images of the belly dancer and the young Israeli women, Alsharif not only draws attention to the regional or global exploitation of women. She also, if indirectly, directs our attention to the need to engage with the archive less as the guardian of the past otherwise lost (a past lost, for example, if Hawal's film had not been recovered), and more with its function as a gatekeeper that limits and blocks our imagination. *O,*

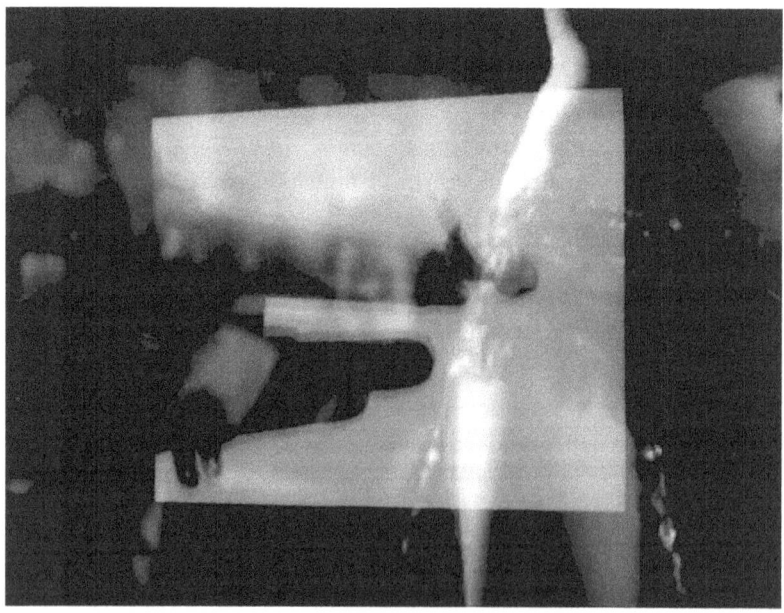

A.2 From Basma Alsharif's *O, Persecuted* (2014). Courtesy of Basma Alsharif.

Persecuted thus follows the figure of belly dancer as the "ghost that lingers beneath the surface" beyond any "particular nostalgic" engagement with the past or a hedonistic escape from it.[9] It is the ghost that reminds us of the archive's real political potential—to draw us closer to the present.

Inspired by this example and the many other critical and creative responses to the question of the archive and to the "Question of Palestine" understood *as* the question of the archive, I strive to demonstrate the power of the archive not primarily as an instrument of repair, restoration, or recovery of lost archives, but rather as a means for facilitating a critical engagement with the very promise of "recovery." Of course, finding, recovering, exhibiting, and engaging lost archives all play important roles in healing dispossessed societies and in creating the basis for a more just future, where everyone's history, past, narrative is known and visible. But I join El-Hassan and Alsharif's concern about archival recovery becoming a goal *in and of itself*—a nostalgic affirmation of peoplehood, nationality, narratives of origins, loss, and triumph. What I think these films and the works I engage with throughout the book teach us is that we must move beyond the investment in saving the past (from being forever lost) and that we must learn to read and engage the present itself as an archive: a set of testimonies of a possible future and a possible *becoming*.

The possibility of becoming, the possibility of *becoming Palestine*, is not simply a theoretical exercise. It is, I stress throughout the book, an urgent political matter. It is "real" just as it is "fiction" because political realities begin with and depend on imagination. This book ought to be read, then, first and foremost as a plea to let go of History with a capital *H*'s monopoly over the archive. It is a call to take advantage of the specific belated colonial configurations of Palestine to replace the historical fixation on *what was* with an investment in imagination and the power to envision and speculate *what may still be*.

Imagination, of course, is what cynics like to make fun of. I don't think we can afford to be cynical any longer. Writing about (postcolonial) cinema in 1985, Gilles Deleuze notes that what must remain missing from the film's frame, while remaining its main concern, are "the people." They are missing, and they must remain missing, because the only collective that matters politically is one that remains always in the process of becoming. The archive, like Deleuze's political cinema, I suggest, must "not address a people, which is presupposed already there, but [must instead] contribute to the invention of a people."[10] For Deleuze, this "people to come [*peuple à-venir*]" does not wait its place in history. It replaces history as we know

it with radical imagination.[11] Palestine today is an archive of colonial violence, but it is also an opportunity to imagine a radically different reality,
a *becoming* as an entirely "different way of knowing the world."[12] Palestine
provides us with an opportunity to enact something seemingly impossible:
the complete undoing of the colonial order, which must include, as such,
going beyond its replacement with anticolonial nationalism.[13]

Epigraph: "Who Will We Be When We Are Free? On Palestine and Futurity," *The Funambulist*, no. 24, "Futurisms" (July–August 2019): 22–27.

1   The New Historians (among them Benny Morris, Ilan Pappé, and Avi Shlaim) have claimed to provide revelations about the 1948 war and *Nakba* that were previously concealed by the Israeli archives. Earlier historians did not have access to an abundance of newly declassified documents, which became available in the 1980s. But there have always been critics who questioned just how *new* these findings really were. Commenting on Benny Morris's "revelation" in particular, Efraim Karsh does not deny the facts revealed (expulsions, violence), but does challenge their newness: "This [accusation against Israeli forces] was made known decades earlier in such works as Jon and David Kimche's *Both Sides of the Hill*; Rony Gabbay's *A Political Study of the Arab-Israeli Conflict*; and Nadav Safran's *From War to War*." What is questioned here is the novelty provided by the archives as the "source" for hidden secret information. Efraim Karsh, *Rethinking the Middle East* (London: Frank Cass, 2003), 175.

2   Gish Amit chronicles the theft of both Palestinian and Mizrahi artifacts and entire libraries in "Salvage or Plunder: Israel's 'Collection' of Private Palestinian Libraries in West Jerusalem," *Journal of Palestinian Studies* 40, no. 4 (2011): 6–23; "The Destruction of Palestinian Libraries," [in Hebrew] *Mita'am: A Review of Literature and Radical Thought* 12 (2007): 41–52; and "Ownerless Objects? The Story of the Books Palestinians Left Behind in 1948," *Jerusalem Quarterly* 33 (2008): 7–20. Rona Sela has exerted great effort to identify and locate missing Palestinian films and other visual archival objects in Israeli archives, where they are sealed away, while declared by Israeli authorities as lost or missing. See Sela's "The Genealogy of Colonial Plunder and Erasure—Israel's Control over Palestinian Archives," *Social Semiotics* 28, no. 2 (2018): 201–29. Sela also made a documentary film about the stolen films and photographs, tracing them back to their original Palestinian owners: *Looted and Hidden—Palestinian Archives in Israel* (2017, 46 min.). Also important in this regard are the artistic efforts of Emily Jacir, particularly her 2010–12 work "ex libris," which is based on Gish Amit's research. Informed by Amit's findings, Jacir made several visits to the National Library of Israel (*ha-sifirya ha-leumit*) in Jerusalem, where looted Palestinian books are held, and made photos of the books using her cell phone. The images were first presented during dOCUMNETA 13, which took place in Kessel, Germany, in the Offenbach Archival Depot, where the largest stolen book redistribution project in history took place, following the end of World War II. The display was thus also a political act of demanding similar restitution

of Palestinian books to their original owners. For details on this project, see Eva Sharrer, "Emily Jacir: ex libris," *Nafas, Universes in Universe*, 2012, accessed April 25, 2020, https://universes.art/en/nafas/articles/2012/emily-jacir-documenta.

3 Ariella Azoulay has created several archives in an attempt to foster alternative historical logic and change the political visual conditions through which the archival material is understood; among these are her photographic exhibitions: *From Palestine to Israel: A Photographic Record of Destruction and State Formation, 1947–1950* (London: Pluto, 2011); *Constituent Violence 1947–1950* (Tel Aviv: Resling, 2009); and *Act of State: A Photographed History of the Occupation 1967–2007*, held at the Minshar Art Gallery in Tel Aviv in June 2007. Another impressive archive attempting to escape the dominant archival conditions in Israel/Palestine is her film *Civil Alliances*. Describing the motivation for making the film, Azoulay notes, "Documenting those civil alliances is an effort to return to that point zero, before the world shared by Arabs and Jews was halved almost irretrievably." See Ariella Azoulay, "Potential History: Thinking through Violence," *Critical Inquiry* 39, no. 3 (2013): 554. This Ground Zero is what I call "the moment before the moment."

4 When the New Historians researched the previously closed Israeli military and government archives during the 1980s, they radically challenged the official Israeli historical narrative about the 1948 war. These scholars found evidence for the forced expulsion of Palestinians, who were previously said to have "fled" by their own free will. The impact of this and other findings that criminalized Israel had a major impact on the Israeli public throughout the 1990s. Publications such as Benny Morris's *Birth of the Palestinian Refugee Problem, 1947–1949* (1987) and later books by Ilan Pappé, Tom Segev, Hillel Cohen, and Idit Zertal, among others, have had a great influence on rendering the Nakba visible and reversing Israel's official and distorted narratives. Palestinian scholars, who have a much harder time accessing Israeli archives, have also continued to expose and document the Nakba through archival research. Among the most influential researchers in this regard are historians Salim Tamari, Adel Manna, and Rashid Khalidi. In addition to scholars struggling with the Israeli archives in search for evidence and details about the Nakba, there are several important *generative* projects that establish alternative and informative archives primarily based on collecting oral testimonies as a form of alternative historical documentation. Among those, I would mention the "Palestinian Oral History Archive (POHA)" at the American University in Beirut (AUB) and available on its website (https://www.aub.edu.lb/ifi/Pages/poha .aspx). *The Christian Palestinian Archive* by Dor Guez is another interesting archival source, comprising digital scans of historical images stored on hard drives; read more about it at https://www.visibleproject.org/blog/project/the-christian -palestinian-archive/.

5 Efraim Karsh, "Debating Israel's History," *Middle East Quarterly* 3, no. 2 (1996): 19.

6 Benny Morris, *The Birth of the Palestinian Refugee Problem, 1947–1949* (Cambridge: Cambridge University Press, 1987).

7   Emphasis added. Ari Shavit, "Survival of the Fittest: Ari Shavit Interviews Benny
    Morris," *Ha'aretz*, January 8, 2004. Morris's account of "destroy" or "be destroyed"
    ignores that the Arabs he accuses of "aim[ing] to kill" were fighting a growing set-
    tler colonial movement, not planning to commit genocide.

8   Saidiya Hartman uses the term *critical fabulation* to describe her approach to the
    archive of the Atlantic slave trade: "I have attempted to jeopardize the status
    of the event, to displace the received or authorized account, and to imagine
    what might have happened or might have been said or might have been done.
    By throwing into crisis 'what happened when' and by exploiting the 'transpar-
    ency of sources' as fictions of history, I wanted to make visible the production
    of disposable lives (in the Atlantic slave trade and, as well, in the discipline of
    history), to describe 'the resistance of the object.'" "Venus in Two Acts," *Small Axe:
    A Caribbean Journal of Criticism* 12, no. 2 (2008): 11. More recently, and following
    Hartman's steps, Tavia Nyong'o has highlighted the importance of mobiliz-
    ing fabulation in keeping the tension and ambivalence between optimism and
    pessimism, as well as between fiction and history as sources of narrating resis-
    tance. See Tavia Nyong'o, *Afro-Fabulations: The Queer Drama of Black Life* (New
    York: NYU Press, 2019).

9   Kiven Strohm, "The Sensible Life of Return: Collaborative Experiments on Art
    and Anthropology in Palestine/Israel," *American Anthropologist* 121, no. 1 (2019):
    249.

10 Edward Said, "Permission to Narrate," *Journal of Palestine Studies* 13, no. 3 (1984):
    27–48.

11 Jumana Manna, "As Told to Lara Atallah," *Artforum*, September 8, 2015, https://
    www.artforum.com/interviews/jumana-manna-speaks-about-her-latest-feature
    -length-film-54890.

12 I thank Nasser Abourahme for engaging in a very productive conversation with
    me about this matter. Reflecting on Palestinian literature, Abourahme (whose
    grandmother Salma Khadra Jayyusi edited and wrote the introduction to the
    1992 *Anthology of Modern Palestinian Literature*—one of the first, if not the first,
    anthologies of modern Palestinian literature) notes that "most of the critics,
    like Said, understood Palestinian literature in its heyday as something defined
    overwhelmingly, beyond genre or style, by a will to narrative: a kind of drive to
    tell the story over and over again until you are recognized" (e-mail exchange,
    February 29, 2020). A similar argument can surely be made about Palestinian
    art post-1948 and until more recently. As acclaimed artist and art critic Samia
    Halaby notes in her landmark book, *Liberation Art of Palestine: Palestinian Painting
    and Sculpture in the Second Half of the 20th Century* (New York: H.T.T.B. Publications,
    2001), Palestinian art since 1948 labored to render visible and knowable a history
    of a people whose story was otherwise muted and silenced. For related arguments
    that trace recent shifts away from the documentary and witnessing and toward
    the experimental and performative in contemporary Palestinian literature and
    art, see Ihab Saloul, "'Performative Narrativity': Palestinian Identity and the

Performance of Catastrophe," *Cultural Analysis* 7 (2008): 5–39; Shir Alon, "No One to See Here: Genres of Neutralization and the Ongoing Nakba," *Arab Studies Journal* 27, no. 1 (2019): 91–117; and Esmail Nashif, "Mawt al-Nas" (Death of the People), [Arabic] *Majallat al-Dirasat al-Filastiniyya* 96 (2013): 96–117.

13 Wendy Brown, "Resisting Left Melancholy," *Boundary 2* 26, no. 3 (1999): 19–27.

Epigraphs: Basel Abbas and Ruanne Abou-Rahme, in conversation with Tom Holert, "The Archival Multitude," *Journal of Visual Culture* 12, no. 3 (December 2013): 353; Ariella Azoulay, *Potential History: Unlearning Imperialism* (New York: Verso, 2019), 186.

1 Carrie Lambert-Beatty, "Make Believe: Parafiction and Plausibility," *October* 129 (2009): 51–84.

2 Avery Gordon, *The Hawthorn Archive: Letters from the Utopian Margins* (New York: Fordham University Press, 2017), x.

3 Umar al-Ghubari and Tomer Gardi, eds., *Awda: Imagined Testimonies from Potential Futures* (Tel Aviv: Zochrot, 2013), 5.

4 Also worth noting are two new literary publications about imagined futures for Palestine. The first is the critical dystopia, *The Book of Disappearance* (*Sifr al-Ikhifaʾ*) by Palestinian writer Ibtisam Azem. The book, depicting the sudden disappearance of all Palestinians from Israel and critically engaging with the Israeli failure to deal with this disappearance, was first published in Arabic in 2014 and has been translated into English by Sinan Antoon. Another book is *Palestine +100: Stories from a Century after the Nakba*, edited by Basma Ghalayini (Manchester, UK: Comma, 2019). This collection of twelve stories from Palestinian writers, like *Awda*, presents a noncoherent image of the future, but overall it seems significantly less optimistic. In the opening story by Saleem Haddad, "Song of the Birds," the narrator anguishes: "We're just another generation imprisoned by our parents' nostalgia" (11). The narrator of Emad El Din Aysha's story "Digital Nation" warns us: "Utopia is a dangerous thing. It had to be stamped out. Hope was contiguous" (81).

5 See their website at http://www.decolonizing.ps/site.

6 As stated on the introductory page of their website: "'Arena of speculation' refers to an intellectual space of critical debate on the spatial futures of Israel-Palestine. . . . This website was established by a group of architects and spatial thinkers with the intention of offering a doorway to this growing sphere of agency, defined here as 'spatial resistance,' by drawing in perspectives encompassing spatial analysis, advocacy, critical speculation and physical intervention. It is hoped that rather than simply offering an echo chamber for debate, this deliberate juxtaposition of speculation with practice may highlight fragments of possible spatial futures that already exist, and how—in the midst of the myriad forces continually reshaping Israel-Palestine—these might represent seeds of an alternative future." See https://arenaofspeculation.org/intro.

7 Over the past decade a number of initiatives began to grapple with the architectural, spatial, and speculative aspect of *awda* ("return"). Among these works are the works of geographer Salman Abu Sitta in his book *Palestinian Right of Return: Sacred, Legal, and Possible,* and DAAR's project "Returns" on their website: http://www.decolonizing.ps/site/site3-returns.

8 Marianne Hirsch, "Stateless Memory," *Critical Times* 2, no. 3 (2019): 417.

9 Hirsch, "Stateless Memory," 417.

10 Hirsch, "Stateless Memory," 419.

11 The full details of the project, the proposal to UNESCO, images of the camp submitted with the proposal, and the responses of various specialists as well as members of the refugee camp are available online on the DAAR website's *Refugee Heritage* section. The introduction section states: "The UNESCO nomination dossier was originally prepared by DAAR (Alessandro Petti, Sandi Hilal, Sandy Rishmawi, Elsa Koehler, Isshaq Al Barbary, Mais Musleh) in consultation with Campus in Camps, Dheisheh Camp Popular Committee, Finiq Cultural Center, Ibdaa Cultural Center, Riwaq Center for Architectural Conservation and Centre for Cultural Heritage Preservation in Bethlehem. Special thanks to the Odah and Al Saifi families. Produced with the support of the Foundation for Art Initiatives and 5th Riwaq Biennale." Alessandro Petti, "Introduction," *Refugee Heritage, Decolonizing Architecture Art Residency,* 2017, accessed April 15, 2020, http://www.decolonizing.ps/site/introduction-4/.

12 UNESCO, Convention Concerning the Protection of the World Cultural and Natural Heritage, the General Conference of the United Nations Educational, Scientific and Cultural Organization meeting in Paris from October 17 to November 21, 1972, at its seventeenth session, https://whc.unesco.org/en/conventiontext.

13 Alessandro Petti, "Architecture of Exile IV.B," 2017, accessed April 10, 2020, https://www.e-flux.com/architecture/refugee-heritage/99756/the-architecture-of-exile-iv-b.

14 Petti, "Architecture of Exile IV.B."

15 Joan Smith, "I Find Myself Instinctively on the Other Side of Power," interview with Edward Said, *The Guardian,* December 10, 2001, https://www.theguardian.com/books/departments/politicsphilosophyandsociety/story/0,6000,616545,00.html.

16 Gilles Deleuze and Félix Guattari, *What Is Philosophy?,* trans. Graham Burchell and Hugh Tomlinson (New York: Columbia University Press, 1994), 110.

17 Antoine L'Heureux, "Art's Utopia: The Geography of Art against (Its) History," in *Art History after Deleuze and Guattari,* ed. Van Tuinen Sjoerd and Zepke Stephen (Leuven, Belgium: Leuven University Press, 2017), 258. Also see Gilles Deleuze and Félix Guattari, *A Thousand Plateaus: Capitalism and Schizophrenia* [1987], trans. Brian Massumi (Minneapolis: University of Minnesota Press, 2017).

18 Patrick Williams and Anna Ball, "Where Is Palestine?" *Journal of Postcolonial Writing* 50, no. 2 (2014): 127–33.

19 Burhan Wazir, "Palestinian Film Denied Oscars Entry," *The Guardian*, December 14, 2002, https://www.theguardian.com/world/2002/dec/15/film.filmnews.

20 Edward Said, *The Question of Palestine* (New York: Vintage, 1992).

21 Mahmoud Darwish, *Palestine as Metaphor*, ed. and trans. Amira El-Zein and Carolyn Forche (London: Interlink, 2019).

22 Said, *The Question of Palestine*, 175.

23 *Pessoptimism* was coined by Palestinian writer Emile Habibi in his 1974 novel, *The Secret Life of Saeed: The Pessoptimist*. The term merges the Arabic words for pessimist (*al-mutasha'im*) and optimist (*al-mutafa'il*).

24 Robin Kelly, *Freedom Dreams: The Black Radical Imagination* (Boston: Beacon, 2002), 10.

25 Ariella Azoulay, "The Imperial Condition of Photography in Palestine: Archives, Looting, and the Figure of the Infiltrator," *Visual Anthropology Review* 33, no. 1 (2017): 10.

26 Jacques Derrida, *Archive Fever: A Freudian Impression* (Chicago: University of Chicago Press, 1996), 36.

27 Basel Abbas and Ruanne Abou-Rahme, in conversation with Tom Holert, "The Archival Multitude," *Journal of Visual Culture* 12, no. 3 (2014): 353.

28 Gregg Burris, *The Palestinian Idea: Film Media and the Radical Imagination* (Philadelphia: Temple University Press, 2019), 18.

29 Ann Laura Stoler, "Colonial Archives and the Arts of Governance," in *Archives, Documentation, and Institutions of Social Memory: Essays from the Sawyer Seminar*, ed. Francis X. Blouin and William G. Rosenberg (Ann Arbor: University of Michigan Press, 2006), 269–71.

30 Derrida, *Archive Fever*. The amount of writing about the nature of the archive after 1995 is tremendous, and I cannot possibly include all references here. The following list mentions just some of the most critical texts. In defense of the "actual archive" (dusty files in a dusty building), see Carolyn Steedman's beautifully written *Dust: The Archive and Cultural History* (New Brunswick, NJ: Rutgers University Press, 2002). For the sensuality of the archive and the importance of historical archival work, see Arlette Farge, *The Allure of the Archives* [1989, French], trans. Thomas Scott-Railton (New Haven, CT: Yale University Press, 2015). Also see Markus Friedrich, *The Birth of the Archive: A History of Knowledge Cultures of Knowledge in the Early Modern World*, trans. John Dillon (Ann Arbor: University of Michigan Press, 2018). About colonial archives, see Antoinette M. Burton, *Dwelling in the Archive: Women Writing House, Home, and History in Late Colonial India* (Oxford: Oxford University Press, 2003); Diana Taylor, *The Archive and the Repertoire: Performing Cultural Memory in the Americas* (Durham, NC: Duke University Press, 2003); Anjali Arondekar, *For the Record: On Sexuality and the Colonial Archive in India* (Durham, NC: Duke University Press, 2009). About Affect Theory and archives, see Ann Cvetkovich, *An Archive of Feelings: Trauma, Sexuality, and Lesbian Public Cultures* (Durham, NC: Duke University Press, 2003); Tina Campt, *Image Matters: Archive, Photography, and the African Diaspora in Europe* (Durham, NC: Duke Univer-

sity Press, 2012). For the importance of archival fabulation, see Saidiya Hartman, *Wayward Lives, Beautiful Experiments: Intimate Histories of Social Upheaval* (New York: W. W. Norton, 2019) and Saidiya Hartman, *Lose Your Mother: A Journey along the Atlantic Slave Road* (New York: Farrar, Straus and Giroux, 2008). Finally, for a broad survey of the different meanings "the archive" carries in different disciplines, see Marlene Manoff, "Theories of the Archive from across the Disciplines," *Portal: Libraries and the Academy* 4, no. 1 (2004): 9–25; Harriet Bradley, "The Seductions of the Archive: Voices Lost and Found," *History of the Human Sciences* 12, no. 2 (1999): 107–22; Achille Mbembe, "The Power of the Archive and Its Limits," in *Refiguring the Archive*, ed. Carolyn Hamilton, Verne Harris, Jane Taylor, Michele Pickover, Graeme Reid, and Razia Saleh (Norwell, MA: Kluwer Academic Publisher, 2002), 19–27; Bhekizizwe Peterson, "The Archives and the Political Imaginary," in *Refiguring the Archive*, ed. Carolyn Hamilton, Verne Harris, Jane Taylor, Michele Pickover, Graeme Reid, and Razia Saleh (Norwell, MA: Kluwer Academic Publisher, 2002), 28–35. Also see Okwui Enwezor, *Archive Fever: Uses of the Document in Contemporary Photography* (New York: International Center of Photography, 2008).

31 Also, see Hal Foster, "An Archival Impulse," *October* 110 (2014): 3–22.

32 A less productive example, but surely widespread and similar in structure, is the feverish archiving of "present moments" on social media (Instagram is a perfect case), where every event posted and archived is generated as *already* a memory.

33 Cvetkovich, *An Archive of Feelings.*

34 Walter Benjamin, "The Work of Art in the Age of Mechanical Reproduction," in *Illuminations*, ed. Hannah Arendt, trans. Harry Zohn (New York: Schocken, 1969), 215.

35 Arjun Appadurai, "The Archive and Aspiration," in *Information Is Alive*, ed. Joke Brouwer and Arjen Mulder (Rotterdam: V_2 Publications, 2003), 15.

36 Michel Foucault, *The Archaeology of Knowledge and the Discourse on Language*, trans. A. M. Sheridan Smith (New York: Pantheon, 1972).

37 See Ariella Azoulay, "Potential History: Thinking through Violence," *Critical Inquiry* 39, no. 3 (2013): 548–74.

38 Abbas and Abou-Rahme, "The Archival Multitude," 353.

39 Abbas and Abou-Rahme, "The Archival Multitude," 353.

40 Walter Benjamin, "Theses on the Philosophy of History," in *Illuminations*, ed. Hannah Arendt, trans. Harry Zohn (New York: Schocken, 1968), 253–64.

41 Benjamin, "Theses," 255.

42 Benjamin, "Theses," 261.

43 Benjamin, "Theses," 255.

44 Derrida writes, "A spectral messianicity works in the concept of the archive and ties it, like religion, like history, like science itself, to a very singular experience of the promise" (*Archive Fever*, 27).

45 Pad.ma, "10 Theses on the Archive," April 2010, accessed April 25, 2020, https://pad.ma/documents/OH.

46 Stephen Best, *None Like Us: Blackness, Belonging, Aesthetic Life* (Durham, NC: Duke University Press, 2018), 15. For more on the significance of "recovery" as the main goal of scholarly engagements with the archive, particularly in the context of Atlantic slavery, see especially pages 13–22.

47 Sigmund Freud, "Mourning and Melancholia," *The Standard Edition of the Complete Psychological Works of Sigmund Freud, Volume XIV (1914–1916): On the History of the Psycho-Analytic Movement, Papers on Metapsychology and Other Works* (London: Hogarth, 1917), 243–58.

48 Best, *None Like Us*, 21. Emphasis in original.

49 Hartman, "Venus in Two Acts," 11.

50 Appadurai, "The Archive and Aspiration," 16, 24.

51 Yehuda Shenhav-Sha'harabani, "Reference," in *Awda: Imagined Testimonies from Potential Futures*, ed. Umar al-Ghubari and Tomer Gardi (Tel Aviv: Zochrot, 2013).

52 Derrida's definition of the archive already includes this destructive element *within* the archive itself. The archive is sustained by two opposed forces, he notes, following Freud's theory of drives; by the preservation drive (to keep, maintain, save from erasure) and its death drive (eliminate, do away with traces, forgetting). Thus, when the archive preserves, it also destroys; when it destroys, it also saves. The very drive that enables archivization to begin with "works to destroy the archive: on the condition of effacing but also with a view of effacing its own 'proper' traces—which consequently cannot be called proper" (*Archive Fever*, 10).

53 Jaimie Baron, "The Archive Effect: Archival Footage," *Projections* 6, no. 2 (2012): 103.

54 In this regard Baron writes: "The archival effect . . . depends on the individual viewer, who may respond to a variety of cues within the appropriated footage as well as to his or her extra textual knowledge about why this footage was made and for who it was originally indented" ("The Archive Effect," 112). In this case, a viewer who doesn't know Dana International or her cultural status within Israel and the pop global scene, or anything about the rave dances in Israel during the 1990s, is unlikely to experience an archival effect by watching the film.

55 Derrida, *Archive Fever*, 4.

56 For research on the centrality of the figure of the archive in modern art, see Ingrid Schaffner and Matthias Winzen, eds., *Deep Storage: Collecting, Storing, and Archiving in Art* (Munich: Prestel, 1998); Rebecca Comay, ed., *Lost in the Archives* (Toronto: Alphabet City Media, 2002); Charles Merewether, ed., *The Archive* (Cambridge, MA: MIT Press, 2006); and Okwui Enwezor, *Archive Fever*.

57 Featuring as a key figure in the archive is Dr. Fadl Fakhouri, a preeminent historian of Lebanon's Civil War, who is Raad's fantastic creation. Through him, and his authority as a "learned historian" and "archivist," Raad has generated multimedia works such as the photographic series *Missing Lebanese Wars, Linguistic* (1996–2002) and *Notebook, Volume 38: Already Been in a Lake of Fire* (1991) and the inkjet print series *My Neck Is Thinner Than a Hair: Engines* (2001). Together, the online archive, the fictional historian, and the fictional collection of videotapes,

along with the artistic multimedia engagements and performative talks by Raad, make for an archive that mainly functions as an intervention into the authoritative status of "the Archive" as a source of reliable information about the past.

58 Gayatri Gopinath, *Unruly Visions: The Aesthetic Practices of Queer Diaspora* (Durham, NC: Duke University Press, 2018), 149.

59 "The Palestinian Museum of Natural History and Humankind" is an ongoing conceptual project/artwork/institution/publication that Rabah established in 2003. The fictive museum is a nomadic entity, first shown internationally at the 2005 Istanbul Biennial, and since then in the New Acropolis Museum in Athens, the Brunei Gallery at London University's School of Oriental and African Studies, at De Appel in Amsterdam, and later also in Beirut, New York, and Venice. The collection brings to mind the kind of museum projects of the nineteenth-century World Fair exhibitions, where African and Native American indigenous people were put on display along with "natural elements" such as stones, fossils, etc. It is both critique of the Western museum and the colonial project and a modality of temporal imagination that invents a present (the museum), a past (the museum's collection), and a future (the possibility that this imagined potentiality will become a reality, if it hasn't already).

60 Hal Foster's discussion of "archival art" or the archival turn in art is limited to examples of art that create archives, stage archives, or create an aesthetic of archives. His examples are limited to European artists who collect, put together, and archive with both a "utopian ambition" and a sense of growing "paranoia" ("An Archival Impulse," 22).

61 Foster, "An Archival Impulse," 4. Also see Tess I. Takahashi, "The Imaginary Archive: Current Practice," *Camera Obscura* 22, no. 3 (2007): 179–84. She writes: "Imaginary archives often envision unrecorded pasts, produce other means of legitimizing information . . . they operate as a prescription and a manifesto—an alternative form of medicine for a sick and feverish culture plagued by forgetting" (180).

62 Emily Jacir is one of the most celebrated Palestinian artists working today. Her work is expansive and widely circulated across the globe. There are numerous reviews and published interviews with her in French, English, Italian (she resides in Italy and Palestine), and Arabic. In comparison to the limited amount of critical material I was able to gather in Arabic about most of the artists under discussion in this book, Arabic reviews and interviews with Jacir are relatively easy to find, even if limited in number. For some central online publications in Arabic, see Katia Haddad, "Palestinian Artist Emily Jacir Presents Her Work in 'Europa' Exhibition," *Al-Arab Al-Yawm* (*ArabsToday.net*), October 6, 2015, https://www.arabstoday.net/495/الفنانة-الفلسطينية-إيميلي-جاسر-تقدّم-أعمالها-في-معرض-أوروبا. Sana Al-Khoury, "Emily Jacir: Returned Safely from 'Where She Came From,'" *Al-Akhbar*, February 23, 2019, https://al-akhbar.com/Archive_People/118502; Ghassan Mafadleh, "Emily Jacir: A Lot from Palestine," *Al-Arabi Al-Jadeed*, January 18, 2015, https://www.alaraby.co.uk/%D8%A5%D9%85%D9%8A%D9%84%D9%8A%D9%8A%D9%8A%D9%8A%D9%8A

-%D8%AC%D8%A7%D8%B3%D8%B1-%D8%A7%D9%84%D9%83%D8%AB%
D9%8A%D8%B1-%D9%85%D9%86-%D9%81%D9%84%D8%B3%D8%B7%D9
%8A%D9%86; Roy Dib, "Emily Jacir Breaches Colonial Discourse," *Al-Akhbar*,
November 25, 2014, https://al-akhbar.com/Literature_Arts/41961.

63 Roland Barthes, "Theory of the Text," in *Untying the Text*, ed. Robert J. C. Young
(London: Routledge, 1981), 39.

64 Niamh Moore, Andrea Salter, Liz Stanley, and Maria Tamboukou, *The Archive
Project: Archival Research in the Social Sciences* (London: Routledge, 2016), 153.

65 See Dalia Karpel, "With Thanks to Ghassan Kanafani," *Ha'aretz*, April 14, 2005.
The review was followed by an official apology from *Ha'aretz*, but the reviewer
herself refused to admit fault or apologize.

66 One must note in this regard that Kanafani's novella is among the most canonical Palestinian narratives, widely read and globally circulated (the novella is
translated into English, French, Spanish, Italian, German, Danish, Swedish,
Norwegian, Hungarian, Polish, Dutch, Czech, Russian, Japanese, and Hebrew).
It is, without doubt, one of the most cited (and staged!) Palestinian literary
narratives of return and resistance, and hardly a text that can be "hidden" in another. The novella has also become well known through several global stage adap-
tations: first a film by Kassem Hawal (1982), then in 2011 a play directed by Israeli
playwright Boaz Gaon and director Sini Patar (with permission from Kanafani's
widow and his son), and more recently a new theatrical version by Ismail Khalidi
and Naomi Wallace (2018).

67 Daniel Boyarin, "The Sea Resists: Midrash and the (Psycho)Dynamics of Intertextuality," *Poetics Today* 10, no. 4 (1989): 662.

68 Wendy Hui Kyong Chun, "Unbearable Witness: Towards a Politics of Listening,"
in *Extremities: Trauma, Testimony, and Community*, ed. Nancy K. Miller and Jason
Tougaw (Urbana: University of Illinois Press, 2002), 159.

69 Quoted in Karpel, "With Thanks to Ghassan Kanafani."

70 Azoulay, "Potential History," 565.

71 Hannah Arendt, *The Origins of Totalitarianism* (New York: Harcourt Brace Jovanovich, 1973), 277.

72 Lila Abu-Lughod, "Palestine: Doing Things with Archives," 2018, 3.

73 Edward Said, "Permission to Narrate," *Journal of Palestine Studies* 13, no. 3 (1984):
27–48.

74 Gish Amit, "Ownerless Objects? The Story of the Books Palestinians Left Behind
in 1948," *Jerusalem Quarterly* 33 (2008): 8.

75 See Gish Amit, "Salvage or Plunder: Israel's 'Collection' of Private Palestinian
Libraries in West Jerusalem," *Journal of Palestinian Studies* 40, no. 4 (2011): 6–23. Also
see the film based on Gish's research: Benny Brunner, dir., *The Great Book Robbery*
(Xela Films, Al Jazeera English, 2011). Also see the exhibition and book created
by Palestinian artist Emily Jacir after she learned about the stolen books from
Amit's research. Emily Jacir, "ex libris," originally shown June 9–September 16,

2012, in Kassel, Germany, at dOCUMENTA (13), https://universes.art/en/nafas /articles/2012/emily-jacir-documenta/. Regarding the looting of Palestinian photography, see Ariella Azoulay, "Photographic Conditions: Looting, Archives, and the Figure of the 'Infiltrator,'" *Jerusalem Quarterly* 61 (2015): 6–22; Rona Sela, *Photography in Palestine/Eretz Israel in the Thirties and Forties* [Hebrew] (Tel Aviv: Muze'on Hertzliya le-omanut and Hakibutz Hameuchad, 2009); Rona Sela, *Made Public: Palestinian Photographs in Military Archives in Israel* (Tel Aviv: Helena Publishing House, 2010). Also see Rona Sela's documentary *Looted and Hidden: Palestinian Archives in Israel* (2017, 46 min.); Wahid Gdoura, "The Violation of Libraries and Books in Occupied Palestine: For the Safeguard of the Palestinian People's Cultural Heritage," in *Libraries of Jerusalem* (Tunis: AFLI, 2003): 36–38; and Aron Shai, "The Fate of Abandoned Arab Villages in Israel on the Eve of the Six-Day War and Its Immediate Aftermath," [Hebrew] *Cathedra* 105 (September 2002): 151–70.

76 See Ann Laura Stoler, *Along the Archival Grain: Epistemic Anxieties and Colonial Common Sense* (Princeton, NJ: Princeton University Press, 2008); James Lowry, ed., *Displaced Archives* (New York: Routledge, 2017); Esther Lezra, *The Colonial Art of Demonizing Others: A Global Perspective* (Oxford: Routledge, 2014).

77 Zionism, Judt writes, "arrived too late" and "has imported a characteristically late nineteenth century separatist project into a world that has moved on . . . the very idea of a 'Jewish state' is rooted in another time and place." Tony Judt, "Israel: The Alternative," *New York Review of Books*, October 23, 2003.

78 Sophia Azeb, "The No State Solution: Power of Imagination for the Palestinian Struggle." Interview recorded with Sophia Azeb in Los Angeles on April 27, 2014, https://thefunambulist.net.

79 On the Birzeit archive collection, see Roger Heacock and Caroline Mall-Dibiasi, "Liberating the Phantom Elephant: The Digitization of Oral Archives," Working Paper Series, Migration and Refugee Studies Module, 2011; and Ann Laura Stoler, "On Archiving as Dissensus," *Comparative Studies of South Asia, Africa, and the Middle East* 38, no. 1 (2018): 43–56. Also see Ahmad Melhem, "Palestinian Museum's Digital Archive Project to Preserve Heritage," *Al-Monitor*, March 11, 2018; and Naima Morelli, "New Directions for the Palestinian Museum: Interview with Director Dr. Adila Laïdi Hanieh," *Middle East Monitor*, June 26, 2019. Information about Guez's Christian Palestinian Archive can be found at https://www .dorguez.com/copy-of-the-architect-1, accessed April 15, 2020. Information about Jacir's project can be found at https://darjacir.com/News-and-Mag, accessed April 15, 2020.

80 See Khazaaen's website at https://www.khazaaen.org.

81 Appadurai, "The Archive and Aspiration," 25.

82 Azoulay, "Potential History," 558. Emphasis added.

83 Azoulay, "Potential History," 565.

84 "Control and Becoming: Gilles Deleuze in Conversation with Antonio Negri," *Funambulist* (1990), accessed April 15, 2020, https://thefunambulist.net/law

/philosophy-control-and-becoming-a-conversation-between-toni-negri-and
-gilles-deleuze.

85 Laurence J. Silberstein, "Becoming Israel, Israeli Becomings," in *Deleuze and the
Contemporary World*, ed. Ian Buchanan and Adrian Parr (Edinburgh: Edinburgh
University Press, 2006), 156.

86 Silberstein, "Becoming Israel," 156. Emphasis added.

87 Frederic Jameson, *Archaeologies of the Future: The Desire Called Utopia and Other Science Fictions* (London: Verso, 2005), 205.

88 Jumana Manna, "As Told to Lara Atallah," *Artforum*, September 8, 2015, artforum
.com/words/id=54890.

89 Michel Foucault, *The Archaeology of Knowledge and the Discourse on Language*, trans.
A. M. Sheridan Smith (New York: Pantheon, 1972), 128–29.

90 Philip Kohl notes that "the association between the development of archaeology
and nation-building was so obvious as to remain largely unquestioned throughout the nineteenth century and most of the twentieth century; the roots of
countries were extended back into the mists of the prehistoric past" (228). He
gives several examples, among them that archaeology helped turn "peasants into
Frenchmen," and propel the German reaction against the universalist ideals of
the Enlightenment: "Germany's pronounced 'cultural obsession' with philhel-
lenism, the glories of ancient Greece, and their subsequent establishment of
exacting standards of scholarship in allied disciplines, such as comparative phi-
lology and Altertumskunde" (229). While nationalist archaeology in Germany
developed largely beyond the borders of Germany, it led to an expanding national imagination into ancient times. Archaeology fits in differently in different
national contexts (the cases examined by Kohl are Spain, Greece, and Italy in
addition to France and Germany, Mexico, the Soviet Union, and China), but in
all of them it serves to solidify, expand, and ground national imagination. See
Philip L. Kohl, "Nationalism and Archaeology: On the Constructions of Nations
and the Reconstructions of the Remote Past," *Annual Review of Anthropology* 27
(1998): 223–46.

91 In *The Archaeology of Knowledge and the Discourse on Knowledge on Language* (1969),
Michel Foucault famously compares the study of archives to archaeological practice. For Foucault the archive is above all an ordering system: The "law of what
can be said" and "the system that governs the appearance of statements as unique
events" (145). Archaeology, according to Foucault, is the discipline that best "describes discourses as practices specified in the element of the archive" (148). One
could say that archaeology is the method that Foucault adopts for understanding
how the archive operates. Above all, "an archaeology of the archive will disclose
how we sculpt and resculpt the materiality of history. The shovel is also part of
the apparatus of social memory creation," to borrow Gabriella Giannachi's words
in *Archive Everything: Mapping the Everyday* (Cambridge, MA: MIT Press, 2015), 35.

92 Laura Marks, *The Skin of the Film: Intercultural Cinema, Embodiment, and the Senses*
(Durham, NC: Duke University Press, 2000), 66.

93 Hartman, "Venus in Two Acts."

94 Sherene Seikaly, "Palestine as Archive," Stanford University Press Blog, August 1, 2014, https://stanfordpress.typepad.com/blog/2014/08/palestine-as-archive .html.

CHAPTER 1: REVISITING THE ORIENTALIST ARCHIVE

Epigraphs: Beshara Doumani, "Archiving Palestine and the Palestinians: The Patrimony of Ihsan Nimr," *Jerusalem Quarterly* 36 (2009): 312; Omar Kholeif, "Focus Interview: Jumana Manna," *Frieze*, May 30, 2014, https://frieze.com /article/focus-interview-jumana-manna.

1 Born in New Jersey in 1987 and raised in Jerusalem, Manna is a sculptor and a video filmmaker currently residing in Berlin, Germany.

2 The Robert Lachmann collection includes 960 ethnographic records and 167 early commercial records of Oriental music recorded in North Africa and in Palestine. The archive also includes Lachmann's lectures about Oriental music, which were aired on the Palestine Broadcasting Service (PBS) between 1936 and 1939.

3 Ruth Katz's *The Lachmann Problem* (2003) is the only published manuscript to date dedicated to Lachmann's work as a musicologist in both Germany and Palestine. The book includes Lachmann's personal and professional letters, as well as a CD with his original recordings in North Africa, including Egypt and Palestine. A more recent publication by Ruth Davis, *Robert Lachmann: The Oriental Music Broadcasts, 1936–1937: A Musical Ethnography of Mandatory Palestine*, introduces Lachmann's radio lectures to readers.

4 According to Ruth Davis, "Lachmann was convinced that it was the inclusiveness of his vision and, in particular, his refusal to focus specifically on Jewish music, that underlay the reluctance of the Hebrew University to support his project" (*Robert Lachmann*, 7).

5 Andrea L. Stanton, *"This Is Jerusalem Calling": State Radio in Mandate Palestine* (Austin: University of Texas Press, 2013), 20.

6 Personal interview with artist, Berlin, July 6, 2016.

7 Robert Lachmann wrote and presented twelve radio programs entitled *Oriental Music*, which were transmitted by the Palestine Broadcasting Service between November 1936 and April 1937.

8 "Interviews: Jumana Manna, as Told to Lara Atallah," *Art Forum*, September 18, 2015, https://www.artforum.com/interviews/jumana-manna-speaks-about-her -latest-feature-length-film-54890.

9 Ruth Davis, "Ethnomusicology and Political Ideology in Mandatory Palestine: Robert Lachmann's 'Oriental Music' Projects," *Music and Politics* 4, no. 2 (2010), 3, accessed April 20, 2020, https://quod.lib.umich.edu/m/mp/9460447 .0004.205/—ethnomusicology-and-political-ideology-in-mandatory?rgn=main; view=fulltext.

10 Rachel Beckles Willson, *Orientalism and Musical Mission: Palestine and the West* (Cambridge: Cambridge University Press, 2013), 111.

11 Lachmann, quoted in Ruth Katz, *The Lachmann Problem*, 183–84.

12 From Jawhariyyeh's memoir, *The Storyteller of Jerusalem: The Life and Times of Wasif Jawhariyyeh, 1904–1948*, edited in English by Salim Tamari and Issam Nassar and translated by Nada Elzeer. For a detailed account of the exchange between Jawhariyyeh and Lachmann, see also Beckles Willson, *Orientalism and Musical Mission*, especially 204–6.

13 Katie Guggenheim, "Interview with Jumana Manna," Chisenhale Gallery London, September 2015.

14 Neta El-Kayam is an Israeli singer of Moroccan heritage. She has played a major role in promoting Moroccan music in Israel. For more information, see her webpage at http://www.netaelkayam.com.

15 Manna could access the Israel State Archives thanks to the fact that she is a Palestinian citizen of Israel; it would likely be impossible for a Palestinian without Israeli citizenship to gain such access. For more about the role of archives in Manna's film, see Asma Jawabreh, "Films, Music and Seeds: Jumana Manna's Means of Preserving Palestinian Heritage," *Al-Fanar*, March 3, 2020, https://www .al-fanarmedia.org/2020/03/artist-preserves-palestinian-heritage-through-film -music-and-seeds/.

16 For a discussion of the relationship between sound and memory ("the sound of memory" and "the memory of sound"), see Leslie Morris, "The Sound of Memory," *The German Quarterly* 74, no. 4 (2001): 368–78. Also see the essay collection, Karin Bijstserveld and José van Dijck, eds., *Sound Souvenirs: Audio Technologies, Memory and Cultural Practices* (Amsterdam: Amsterdam University Press, 2009). There has been a growing interest among scholars over the past years in the role of "sound" in our understanding of history. See in this regard Fahmy Ziad, "Coming to Our Senses: Historicizing Sound and Noise in the Middle East," *History Compass* 11, no. 4 (2013): 305–15; and Edwin Seroussi, "Nostalgic Soundscapes: The Future of Israel's Sonic Past," *Israel Studies* 19, no. 2 (2014): 35–50.

17 Robert Lachmann, from a lecture broadcasted on PBS, November 18, 1936. Quoted in Ruth Katz, *The Lachmann Problem: An Unsung Chapter Comparative Musicology* (Jerusalem: Hebrew University Magnes Press, 2003), 333.

18 Robert Lachmann, "Letter to Judea Magnes," November 14, 1937, quoted in Katz, *The Lachmann Problem*, 198.

19 For an excellent overview of the impact of Orientalist approaches to the study of Arab music by European musicologists who sought to "conserve" authentic local music in Palestine, see Beckles Willson, *Orientalism and Musical Mission*.

20 Jumana Manna, quoted in Daryl Meador, "Music Floats above Zionism's Barrier," *Electronic Intifada*, May 31, 2016.

21 Christine Antaya, "Ten Questions to Jumana Manna," *Kunstkrikk: Nordic Journal*, January 28, 2016, https://kunstkritikk.com/ten-questions-jumana-manna.

22 See Ruth F. Davis, "Robert Lachmann's Oriental Music: A Broadcasting Initiative in 1930s Palestine," in *The Mediterranean in Music: Critical Perspectives, Common Concerns, Cultural Differences*, ed. David Cooper and Kevin Dawe (Lanham, MD: Scarecrow, 2005), 79–95. Also see Ruth Davis, *Robert Lachmann: The Oriental Music Broadcasts, 1936–1937*, xxvi. For more information on the special status of Mount Scopus as a demilitarized zone placed under UN control and the Israeli convoy system, which, among other things, facilitated the movement of books, archival materials, and lab tools back into Israel, see Raphael Israeli, *Jerusalem Divided: The Armistice Regime, 1947–1967* (London: Routledge, 2002), 70–71.

23 "He was a Jewish, gay man escaping the Nazis, arriving to Jerusalem with his German partner," Manna comments, and "was unable to get funding because his work did not coincide with the political formations that triumphed." I was unable to find any further material about Robert Lachmann's partner or about him being gay (Antaya, "Ten Questions").

24 For a broader account of Israeli archival politics, see the important work of Gish Amit, which chronicles the theft of both Palestinian and Mizrahi artifacts and entire libraries: "Salvage or Plunder? Israel's Collection of Private Palestinian Libraries in West Jerusalem," *Journal of Palestine Studies* 40, no. 4 (2011): 6–23; "The Destruction of Palestinian Libraries," [in Hebrew] *Mita'am: A Review of Literature and Radical Thought* 12 (2007): 41–52; and "Ownerless Objects? The Story of the Books Palestinians Left Behind in 1948," *Jerusalem Quarterly* 33 (2008). Also see Rona Sela, "The Genealogy of Colonial Plunder and Erasure—Israel's Control over Palestinian Archives," *Social Semiotics* 28, no. 2 (2018): 201–29. Sela's essay adds to Amit's in discussing two later cases of Palestinians archives plundered by Israelis in Beirut in the 1980s: the Research Center of the Palestine Liberation Organization (PLO) and the Archive of Palestinian Films. Finally, see the film *The Great Book Robbery* (dir. Benny Brunner, 2013; Xela Films, Al Jazeera English), which documents the illegal confiscation of Palestinian books by Israeli army personnel in 1948 and the archiving of these books, still ongoing today in the National Library of Israel at the Hebrew University of Jerusalem.

25 Cheryl McEwan, "Building a Postcolonial Archive? Gender, Collective Memory, and Citizenship in Post-Apartheid South Africa," *Journal of Southern African Studies* 29, no. 3 (2003): 739–57.

CHAPTER 2: LOST AND FOUND IN ISRAELI FOOTAGE

Epigraph: DAAR (Decolonializing Architecture Art Residency), "A Demolition," accessed April 15, 2020, http://www.decolonizing.ps/site/a-demolition.

1 Amnon Niv, Amnon Schwartz, and Danny Schwartz.

2 DAAR, "A Demolition."

3 Kamal Aljafari, Palestinian film director, was born in 1972 and grew up in Ram-
   lah and Jaffa (in Israel/Palestine). He studied film at the Hebrew University in
   Jerusalem, and later in Berlin, where he resides today. His three films, *The Roof*
   (2006), *Port of Memory* (2009), and *Recollection* (2015), center on Jaffa, his childhood town.

4 Nathalie Handal, "Kamal Aljafari: Unfinished Balconies in the Sea: Interview
   with the Filmmaker," *Guernica: A Magazine of Art and Politics*, February 18, 2016.

5 David Pendleton, The Harvard Film Archive, 2010, from the abstract for the collection, *The Films of Kamal Aljafari* (2011).

6 Tel Aviv was established in 1909 as a "Jewish town" after the second wave of Jewish immigration into Palestine (*Aliya Shniya*), and as a response to the lack of
   housing in Jaffa. Approximately sixty families first moved to the newly created
   town bordering Jaffa. In effect, Tel Aviv was a Zionist city that preceded the establishment of the Zionist state. The idea of the founders of the city was to create
   a modern, European, ordered, and clean town suitable for the renewal of Hebrew
   life in the land of Israel.

7 Or Aleksandrowicz, "The Camouflage of War: Planned Destruction in Jaffa and
   Tel Aviv, 1948," *Planning Perspective* 32, no. 2 (2017): 2.

8 Hanna Hamdan-Saliba, "Urban Planning and the Everyday Experience of Palestinian Women in Jaffa," *Documents d'Anàlisi Geogràfica* 60, no. 1 (2014): 120.

9 Salim Tamari, "Treacherous Memories: Electronic Return to Jaffa," *Palestine-
   Israel Journal: Of Politics, Economic, and Culture* 5, no. 1 (1998), accessed April 15,
   2020, https://pij.org/articles/435.

10 Daniel Monterescu, "Heteronomy: The Cultural Logic of Urban Space and Sociality in Jaffa," in *Mixed Towns, Trapped Communities: Historical Narratives, Spatial
   Dynamics, Gender Relations and Culture Encounters in Palestinian-Israeli Towns*, ed. Daniel Monterescu and Dan Rabinowitz (Hampshire, UK: Ashgate, 2007), 157–78; and
   Daniel Monterescu, "The Bridled Bride of Palestine: Orientalism, Zionism, and
   the Troubled Urban Imagination," *Identities: Global Studies in Culture and Power* 16
   (2009): 643–77.

11 Eduardo Cadava writes beautifully about the image and the ruin and about the
   image of the ruin. The particular poetics of ruination: "The image, then: this
   means 'of ruin'—composed of ruin, belonging to ruin, taking its point of departure from ruin, seeking to speak of ruin . . . the emergence and survival of an
   image that, telling us it can no longer show anything, nevertheless shows and
   bears witness." In "Lapsus Imaginis: The Image in Ruins," *October* 96 (2001): 36.

12 Kamal Aljafari, *The Roof* (2006).

13 Shammas, an Israeli citizen, was very involved in both the Hebrew and Arabic
   literature scene in Israel until the late 1980s. He has long since left the country,
   stopped writing in Hebrew, and no longer identifies as an Israeli. He has, however, continued his remarkable translating work from Arabic to Hebrew. He
   currently resides in Ann Arbor, Michigan, where he also teaches in the Depart-
   ment of Comparative Literature at the University of Michigan.

14 Nadia Yaqub, "Refracted Filmmaking in Muhammad Malas's *The Dream* and Kamal Aljafari's *The Roof*," *Middle East Journal of Culture and Communication* 7 (2014): 164.

15 Handal, "Kamal Aljafari: Unfinished Balconies in the Sea."

16 Mark LeVine, *Overthrowing Geography: Jaffa, Tel Aviv, and the Struggle for Palestine, 1880-1948* (Berkeley: University of California Press, 2005), 220. Also see Andre Mazawi, "Film Production and Jaffa's Predicament," *Jaffa Diaries*, February 9, 1998.

17 Building on Barthes's theory of the studium and punctum in *Camera Lucida*, Yara Saadi analyzes Aljafari's use of artifacts from the Israel Film Archive as references stripped of their original narrative frame. See Yara Saadi, "Kamal Aljafari's 'Recollection': Tell Us, Tell Us about Jaffa," *7iber*, May 7, 2017, https://www.7iber .com/culture/recollection-review. For a comparative reading of the use of silence to challenge the authority of the Israeli archive in Aljafari's *Recollection* and Elia Sulieman's *Chronicle of a Disappearance* (1996), see Zeina Halabi, "When Kamal Aljafari Erased Chuck Norris from Jaffa," *Jadaliyya*, May 31, 2015, https://www .jadaliyya.com/Details/32115.

18 Ella Shohat, *Israeli Cinema: East/West and the Politics of Representation* (Austin: University of Texas Press, 1989), 127, 128, 134-35. Shohat notes that the "Charming gangster, Kasablan, the film slowly reveals, is a hero of the 1967 war who risked his life for his upper-class commander. When the Polish/Sabra woman and her family become aware of [his] patriotic nature, his ascendance on the social ladder is legitimized" (135).

19 Personal interview with the director, Berlin, June 6, 2016.

20 I am referring to a vast postcolonial discourse that has embraced the idea of irony and mimicry as the postcolonial aesthetic mode of representation par excellence. The most influential text in this regard remains Homi Bhabha, "Of Mimicry and Man," in *The Location of Culture* (New York: Routledge, 1994), 85-92.

21 Peter Limbrick, "Contested Spaces: Kamal Aljafari's Transnational Palestinian Films," in *A Companion to German Cinema*, ed. Terri Ginsberg and Andrea Mensch (West Sussex, UK: Wiley-Blackwell, 2012), 240.

22 I am, of course, alluding to Freud's definition of "the uncanny" in his essay by the same name, highlighting the double meaning of the German name *heimlich*, which stands for both belonging and familiar *and* concealed and invisible. Freud writes: "In general we are reminded that the word *heimlich* is not unambiguous, but belongs to two sets of ideas, which without being contradictory are yet very different: on the one hand, it means that which is familiar and congenial, and on the other, that which is concealed and kept out of sight." Sigmund Freud, "The Uncanny," in *Writings on Art and Literature* (Palo Alto, CA: Stanford University Press, 1997), 193-233.

23 Plenty of Israeli films were shot in Jaffa from the early 1960s through to the present. Judging by these films, one can conclude that Jaffa provided the perfect setting to construct new Israeli narratives on top of emptied Palestinian ruins.

Indeed, Jaffa served as a blank canvas onto which various fantasies could be played out: a "forbidden love" between a Mizrahi thug and an Ashkenazi woman (*Kazablan*, dir. Menachem Golan, 1973), a war between American soldiers and Arab terrorists taking place in Beirut (*Delta Force*, dir. Menachem Golan, 1986), stories of petty crimes, poverty, and prostitution (*Queen of the Streets*, dir. Menachem Golan, 1972), an impossible love of a Jewish man for a Christian woman (*Nini*, dir. Shlomo Suriano, 1963), a story of a policeman who falls in love with a prostitute (*The Policeman Azoulay*, dir. Efrain Kishon, 1971), and many more. For more details on these and other similar movies, see Shohat, *Israeli Cinema*, and LeVine, *Overthrowing Geography*.

24 Personal interview with the director, October 26, 2016, Los Angeles.

25 Personal interview with the director, October 26, 2016, Los Angeles.

26 Personal interview with the director, October 26. 2016, Los Angeles.

27 Handal, "Kamal Aljafari: Unfinished Balconies in the Sea."

28 Saree Makdisi, "The Architecture of Erasure," *Critical Inquiry* 36, no. 3 (2010): 527.

CHAPTER 3: "SUSPENDED BETWEEN PAST AND FUTURE"

Epigraphs: This text is originally from the Anglo-American Committee of Inquiry Report to the United States Government and His Majesty's Government in the United Kingdom, Lausanne, Switzerland, April 20, 1946, 38. The report concluded that Palestine was never colonized but was rather protected and taken by Western forces because it was necessary to ensure free access to the domain of archaeology. "Archive archaeology: Archiving and Collecting the Past," PhD course, Aarhus University, November 16–17, 2015, Nordic Graduate School in Archaeology in collaboration with the School of Culture and Society, Aarhus University, https://www.hf.uio.no/iakh/english/research/dialogues-with-the-past/courses/archive-archaeology-archiving-and-collecting-the.html; Nadia Abu El-Haj, *Facts on the Ground: Archaeology Practice and Territorial Self-Fashioning in Israeli Society* (Chicago: University of Chicago Press, 2001).

1 While the archaeological activities of digging, finding, and identifying go back centuries, the perception of archaeology as a "science" with growing credibility in mapping, cataloging, archiving, and verifying the historical identity of its findings can be traced back to the late eighteenth century. Such accreditation grows dramatically after the Darwinian evolutionary turn in the mid-nineteenth century and yet again in the mid-twentieth century with the development of chemical composition and DNA identification of deceased individuals. For more on this, see Paul G. Bahn, *Cambridge Illustrated History of Archaeology* (Cambridge: Cambridge University Press, 1996); Bruce Trigger, *A History of Archaeological Thought* (Cambridge: Cambridge University Press, 1989); Bruce Trigger, "Romanticism, Nationalism and Archaeology," in *Nationalism, Politics, and the Practice of Archaeology*, ed. Philip Kohl and C. Fawcett (Cambridge: Cambridge University

Press, 1995), 263–79; Christopher Evans, "'Delineating Objects': Nineteenth-Century Antiquarian Culture and the Project of Archaeology," in *Visions of Antiquity: The Society of Antiquaries of London 1707-2007*, ed. Susan Pearce (London: Society of Antiquaries of London, 2007), 267–305; Tim Murray, *From Antiquarian to Archaeologist: The History and Philosophy of Archaeology* (Barnsley, UK: Pen and Sword Archaeology, 2014).

2 See Sommer Ulrike, "Archaeology and Nationalism," in *Key Concepts in Public Archaeology*, ed. Moshenska Gabriel (London: UCL Press, 2017), 166–86; Victor A. Shnirel'man, "Nationalism and Archaeology," *Anthropology and Archaeology of Eurasia* 52, no. 2 (2013): 13–32; Margarita Díaz-Andreu, "Nationalism, Ethnicity and Archaeology: The Archaeological Study of Iberians through the Looking Glass," *Journal of Mediterranean Studies* 7, no. 2 (1997): 155–68; Rafael P. Curtoni and Gustavo G. Politis, "Race and Racism in South American Archaeology," *World Archaeology* 38, no. 1 (2006): 93–108; Chris Gosden, "Race and Racism in Archaeology: Introduction," *World Archaeology* 38, no. 1 (2006): 1–7.

3 C. W. Ceram, *Gods, Graves, and Scholars: The Story of Archaeology* (New York: Knopf, 1952), 20. C. W. Ceram is a pseudonym used by German journalist and author Kurt Wilhelm Marek.

4 Nadia Abu El-Haj, *Facts on the Ground: Archaeology Practice and Territorial Self-Fashioning in Israeli Society* (Chicago: University of Chicago Press, 2001), 48.

5 Sir Charles Moore Watson and Palestine Exploration Fund, *Fifty Years' Work in the Holy Land: A Record and a Summary, 1865-1915* (London: Committee of the Palestine Exploration Fund, 1915), 80.

6 Pablo Garcia, "Ruins in the Landscape: Tourism and the Archaeological Heritage of Chinchero," *Journal of Material Culture* 22, no. 3 (2017): 317–33.

7 Paul Carter, *The Road to Botany Bay: An Exploration of Landscape and History* (New York: Knopf, 1988), 69.

8 Suzanne Cassirer Bernfeld, "Freud and Archaeology," *American Imago* 8, no. 2 (1951): 125. She writes: "Archaeology represented for Freud not only the mastery of the death problem. Already in Freiberg he had identified the grave with his mother's womb, had united the dead and the not yet living" (125).

9 Sigmund Freud, "Constructions in Analysis," in *The Standard Edition of the Complete Psychological Works of Sigmund Freud, Volume XXIII (1937-1939): Moses and Monotheism: An Outline of Psycho-Analysis and Other Works* (London: Hogarth, 1964), 259.

10 Joanna Montgomery Byles, "Archaeology and Psychoanalysis," in *Méditerranée: Ruptures et Continuités*. Actes du colloque tenu à Nicosie les 20–22 Octobre 2001, Université Lumière-Lyon 2, Université de Chypre (Lyon: Maison de l'Orient et de la Méditerranée Jean Pouilloux, 2003), vol. 37, 60.

11 Most famously, Freud makes a clear tie between archaeology and psychoanalysis in his reading of Wilhelm Jensen's novella *Gradiva: A Pompeiian Fantasy* (1903). His "Delusions and Dreams in Jensen's 'Gradiva'" (1907) is a psychoanalysis of Norbert Hanold, the archaeologist and protagonist of the novella, who was himself

(in Freud's reading) Gradiva's analysand. In the novella, Hanold, in search of his own repressed desires, falls in love with a plaster cast of an ancient Roman marble relief of Gradiva, "The girl splendid in walking," from Pompeii. His passion for archaeology leads him to believe that the statue represents a real woman, who lived and died in Pompeii, and he is determined to find her traces: literally to search for her footprints in the volcanic dust of Pompeii. He finally encounters her as a ghost, walking through the ruins of the buried city, speaking German, before realizing that she is not a ghost at all, nor is she a statue come-to-life, but rather a woman he knows: Zoe Bertgang, a childhood friend who appears to be on a vacation in Pompeii with her zoologist father. This discovery leads to the end of Hanold's fascination with Gardiva and the beginning of a real love affair with Zoe. Freud's reading of the novella suggests that Hanold's archaeological interest was an outcome of his complex hysterical delusion, serving as an intellectual pretext for unconscious erotic desires for Zoe. In Freud's reading, Gardiva is the psychoanalyst who comes to rescue the archaeologist. Her "techniques are . . . surprisingly modern in their subtlety and their similarity to the contemporary fifty-minute hour [psychoanalytic session]" (Mary Bergstein, "Gradiva Medica: Freud's Model Female Analyst as Lizard-Slayer," *American Imago* 60, no. 3 [2003]: 291). Returning to Freud's reading of Jensen's novella, Jacques Derrida discusses both Hanold's attempt to find the original footsteps of a Pompeiian girl and Freud's efforts to analyze the story in terms of "archive fever": the desire to find the original (moment) and "the unique instant where they [the pressure and the trace] are not yet distinguished the one from the other" (Jacques Derrida, *Archive Fever: A Freudian Impression* (Chicago: University of Chicago Press, 1995), 99; Okwui Enwezor, *Archive Fever: Uses of the Document in Contemporary Photography* (New York: International Center of Photography, 2008).

For our part, the interesting part about Derrida's text is that it brings psychoanalysis and archaeology together under the discussion of the archive and the archival impulse. For Derrida, both archaeology and psychoanalysis bury just as much as they try to dig up. This is the paradoxical nature of the failed attempt to find a point of departure, a pure origin, a ground zero in the archive. Psychoanalysis's psychic archive may be approached by archaeological methods, but by the same token archaeology can no longer be thought of but through psychoanalysis. If archaeology is a mode of archivization, it is, as we learn from psychoanalysis, inevitably haunted by its invisible, repressed, and ghostly margins. The archive (any archive) can never *only* reveal or conceal. The very act of "digging" is always also an act of burying.

12 Freud's attraction to archaeology and antiques is well known. The man who became known as the father of psychoanalysis was drawn to archaeology not only because it offered him a structure and metaphoric language with which to discuss psychoanalysis's new methods of exposing and unveiling repressed memories, but also because this new science of excavating presented him with a language with which to imagine the psychic itself as an archive of memories.

13 Sansour and Søren Lind's *In the Future They Ate from the Finest Porcelain* (2016, 29 min.) is third in a trilogy of short sci-fi films she directed. Preceding it are *A Space Exodus* (2008, 5 min.) and *Nation Estate* (2012, 9 min.). Born in Jerusalem, Sansour studied art in Copenhagen, London, and New York. Her early work, preceding the trilogy, includes mainly short documentary films about everyday life in Palestine. With the trilogy, Sansour shifted from the documentary medium to fantasy, futurism, and dystopia. Viewed together, the three films progress from utopia to dystopia, and from irony to a more solemn mode of critique. About the trilogy as a work in dialogue with other postcolonial, non-Western sci-fi, see my essay: "Jerusalem, We Have a Problem: Larissa Sansour's Sci-Fi Trilogy and the Impetus of Dystopic Imagination," *Arab Studies Journal* 26, no. 1 (2018): 34–57.

14 Most classic works on sci-fi remain Euro- and US-centric. This is still the case for many contemporary scholars of sci-fi, for whom the Western canon remains the only source for imagining an alternative future. See, for instance, Louisa Kay Demerjian, ed., *The Age of Dystopia: One Genre, Our Fears, and Our Future* (Newcastle, UK: Cambridge Scholars Publishing, 2016), which speaks about dystopia as a genre of *our* time that focuses on *our* fears and *our* future, as if this is a global phenomenon. But a closer look at the book reveals that the texts discussed are limited to primarily well-known Western novels and young adult literature (*Hunger Games*). Many other canonical theoretical texts on science fiction, which are otherwise quite helpful and informative, remain of little use to those who wish to theorize science fiction from a non-Western point of view. This is also true for key theoretical texts such as Andrew Milner, ed., *Tenses of Imagination: Raymond Williams on Science Fiction, Utopia, and Dystopia* (Bern, Switzerland: Peter Lang AG, 2010); Tom Moylan and Raffaella Baccolini, eds., *Dark Horizons: Science Fiction and the Dystopian Imagination* (New York: Routledge, 2013); and, more recently, Gregory Claeys's *Dystopia: A Natural History* (Oxford: Oxford University Press, 2017). Recent attempts to challenge this Eurocentrism include Jessica Langer, *Postcolonialism and Science Fiction* (New York: Palgrave Macmillan, 2011); and Ericka Hoagland and Reema Sarwal, eds., *Science Fiction, Imperialism, and the Third World* (Jefferson, NC: McFarland, 2011).

15 The final scene, to which I return later, presents an alternative imagery for the iconic "Last Supper" image.

16 The essay-film genre incorporates text and image, following what can be loosely defined as an essay format. The genre is commonly characterized by fragmentation and a distinct lack of closure. Most film scholars agree that the attempts to define the essay film have so far only been partially successful, mainly due to the hybrid nature of the genre itself, which crosses between fiction and nonfiction cinema, and between cinematic and noncinematic qualities. Among the originators of this cinematic genre are Chris Marker, Alain Resnais, Agnès Varda, and Jean-Luc Godard. Later directors working in the genre include Chantal Ackerman, Werner Herzog, Harun Farocki, and Isaac Julian, among many others.

17 The text, written by Sansour and Søren Lind, is read as a dialogue between the
    narrator and her therapist. It is spoken in a Palestinian dialogue rather than
    classical (formal) Arabic. English subtitles appear on the screen, making the
    process of focusing attention even harder as one listens to the Arabic, follows
    the images, while all the time also being aware of the process of translation tak-
    ing place between the oral/audio and the written, the Arabic and the English.
    That viewing this film is an ongoing work of translation befits the general prem-
    ise of film, which both invites interpretation and negates the possibility of inter-
    pretation, presenting the latter as always already partial, violent, and misguided.

18 In a personal interview, Sansour shared with me the following comments about
    creating her frames: "All these archival images are taken from different colonial
    moments from Palestine's history . . . images from the Ottoman era, the British
    mandate and the early days of the Israeli state. The biblical [looking] figures are of
    a Samaritan from the late 19th century and of a Bedouin. The figures in modern
    clothes are from actual archival photos of Palestinians before 1948, before the
    Nakba. The image of the two girls is based on an actual archival image of two
    young Bethlehem girls from the late 19th century" (June 12, 2017).

19 Freud is following German psychiatrist Ernst Jentsch when he writes that the
    source of doubt the uncanny raises is about "whether an apparently animate
    being is really alive; or conversely, whether a lifeless object might not be in fact
    animate." See Sigmund Freud, "The Uncanny" [1919], in *Fantastic Literature a
    Critical Reader*, ed. David Sandner (Westport, CT: Praeger, 2004), 80.

20 Freud first develops the idea of "working through" when he observes resistance
    to therapy among patients and discusses the impact of this resistance on the
    patients' ongoing neuroses. He writes: "'Working through' of the resistances may
    in practice amount to an arduous task for the patient and a trial of patience
    for the analyst. Nevertheless, it is the part of the work that effects the greatest
    changes in the patient and that distinguishes analytic treatment from every kind
    of suggestive treatment. Theoretically one may correlate it with the 'abreaction' of
    quantities of affect pent-up by repression, without which the hypnotic treatment
    remained ineffective" (376). See Sigmund Freud, "Further Recommendations
    in the Technique of Psycho-analysis: Recollection, Repetition, and Working
    Through" [1914], in *Collected Papers Volume II* (London: Hogarth, 1948), 366–76.

21 The United Nations Relief and Works Agency for Palestine Refugees in the Near
    East (UNRWA) was founded in 1949 by United Nations General Assembly Resolu-
    tion 302 (IV) of December 8, 1949, to carry out direct relief and works programs
    for Palestine refugees. The agency began operations on May 1, 1950. The Gen-
    eral Assembly has repeatedly renewed UNRWA's mandate, most recently extend-
    ing it until June 30, 2020. For details see "Communiqué Ministerial Strategic
    Dialogue on UNRWA," April 12, 2019, https://www.unrwa.org/newsroom/official
    -statements/communiqu% C3% A9-ministerial-strategic-dialogue-unrwa.

22 Personal e-mail interview with the director, June 12, 2017.

23 "It was important for me to have the actors in clothing that was a complete rep-
    lica to what you see in the archives," Sansour comments on the two girls featured

in the center of the opening few scenes. "I worked with a Palestinian fashion de-
signer and tailor who has an extensive knowledge in Palestinian historical dress"
to make sure the images are modeled on the archive and that the acting parts
"blend" with the archival photographs (personal e-mail interview, June 12, 2017).

24 Labocine, "Envisioning Future States with Science Fiction," *Journal of Labocine*,
February 21, 2017, https://medium.com/labocine/envisioning-future-states-with
-science-fiction-7a4ea54e00ca.

25 For more on this, see Philip L. Kohl and Clare Fawcett, eds., *Nationalism, Politics
and the Practice of Archaeology* (Cambridge: Cambridge University Press, 1996);
Philip L. Kohl, "Nationalism and Archaeology: On the Constructions of Nations
and the Reconstructions of the Remote Past," *Annual Review of Anthropology* 27
(1998): 223–46; Effie-Fotini Athanassopoulos, "An 'Ancient' Landscape: European
Ideals, Archaeology, and Nation Building in Early Modern Greece," *Journal of
Modern Greek Studies* 20, no. 2 (2002): 273–305.

26 Nadia Abu El-Haj, *Facts on the Ground: Archaeological Practice and Territorial Self-
Fashioning in Israeli Society* (Chicago: University of Chicago Press, 2001), 1.

27 As noted by Nadia Abu El-Haj, archaeology has a special political theological
power given that "antiquities . . . are a distinctive breed of historical fact. They
are facts that can be seen and that were long understood to embody a kind of
ancient immediacy . . . biblical archaeology as a scientific field in the nineteenth
century [would use artifacts as] the empirical basis [on which] *knowledge* of biblical geography and history would be built. In turn, the geographies and artifacts
produced through archaeology's work could be used to evaluate—to confirm, in
effect—the historicity of biblical tales" (*Facts on the Ground*, 15).

28 Joseph P. Free and Howard F. Vos, *Archaeology and Bible History* (Grand Rapids,
MI: Zondervan, 1992); Alfred J. Hoerth, *Archaeology and the Old Testament* (Grand
Rapids, MI: Baker Books, 1998); P. R. S. Moorey, *A Century of Biblical Archaeol-
ogy* (Louisville, KY: Westminster/John Knox, 1991); Nur Masalah, *The Bible and
Zionism: Invented Traditions, Archaeology and Post-Colonialism in Palestine-Israel*
(London: Zed, 2007); Israel Finkelstein, *The Archaeology of the Israelite Settle-
ment*, trans. Daniella Saltz (Jerusalem: Israel Exploration Society, 1988); Raz
Kletter, *Just Past? The Making of Israeli Archaeology* (London: Equinox, 2006); Yael
Zerubavel, *Recovered Roots: Collective Memory and the Making of Israeli National Tra-
dition* (Chicago: University of Chicago Press, 1995).

29 Abu El-Haj, *Facts on the Ground*, 3.

30 Abu El-Haj, *Facts on the Ground*, 44.

31 From the Greek *outopos*, meaning "no place" or "nowhere," and the almost identical *eutopos*, meaning "a good place."

32 Frederic Jameson, *Archaeologies of the Future: The Desire Called Utopia and Other Science Fictions* (London: Verso, 2005), 205.

33 Jameson, *Archaeologies of the Future*, 205. Joan Gordon, following Jameson, argues
that utopia always excludes the imperfect and annihilates "the contamination of
difference." See Joan Gordon, "Utopia, Genocide, and the Other," in *Edging into
the Future: Science Fiction and Contemporary Cultural Transformation*, ed. Veronica

Hollinger and Joan Gordon (Philadelphia: University of Pennsylvania Press, 2002), 210. Jameson also adds that the utopia is "very much the prototype of the settler colony" (*Archaeologies of the Future*, 25).

34 Mark Dery, "Black to the Future: Interviews with Samuel R. Delany," in *Flame Wars: The Discourse of Cyberculture*, ed. Mark Dery, Greg Tate, and Tricia Rose (Durham, NC: Duke University Press, 1994), 8.

35 See Sami Schalk, *Bodyminds Reimagined: (Dis)ability, Race, and Gender in Black Women's Speculative Fiction* (Durham, NC: Duke University Press, 2018); and Justin Louis Mann, "Pessimistic Futurism: Survival and Reproduction in Octavia Butler's Dawn," *Feminist Theory* 19, no. 1 (2017): 61–76. *Pessoptimism* refers to the term coined by Palestinian writer Emile Habibi in his 1974 novel, *The Secret Life of Saeed: The Pessoptimist*. The term merges the Arabic words for pessimist (*al-mutasha'im*) and optimist (*al-mutafa'il*). See Emile Habibi, *The Secret Life of Saeed: The Pessoptimist*, trans. Trevor Le Gassick (London: Arabia Books, 2010).

36 In this sense, Sansour's film joins other Palestinian artistic projects that focus on a fictive future as a setting for discussing Palestine-in-becoming. One such example is Khaled Jarrar's 2011 passport stamp performative project, "Live and Work in Palestine." The project began with Jarrar inviting foreign visitors to Ramallah to stamp their passports with a Palestinian border patrol stamp he created. Jarrar first performed the act in Ramallah and later in various locations around the world. His stamp performance highlights the fictional existence of the state of Palestine, but also its potential, if contested, becoming. But there is a significant difference between the nature of Jarrar's futuristic project and Sansour's film. While Jarrar's project highlights the fictiveness of the Palestinian state at present, it nevertheless stages the state (the stamp granter) as the valid or representative agency of a future Palestine. Sansour's futurity, on the other hand, operates outside the temporality of the nation-state. It is a much less predictable future that replaces state-oriented hopes with a dystopic-utopic reflection on the nation's own fantastic status in a postfactual world.

37 Daniel Orrells, "Derrida's Impression of Gradiva Archive Fever and Antiquity," in *Derrida and Antiquity*, ed. Miriam Leonard (Oxford: Oxford University Press, 2010), 174.

38 I borrow the term from Reem Fadda, "Not-Yet-Ness," in *Liminal Spaces 2006–2009*, ed. Eyal Danon and Galit Eilat (Holon, Israel: The Center for Digital Art, 2009), 227.

CHAPTER 4: "FACE TO FACE WITH THE ANCESTORS OF CIVILIZATION"

Epigraphs: Azmi Bishara, "Bein makom le-merhav," [Hebrew] *Studio* 37 (1992): 6–9 (author's translation from Hebrew); "Ruanne Abou-Rahme and Basel Abbas in Conversation with Fawz Kabra," *Ocula Magazine*, January 18, 2018, https://ocula.com/magazine/conversations/basel-abbas-and-ruanne-abou-rahme/.

1 Personal interview recorded via videoconference call between artists and author in Ramallah and New York, respectively, August 26, 2019.

2 Palestinians have long engaged in various performed "acts of return," partly in a direct confrontation with the temporality of the Israeli state that marks the ruins as symbols of a past with no future. Among these acts of return and contemplation of the ruins and their temporality are, most notably, the case of al-Araqib—the village in the south part of Israel, the Negev, which has never been formally recognized by the Israeli state and has been demolished over ninety times, but continues to be rebuilt. See Silvia Boarini, "Village Refuses to Be Wiped Off the Map," *Electronic Intifada*, November 11, 2015, https://electronicintifada.net /content/village-refuses-be-wiped-map/14993; and "Among the Ruins of Bedouin Al-Araqib," Palestinian Return Centre website, September 11, 2012, https://prc.org .uk/en/post/2742/among-the-ruins-of-bedouin-al-araqib. Also see John Halaka's film *The Presence of Absence in the Ruins of Kafr Bir'im* (2007) about the Palestinian village Kafr Bir'im, the ethnic cleansing of Palestine during the 1948 Catastrophe, and the insistence of return to the ruins. There are also several films about returns to destroyed villages, among them, most notably, is Michel Kheleifi's *Ma'lul Celebrates Its Destruction* (Palestine, 1985, 30 min.). The film follows a yearly ritual that takes place on Nakba Day, in which elders take their grandchildren to their ancestral grounds to explore the remains and flora.

3 For a detailed account, see Yifat Gutman, *Memory Activism: Reimagining the Past for the Future in Israel-Palestine* (Nashville, TN: Vanderbilt University Press, 2017).

4 See the description on the artists' website, accessed April 20, 2020, https:// baselandruanne.com/And-yet-my-mask-is-powerful-Part-2. Also see Basel Abbas and Ruanne Abou-Rahme, in conversation with Tom Holert, "The Archival Multitude," *Journal of Visual Culture* 12, no. 3 (2014): 345–63.

5 In the 1950s, Israel's policy toward the remaining ruins of depopulated villages was mainly focused on the elimination of any visible signs that would "serve as a reminder to the Palestinian refugee problem" (Noga Kadman, *Be-tsidai ha-derekh u-be-shulai ha-toda'a: dehikat ha-kfarim ha-'arviim sh-hitroqnu be-1948 me-hasiah ha-yisraeli* [Hebrew] [*Erased from Space and Consciousness: Depopulated Palestinian Villages in the Israeli Zionist Discourse*] (Jerusalem: November Books, 2008), 30. In the 1960s and 1970s, erasure of ruins was still prevalent, but a competing trend of preservation emerged and was informed by the idea that the return of Jews to the Promised Land meant not just the redemption of the people but also the redemption of the land. Within this mindset, the redemption of the land meant, among other things, "a revival of the landscape which has been said to be destroyed and neglected by the previous inhabitants of the land" (Kadman, 38). As I will argue, archaeology functions in the service of the Zionist narrative about Jewish protection not only of the land but also of human civilization and the history of human presence in the land; hence the attentiveness to "ruins" *as ruins*, that is to say, as markers of a lost destroyed past that is turned into a site of memory. According to *Zochrot*, "More than two-thirds of KKL forests and sites—46 out of 68—conceal

or are located on the ruins of Palestinian villages demolished by Israel." Eitan
Bronstein Aparicio, "Most JNF-KKL forests and sites are located on the ruins
of Palestinian villages," *Zochrot*, April, 2014, https://www.zochrot.org/en/article
/55963.

6 The Israel Nature and Parks Authority (Rashut Hateva' Ve-haganim), a govern-
mental organization set up in 1998, runs several so-called archaeological parks
in Israel. Many of these spaces are constructed on the ruins of Palestinian villages destroyed in 1948. The incorporation of the ruins of Palestinian villages
into the Israeli landscape by means of resignification has been the topic of several studies to date, including Walid Khalidi, *All That Remains: The Palestinian
Villages Occupied and Depopulated by Israel in 1948* (Beirut: Institute for Palestine
Studies, 1992); Meron Benvinisti, *Sacred Landscape: The Buried History of the Holy
Land Since 1948*, trans. Maxine Kaufman-Lacusta (Berkeley: University of California Press, 2000); Susan Slyomovics, *The Object of Memory: Arab and Jew Narrate
the Palestinian Village* (Philadelphia: University of Pennsylvania Press, 2000); and
Kadman, *Erased from Space and Consciousness*. Also important in this regard is the
Hebrew-Arabic guidebook, Tomer Gardi, Umar al-Ghubari, and Noga Kadman,
eds., *Once Upon a Land: A Tour Guide* [in Hebrew and Arabic] (Tel Aviv: Zochrot/
Pardes, 2012). The book features walks through ruins of Palestinian villages and
urban neighborhoods, many of which have been "converted" into Israeli sites.

7 For a detailed account, see Nur Masalha, "Settler-Colonialism, Memoricide, and
Indigenous Toponymic Memory: The Appropriation of Palestinian Place Names
by the Israeli State," *Journal of Holy Land and Palestine Studies* 14, no. 1 (2015): 3–57.

8 "Ruanne Abou-Rahme and Basel Abbas in Conversation with Fawz Kabra," 2018.

9 Walter Benjamin, "Theses on the Philosophy of History," in *Illuminations: Essays
and Reflections*, ed. Hannah Arendt, trans. Harry Zohn (New York: Schocken,
1968), 257–58.

10 Personal interview, with Abou-Rahme and Abbas, August 26, 2019.

11 Abbas and Abou-Rahme, "The Archival Multitude," 352. My emphasis.

12 Abou-Rahme and Abbas's investment in new forms of archiving and archives
is not unconditional. They are well aware, as they mention themselves, of the
potential dangers involved in the process of "accessibility": "For us the potential
for archival activity, or the 'archival multitude' to produce subversive discourses,
in terms of both content and form, is only one current that is shaping the field of
possibilities for the archives to come. Another current is in many ways connected
to the logic of contemporary capital, the speed of the feed as we have mentioned
creates an incomprehensible overflow at points. Significantly it re-produces contemporary capitalism's obsession with the 'now,' the immediate, producing a vast
amount of material only to render it obsolete the very next moment in a continu-
ous stream of information" ("The Archival Multitude," 356).

13 Arjun Appadurai, "The Archive and Aspiration," in *Information Is Alive*, ed. Joke
Brouwer and Arjen Mulder (Rotterdam: v_2 Publications, 2003), 25.

14 Abbas and Abou-Rahme, "Archival Multitude," 353.

15 Ruanne Abou-Rahme and Morgan Cooper, "Invasions, Incarcerations, and Insurgent Imagination: Incidental Insurgents: An Interview," *Biography* 37, no. 2 (2014): 507–15.

16 Hal Foster, "An Archival Impulse," *October* 110 (fall 2004): 3–22.

17 Earlier works by the artists include *Contingency* (2010) and *The Zone* (2011), both of which also explore the relationship between artistic practices and acts of archiving, in terms of an exchange between fiction and history, the temporality of historical investigation, and that of poetic imagination.

18 Personal interview, August 26, 2019.

19 Adrienne Rich, *Poems 1971–1972* (New York: W. W. Norton), 62.

20 In general, Google searches are prominent components of the duo's creative process and aesthetics, and a documentation of their online searches is, in this case and many others, included in the final exhibition form of their work.

21 For more on the masks, see "Pictures of the Day: 6 April 2018," *The Telegraph*, April 6, 2018, https://www.telegraph.co.uk/news/2018/04/06/pictures-day-6-april-2018/group-palestinian-women-protester-guy-fawkes-masks-palestinian.

22 See the virtual tour, accessed April 20, 2020, http://s3-eu-west-1.amazonaws.com/shai-s.vr.face-to-face.eng/face_to_face_eng.html.

23 All quotations are taken from the exhibit's catalog.

24 See the virtual tour, accessed April 20, 2020, http://s3-eu-west-1.amazonaws.com/shai-s.vr.face-to-face.eng/face_to_face_eng.html.

25 Nadia Abu El-Haj, *Facts on the Ground: Archaeological Practice and Territorial Self-Fashioning in Israeli Society* (Chicago: University of Chicago Press, 2001); Uzi Baram, "Appropriating the Past: Heritage, Tourism, and Archaeology in Israel," in *Selective Remembrances: Archaeology in the Construction, Commemoration, and Consecration of National Past*, ed. Philip L. Kohl, Mara Kozelsky, and Nachman Ben-Yehuda (Chicago: University of Chicago Press, 2007), 299–325; Michael Feige, "Recovering Authenticity: West-Bank Settlers and the Second Stage of National Archaeology," in *Selective Remembrances: Archaeology in the Construction, Commemoration, and Consecration of National Past*, ed. Philip L. Kohl, Mara Kozelsky, and Nachman Ben-Yehuda (Chicago: University of Chicago Press, 2007), 277–98; Neil Asher Silberman, "Promised Lands and Chosen Peoples: The Politics and Poetics of Archaeological Narrative," in *Nationalism, Politics, and the Practice of Archaeology*, ed. Philip L. Kohl and Clare Fawcett (Cambridge: Cambridge University Press, 1995), 249–62.

26 On the modernity of archaeology and the national character of most archaeological projects, see Philip L. Kohl, "Nationalism and Archaeology: On the Constructions of Nations and the Reconstructions of the Remote Past," *Annual Review of Anthropology* 27 (1998): 223–46. Also see Siân Jones, *The Archaeology of Ethnicity: Constructing Identities in the Past and Present* (London: Routledge, 1997); Don D. Fowler, "Uses of the Past: Archaeology in the Service of the State," *American Antiquity* 52, no. 2 (1987): 229–48; Oleg Grabar and Benjamin Z. Kedar, eds., *Where Heaven and Earth Meet: Jerusalem's Sacred Esplanade* (Austin: University of

Texas Press, 2009); and Yannis Hamilakis, "Lives in Ruins: Antiquities and National Imagination in Modern Greece," in *The Politics of Archaeology and Identity in
a Global Context*, ed. Susan Kane (Boston: AIA, 2007), 51–78.

27 Ariel David, "Archeologists Recover Rare 9,000-Year-Old Mask Found by West
Bank Settler," *Ha'aretz,* November 28, 2018.

28 Despite agreements made during the Oslo negotiation period, Israeli archaeological activities throughout the West Bank remain a matter of daily business. While
most of these activities are performed by professional archaeologists, many amateurs are incorporated into the national project of digging. Hence, there seems
to have been no surprise or problem with the narrative about a Jewish settler
"taking a walk" and "bumping into" a nine thousand-year-old Neolithic mask on
the hills near Hebron. For more information on the post-Oslo agreements, see
Ziv Stahl, "Appropriating the Past: Israel's Archaeological Practices in the West
Bank," report by NGOs Emek Shaveh and Yesh Din, December 2017, accessed
April 25, 2020, http://alt-arch.org/en/wp-content/uploads/2017/12/Menachsim
-Eng-Web.pdf. Also see Dylan Bergeson, "The Biblical Pseudo-Archeologists Pillaging the West Bank," *Atlantic*, February 28, 2013, https://www.theatlantic.com
/international/archive/2013/02/the-biblical-pseudo-archeologists-pillaging-the
-west-bank/273488. Also see Diakonia International Humanitarian Law Resource
Centre, "Occupation Remains a Legal Analysis of the Israeli Archeology Policies
in the West Bank: An International Law Perspective," 2015, accessed April 25,
2020, https://www.diakonia.se/globalassets/documents/ihl/ihl-resources
-center/archeology-report-report.pdf. For a broader analysis of the politics
of Israeli archaeology, see Aharon Kempinski, "The Influence of Archaeology
on Israeli Society and Culture," [Hebrew] *Ariel* 100–101 (1994): 179–90; Yaacov
Shavit, "The Bible as History and the Controversy over the Historical Truth in
the Bible," [Hebrew] in *New Jewish Time: Jewish Culture in a Secular Era* (Jerusalem:
Keter, 2007): 129–34.

29 See references to Nadia Abu El-Haj, and Uzi Baram, under note 25.

30 Alex Shams, "Interview: Nadia Abu El-Haj on Archaeology and the Zionist Project," *Ma'an News Agency*, April 9, 2014.

31 Israel Finkelstein and Neil Asher Silberman, *The Bible Unearthed: Archaeology's
New Vision of Ancient Israel and the Origin of Its Sacred Texts* (New York: Free Press,
2001). Also see Feige, "Recovering Authenticity."

32 Mizrachi is quoted in Isabella Creatura, "Digging for the Holy Land: The Politicization of Archaeology along the Israel-Palestine Border," *Brown Political Review*,
November 6, 2015, http://www.brownpoliticalreview.org/2015/11/digging-for-the
-holy-land-the-politicization-of-archaeology-along-the-israel-palestine-border/.

33 I am thinking, for example, of W. E. B. Du Bois's famous words: "Every child
knows that ancient Jewish civilization centered in Palestine . . . everybody knows
the way in which the history of the Jewish religion is wound about Palestine and
from there how the thread runs through all modern history . . . finally after a
bitter fight there arouse with increasing voice a demand on the part of the Jews

themselves that they should go back to Zion and refound the state which they have lost." W. E. B. Du Bois, "The Ethics of the Problem of Palestine," ca. 1948, W. E. B. Du Bois Papers (MS 312), Special Collections and University Archives, University of Massachusetts Amherst Libraries, accessed April 20, 2020, http://credo.library.umass.edu/view/full/mums312-b209-i090.

34 Israel Ministry of Foreign Affairs, "Culture: Archaeology," 2013, accessed April 25, 2020, https://mfa.gov.il/mfa/aboutisrael/culture/pages/culture-% 20archeology .aspx, emphasis added.

35 Dayan was minister of defense during the 1967 war, and Israel's victory made him a mythical hero. During three decades between 1951 and 1981, Dayan established a vast collection of antiquities acquired through illicit excavations, as well as bought, exchanged, and sold antiquities in Israel and abroad. These activities seem to be an open secret in Israel. But often these activities have been justified as an act of saving antiquities from those who do not appreciate their scientific and cultural merits. Thus, for example, Dayan's biographer writes that Dayan was a learned explorer of sites, "who saved antiquities from destruction, a sort of Robin Hood who fought stupid bureaucracy." See Ben Ezer, *Courage: The Story of Moshe Dayan* [Hebrew] (Jerusalem: Ministry of Defense, 1997): 121, 218–19. For a critical and detailed account of Dayan's archaeological activities, see Raz Kletter, "A Very General Archaeologist: Moshe Dayan and Israeli Archaeology," *The Journal of Hebrew Scriptures* 4, no. 5 (2003). Kletter documents thirty-five cases in which there is solid evidence of robbing and illegal digging by Dayan. Also see Y. Ariel, "The Antiquity Robbery and Dayan's Collection," [Hebrew] *Ha'aretz*, April 13, 1986.

36 Abou-Rahme and Abbas, "Artist Statement," *And Yet My Mask Is Powerful*, 2017, accessed April 25, 2020, emphasis added. In a follow-up group exhibit, "Jerusalem Life," some of these masks were displayed at the Palestinian Museum in Ramallah (curated by Reem Faada, 2017); see https://www.palmuseum.org/ehxibitions /participating-artists-jerusalem-lives.

37 Becoming other for Deleuze is established via "diversity, multiplicity [and] the destruction of identity" (*Negotiations 1972–1990*, trans. M. Joughin [New York: Columbia University Press, 1995], 44); it presupposes breaking out of common ways of being so as to "bring into being that which does not yet exist" (*Difference and Repetition*, trans. P. Patton [New York: Columbia University Press, 1994], 147).

38 Personal interview, Skype recorded August 26, 2019.

39 Personal interview, Skype recorded August 26, 2019.

40 This is not the same as articulating a political plan in terms of "rights of return" understood as the establishment of Palestinian statehood. As recently noted by Rana Baker, "The problem with the present pro-Palestinian discourse is its fixation on statehood. Our primary aim must be the downfall of Zionism, its thudding defeat, before statehood. After all, post-colonial nation states do not seem to have fared well. Palestine need not follow their example." See Rana Baker, "Re-

turn to What? Against Misreadings of Gaza's Great March," *Mada*, October 14, 2019, https://madamasr.com/en/2019/10/14/opinion/u/return-to-what-against -misreadings-of-gazas-great-march/?fbclid=IwAR3sWF4qLQobHFRfK1zkxE3 XQqUKpnRQdIxtSz3pRfpPEI3Du4ak46rLqI.

41   Archaeological wars between Israelis and Palestinians have centered on the simple central question: "Who was here first?" Recent DNA studies of found skulls in archaeological diggings have similarly fixed on the identity of the Canaanites. Recently, for example, Palestinian Authority president, Mahmoud Abbas, stated, "We are the Canaanites," and concluded that "this land is for its people . . . who were here 5,000 years ago." The investment in the copy offers a radically differ-ent response to the Zionist archaeological fever. See Andrew Lawler, "DNA from Biblical Canaanites Lives on in Modern Arabs and Jews," *National Geographic*, May 28, 2020, https://www.nationalgeographic.com/history/2020/05/dna-from -biblical-canaanites-lives-modern-arabs-jews/.

42   In *"Incidental Insurgents,"* Abou-Rahme and Abbas follow a similar line of thought by staging the work as an act of "hacking archives": making everything that the archive presents as singular and precious into an infinite copy that can and does travel anywhere, always, and to everyone. Copy, mutation, replication—the ar-chive spills out if any attempt is made to fence and gate it. See Homi Bhabha, "Of Mimicry and Man: The Ambivalence of Colonial Discourse," *October* 28 (1984): 85–92.

43   Basel Abbas and Ruanne Abou-Rahme, *And Yet My Mask Is Beautiful* (New York: Printed Matter, 2017).

44   The work originally showed in 2016 in Carroll/Fletcher, London. It was later shown in 2017 in Kevin Space Kunstverein, Vienna; Art Jameel Project Space, Dubai; and Alt Bomontiada, Istanbul. In 2018 the work was exhibited in Kun-stverein in Hamburg, and in the Krannert Art Museum, Urbana-Champaign, Illinois.

45   Commenting on the aesthetics of the show, one reviewer astutely noted: "The format is accessible and familiar: a late-night dive into associative thinking, dense with layered, repetitive images and referential tangents, rubbing up against an intimately narrated sequence of handwritten notes—a detective's notebook at the scene of a crime." See Lynn Maliszewski, "Basel Abbas and Ru-anne Abou-Rahme's *And Yet My Mask Is Powerful*," BOMB *Magazine* (2017), accessed April 25, 2020, https://bombmagazine.org/articles/basel-abbas-and-ruanne-abou -rahmes-and-yet-my-mask-is-powerful/. Another reviewer described it as a "vir-tual museum." See Phillip Griffith, "Basel Abbas and Ruanne Abou-Rahme's *And Yet My Mask Is Powerful*," *The Brooklyn Rail* (2018), accessed April 25, 2020, https:// brooklynrail.org/2018/02/art_books/Basel-Abbas-and-Ruanne-Abou-Rahme -And-Yet-My-Mask-Is-Powerful.

46   Dieter Roelstraete, "The Way of the Shovel," *e-flux*, March 4, 2009, https:// www.e-flux.com/journal/04/68582/the-way-of-the-shovel-on-the-archeological -imaginary-in-art/.

47 This process of imagination is not presented as a negation of more practical at-
    tempts of return and reconstruction, such as demonstrated in the Palestinian
    ruins of Lifta (by Jerusalem) or Iqrit (north of Acai). Nor does the incentive to
    imagine otherwise stand in opposition to the "right of return," as it is discussed
    in international law. It does, however, suggest that the law in and of itself can-
    not provide a radical enough shift in political framework, in this case and more
    generally speaking.

48 Personal interview, Skype recording, August 26, 2019.

49 Ariella Azoulay, *Potential History: Unlearning Imperialism* (New York: Verso, 2019), 56.

50 Nasrin Himada, "For Many Returns," *Feature #3*, January 21, 2018, https://
    contemptorary.org/for-many-returns/? auth=req/.

51 Many scholars and activists today are thinking and rethinking the idea of "re-
    turn" in radical ways, not doing away with the importance of "the right of re-
    turn" for Palestinians but reimagining the meaning of "return" in the context
    of present-day and future politics. Consider, for example, the artistic project of
    "Permanent Temporalities" by Alessandro Petti and Sandi Hilal (and the DAAR
    collective), which highlights the permanency of the Palestinian refugee camp
    as a condition from which to think anew the meaning of "return." See Ales-
    sandro Petti, "Introduction," *Refugee Heritage*, Decolonizing Architecture Art
    Residency (DAAR), 2017, accessed April 25, 2020, http://www.decolonizing.ps/site
    /introduction-4/. Also see Nasser Abourahme and Sandi Hilal, "Intervention:
    (Self) Urbanization and the Contours of Political Space in Dheisheh Refugee
    Camp," *Jerusalem Quarterly* 38, no. 2 (2009): 59-77.

CHAPTER 5: GESTURING TOWARD RESISTANCE

Epigraphs: Quoted in André Lepecki, "Choreopolice and Choreopolitics: Or,
the Task of the Dancer," *The DraReview* 57, no. 4 ([1993] 2013): 13. Lepecki brings
the original German: "Sie zeigen an, dass wir in eine Situation geraten sind,
in der wir uns gerade politisch nicht oder noch nicht zu bewegen verstehen"
and compares it to the English translation from the 2005 collection of Arendt's
essays edited by Jerome Kohn. This sentence is translated by John E. Woods:
"They indicate that we have stumbled into a situation in which we do not know,
or do not yet know, how to function in just such political terms" (Arendt, *The
Promise of Politics*, 96). As Lepecki makes clear, the translation of "*zu bewegen*"
(to move) as "to function" deeply forecloses the kinetic dimension in Arendt's
formulation. I am thankful to Lepecki for his illuminating reading of Arendt:
"Performatively, Arendt's fragment persists, resonates, unsettles, stirs. Its afterlife expresses and beckons a challenge and a provocation that are both political
and kinetic—in one word, choreopolitical—a challenge we must answer" (14).
Hannah Arendt, *The Promise of Politics*, ed. Jerome Kohn (New York: Schocken,
2005). Renan Benyamina, "Archive: Interview with Arkadi Zaides," Festival

D'Avignon, 68th edition, 2014, accessed April 20, 2020, http://www.festival
-avignon.com/fr/spectacles/2014/archive. Farah Saleh, "Archiving Gestures
of Disobedience," *Contemporary Theatre Review* 27, no. 1 (2017): 145, accessed
April 20, 2020, https://hcommons.org/deposits/objects/hc:13884 /datastreams/
CONTENT/content.

1 Diana Taylor, *The Archive and the Repertoire: Performing Cultural Memory in the Americas* (Durham, NC: Duke University Press, 2003), 19–20.

2 Farah Saleh is a Palestinian dancer and choreographer active in Palestine, Eu-
rope, and the United States. Since 2010, she has taken part in local and interna-
tional projects with Sareyyet Ramallah Dance Company (Palestine), the Royal
Flemish Theatre and Les Ballets C de la B (Belgium), Mancopy Dance Company
(Denmark/Lebanon), Siljehom/Christophersen (Norway), and Candoco Dance
Company (UK). In 2016 she cofounded Sareyyet Ramallah Dance Summer
School, which runs on a yearly basis. She is currently an associate artist at Dance
Base in Edinburgh, UK.

3 See Basel Abbas and Ruanne Abou-Rahme, in conversation with Tom Holert,
"The Archival Multitude," *Journal of Visual Culture* 12, no. 3 (2014).

4 Marianna Liosi, "Speculations for Collective Transformations: Farah Saleh in
Conversation with Marianna Liosi," IBRAAZ: *Contemporary Visual Culture in North
Africa and the Middle East* 10, no. 5 (2016), accessed April 20, 2020, https://www
.ibraaz.org/interviews/204.

5 Biliana Vassileva, "Dramaturgies of the Gaga Bodies: Kinesthesia of Pleasure/
Healing," *Danza e Ricerca* 7, no. 8 (2016): 77, 93.

6 Gia Kourlasaug, "Twisting Body and Mind," *New York Times*, August 12, 2011.

7 For Naharin on Gaga and pleasure, see Deborah Friedes Galili, "Gaga: Moving
beyond Technique with Ohad Naharin in the Twenty-First Century," *Dance
Chronicle* 38, no. 3 (2015): 360–92.

8 Liosi, "Speculations for Collective Transformations."

9 Farah Saleh, "Archiving Gestures of Disobedience," *Contemporary Theatre Review* 27, no. 1 (2017): 145, accessed April 20, 2020, https://hcommons.org/deposits
/objects/hc:13884/datastreams/CONTENT/content.

10 Ariella Azoulay, *Potential History: Unlearning Imperialism* (New York: Verso, 2019), 286.

11 Azoulay, *Potential History*, 163.

12 Azoulay, *Potential History*, 187.

13 The epigraph is from Kathleen Stewart, *Ordinary Affects* (Durham, NC: Duke
University Press, 2007), 84.

14 Gabi Baramki, *Peaceful Resistance: Building a Palestinian University under Occupation*
(London: Pluto, 2009), 80–81.

15 E-mail interview with Saleh, November 12, 2019.

16 Simone Osthoff, *Performing the Archive: The Transformation of the Archive in Contemporary Art from Repository of Documents to Art Medium* (New York: Artopos,
2009), 11.

17 Saleh, "Archiving Gestures of Disobedience," 143

18 Saleh, "Archiving Gestures of Disobedience," 143.

19 During the late 1980s, performative acts such as the postcard projects by Birzeit University students and the secret study cells received considerable global media attention and were joined by activism across the globe. However, these acts have been largely forgotten, and they continue to be marginalized if not altogether erased from both the local and global political imaginary. Saleh's work confronts this contemporary erasure by not only reinserting these acts of resistance back into the public domain as a forgotten chapter in the history of Palestinian resistance, but by further examining them as living legacies of resistance with a potential to impact the present and future.

20 Saleh, "Archiving Gestures of Disobedience," 144.

21 *Gesture* derives from the Latin words *gestural*, meaning "bearing," "way of carrying," or "mode of action," and the infinitive form *gerere*, which means "to carry, to behave, to take on oneself, to take charge of, to perform or to accomplish." According to the Oxford English Dictionary, "gesture," as a noun, signifies "the manner of carrying the body," "grace of manner," "the employment of bodily movement," "position," "posture," or "attitude"; and, as a verb, "to order the attitudes of movements of (the body, oneself)." Andrew Colman explores the etymology of the word *gesture* in *A Dictionary of Psychology* (Oxford: Oxford University Press, 2001) and Adam Kendon does so in "The Study of Gesture: Some Observations on Its History," *Semiotic Inquiry* 2, no. 1 (1982): 44–62.

22 Carrie Noland and Sally Ann Ness, eds., *Migrations of Gesture* (Minneapolis: University of Minnesota Press, 2008), xiii. In the introduction Noland describes the numerous and often conflicting accounts of "gesture," centering on the main tension that shapes these debates between "two positions—gestures as indexical of subjectivity and presence versus gestures as signifiers for meanings generated by the mechanics and conditions of signification itself" (iv).

23 Noland and Ness, *Migrations of Gesture*, xiv.

24 For a magnificent talk/performance about the subordination of bodies to writing and the misconception of gesture as mere movement (not sign), see Susan Leigh Foster, "Choreographies of Writing," Susan Foster! Susan Foster! Three Performed Lectures, March 22, 2011, http://danceworkbook.pcah.us/susan-foster/choreographies-of-writing.html.

25 Marcel Mauss, *The Gift: The Form and Reason for Exchange in Archaic Societies* (London: Routledge, 1973).

26 Pierre Bourdieu, "Structures, Habitus, Practices," in *The Logic of Practice* (Cambridge: Polity, 1990), 73.

27 A work that could be compared to this is "Archive" (2015), by the Israeli dancer Arkadi Zaides.

28 Michel Foucault, *Discipline and Punish: The Birth of the Prison* (New York: Pantheon, 1977), 152.

29 Judith Butler, "When Gesture Becomes Event," Plenary Lecture, "Crossings and Transfers in Contemporary Anglo-American Thought," Theater Performance Philosophy International Conference, June 26–28, 2014, https://www.youtube.com/watch?v=iuAMRxSH—s.

30 Butler, "When Gesture Becomes Event."
31 Lepecki, "Choreopolice and Choreopolitics," 22. Emphasis added.
32 Lepecki, "Choreopolice and Choreopolitics," 25.

AFTERWORD

1 There is a great deal of writing on the erasure of the Palestinian narrative and
   the destruction of Palestinian archives. Among others, see Ahmad H. Sa'di and
   Lila Abu-Lughod, eds., *Nakba: Palestine, 1948, and the Claims of Memory* (New York:
   Columbia University Press, 2007); Nur Masalha, *The Palestine Nakba: Decolonising History, Narrating the Subaltern, Reclaiming Memory* (London: Zed, 2012); Rona
   Sela's documentary film *Looted and Hidden: Palestinian Archives in Israel* (2017) and
   her essay, "The Genealogy of Colonial Plunder and Erasure: Israel's Control over
   Palestinian Archives," *Social Semiotics* 28, no. 2 (2018): 201–29; Ilan Pappé, "Israel's Latest Attempt to Erase Palestine," *Electronic Intifada*, July 25, 2019, https://
   electronicintifada.net/content/israels-latest-attempt-erase-palestine/27941; Ofer
   Aderet, "Why Are Countless Palestinian Photos and Films Buried in Israeli Archives?" *Ha'aretz*, July 1, 2017, https://www.haaretz.com/israel-news/.premium
   .MAGAZINE-why-are-palestinian-photos-and-films-buried-in-israeli-archives-1
   .5490325; Ann Laura Stoler, "On Archiving as Dissensus," *Comparative Studies of
   South Asia, Africa and the Middle East* 38, no. 1 (2018): 43–56.
2 The Palestinian Cinema Institute (PCI) archive in Beirut, *The Culture and Arts Section*, directed by Palestinian artist Ismail Shammout, was destroyed by the Israeli
   army in 1982, but not all materials have been declared lost. This explains why
   there have been ongoing attempts to find and restore archival materials. These
   efforts include but are not limited to Rona Sela's article and film cited in the first
   note; Kais al Zubaidi, *Filastin fi al-Sinima* (Beirut: Institute for Palestinian Studies,
   2006) [Arabic]; and Emily Jacir and Monica Maurer's project to digitalize found
   Palestinian films and create a digital archive, described in Maureen Clare Murphy, "1970s Film of Palestinian Struggle in Lebanon Restored," *Electronic Intifada*,
   November 17, 2013, https://electronicintifada.net/content/1970s-film-palestinian
   -struggle-lebanon-restored/12914. Subversive Films and the Palestine Film Foundation have also done much work of cataloging, exhibiting, and circulating archival cinematic material from the 1970s. Finally, Nadia Yaqub's *Palestinian Cinema in the Days of Revolution* (Austin: University of Texas Press, 2018) documents
   restoration efforts and adds an important historical study of early Palestinian
   cinema.
3 Yaqub, *Palestinian Cinema in the Days of Revolution*, 199.
4 Yaqub, *Palestinian Cinema in the Days of Revolution*, 199.
5 *Our Small Houses* (24 min.) by the Iraqi writer and director Kassem Hawal is one of
   the few surviving films made by the cinema group Hawal, founded and led under
   the Central Information Committee of the Popular Front for the Liberation of

Palestine (PFLP). The film was damaged, and until recently it was overlooked in histories of revolutionary film. For more about the film, see Yaqub, *Palestinian Cinema in the Days of Revolution*, 145–47.

6 Aily Nash, "Working With, and Through, Conflict: Interview with Basma Alsharif," *BOMB Magazine*, March 12, 2015, https://bombmagazine.org/articles /basma-alsharif/.

7 Daryl Meador, "A Cinematic Rejection of Gaza's Isolation," *Electronic Intifada*, July 20, 2017, https://electronicintifada.net/content/cinematic-rejection-gazas -isolation/21131.

8 Gautam Valluri, "The Wanderer's Home Movies: An Interview with Basma Alsharif," *Projectorhead*, June 2016, accessed April 25, 2020, https://projectorhead .in/an-interview-with-basma-alsharif/.

9 Nash, "Working With, and Through, Conflict."

10 Gilles Deleuze, *Cinema 2: The Time-Image*, trans. Hugh Tomlinson and Robert Galeta (Minneapolis: University of Minnesota Press, 1989), 217.

11 Deleuze, *Cinema 2*, 223.

12 Sophia Azeb, "The No State Solution: Power of Imagination for the Palestinian Struggle," interview recorded with Sophia Azeb in Los Angeles on April 27, 2014, https://thefunambulist.net/podcast/sophia-azeb-the-no-state-solution-power-of -imagination-for-the-palestinian-struggle.

13 Along these lines, see Rana Baker, "Return to What? Against Misreadings of Gaza's Great March," *Madamasr*, October 14, 2019, https://madamasr.com/en/2019 /10/14/opinion/u/return-to-what-against-misreadings-of-gazas-great-march/ ?fbclid=IwAR18IxJWWEHSofpQttpkMtEUfuGh9W8w33KiEu7CIdjWWiZw LFr_CtcbXXc. She writes: "The problem with the present pro-Palestinian discourse is its fixation on statehood. Our primary aim must be the downfall of Zionism, its thudding defeat, before statehood. After all, post-colonial nation states do not seem to have fared well. Palestine need not follow their example."

Abbas, Basel, and Ruanne Abou-Rahme. *And Yet My Mask Is Beautiful*. New York: Printed Matter, 2017.

Abbas, Basel, and Ruanne Abou-Rahme, in conversation with Tom Holert. "The Archival Multitude." *Journal of Visual Culture* 12, no. 3 (2014): 345–63.

Abou-Rahme, Ruanne, and Basel Abbas. "Artist Statement." *And Yet My Mask Is Powerful* (2017). Accessed April 25, 2020.

Abou-Rahme, Ruanne, and Morgan Cooper. "Invasions, Incarcerations, and Insurgent Imagination: Incidental Insurgents: An Interview." *Biography* 37, no. 2 (2014): 507–15.

Abourahme, Nasser, and Sandi Hilal. "Intervention: (Self) Urbanization and the Contours of Political Space in Dheisheh Refugee Camp." *Jerusalem Quarterly* 38, no. 2 (2009): 59–77.

Abu El-Haj, Nadia. *Facts on the Ground: Archaeology Practice and Territorial Self-Fashioning in Israeli Society*. Chicago: University of Chicago Press, 2001.

Abu Sitta, Salman. *Palestinian Right of Return: Sacred, Legal, and Possible*. London: PRC, 1999.

Abu-Lughod, Lila. "Imagining Palestine's Alter-Natives: Settler Colonialism and Museum Politics." *Critical Inquiry* 47, no. 1 (2020): 1–27.

Abu-Lughod, Lila. "Palestine: Doing Things with Archives." *Comparative Studies of South Asia, Africa, and the Middle East* 38, no. 1 (2018): 3–5.

Aderet, Ofer. "Why Are Countless Palestinian Photos and Films Buried in Israeli Archives?" *Ha'aretz*, July 1, 2017. https://www.haaretz.com/israel-news/.premium.MAGAZINE-why-are-palestinian-photos-and-films-buried-in-israeli-archives-1.5490325.

Al-Azhari, Nada. "Paris: A Reference for Documentary Cinema." [Arabic] *Aljazeera Documentary*, April 3, 2018. https://bit.ly/366xUwU.

Aleksandrowicz, Or. "The Camouflage of War: Planned Destruction in Jaffa and Tel Aviv, 1948." *Planning Perspective* 32, no. 2 (2017): 175–98.

al-Ghubari, Umar, and Tomer Gardi, eds. *Awda: Imagined Testimonies from Potential Futures*. Tel Aviv: Zochrot, 2013.

Aljafari, Kamal. *The Roof*. 2006.

Al-Khoury, Sana. "Emily Jacir: Returned Safely from 'Where She Came From.'" *Al-Akhbar*, February 23, 2019. https://alakhbar.com/Archive_People/118502.

Alon, Shir. "No One to See Here: Genres of Neutralization and the Ongoing Nakba." *Arab Studies Journal* 27, no. 1 (2019): 91–117.

al Zubaidi, Kais. *Filastin fi al-Sinima*. [Arabic] Beirut: Institute for Palestinian Studies, 2006.

Amit, Gish. "The Destruction of Palestinian Libraries." [Hebrew] *Mita'am: A Review of Literature and Radical Thought* 12 (2007): 41–52.

Amit, Gish. "Ownerless Objects? The Story of the Books Palestinians Left Behind in 1948." *Jerusalem Quarterly* 33 (2008): 7–20.

Amit, Gish. "Salvage or Plunder: Israel's 'Collection' of Private Palestinian Libraries in West Jerusalem." *Journal of Palestinian Studies* 40, no. 4 (2011): 6–23.

"Among the Ruins of Bedouin Al-Araqib." Palestinian Return Centre, September 11, 2012. https://prc.org.uk/en/post/2742/among-the-ruins-of-bedouin-al-araqib.

Anglo-American Committee of Inquiry Report to the United States Government and His Majesty's Government in the United Kingdom. Lausanne, Switzerland, April 20, 1946.

Antaya, Christine. "Ten Questions to Jumana Manna." *Kunstkrikk: Nordic Journal*, January 28, 2016. https://kunstkritikk.com/ten-questions-jumana-manna/.

Appadurai, Arjun. "The Archive and Aspiration." In *Information Is Alive*, edited by Joke Brouwer and Arjen Mulder, 14–25. Rotterdam: V_2 Publications, 2003.

"Archive Archaeology: Archiving and Collecting the Past." PhD course description. Nordic Graduate School in Archaeology in collaboration with the School of Culture and Society, Aarhus University, November 16–17, 2015. https://www.hf.uio.no/iakh/english/research/dialogues-with-the-past/courses/archive-archaeology-archiving-and-collecting-the.html.

Arendt, Hannah. *The Origins of Totalitarianism.* New York: Harcourt Brace Jovanovich, 1973.

Arendt, Hannah. *The Promise of Politics*, edited by Jerome Kohn. New York: Schocken Books, 2005.

Ariel, Y. "The Antiquity Robbery and Dayan's Collection." [Hebrew] *Ha'aretz*, April 13, 1986.

Arondekar, Anjali. *For the Record: On Sexuality and the Colonial Archive in India.* Durham, NC: Duke University Press, 2009.

Athanassopoulos, Effie-Fotini. "An 'Ancient' Landscape: European Ideals, Archaeology, and Nation Building in Early Modern Greece." *Journal of Modern Greek Studies* 20, no. 2 (2002): 273–305.

Aysha, Emad El Din. "Digital Nation." In *Palestine +100: Stories from a Century after the Nakba*, edited by Basma Ghalayini, 77–94. Manchester, UK: Comma, 2019.

Azeb, Sophia. "The No State Solution: Power of Imagination for the Palestinian Struggle." Interview recorded with Sophia Azeb in Los Angeles, April 27, 2014. https://thefunambulist.net.

Azeb, Sophia. "Who Will We Be When We Are Free? On Palestine and Futurity." *Funambulist* 24, "Futurisms" (July–August 2019): 22–27.

Azem, Ibtisam. *The Book of Disappearance.* Translated by Sinan Antoon. New York: Syracuse University Press, 2019.

Azem, Ibtisam. *Sifr al-Ikhifa'* (*The Book of Disappearance*). [Arabic] Beirut: Dal al-Jamal, 2014.

Azoulay, Ariella. *Constituent Violence 1947–1950.* Tel Aviv: Resling, 2009.

Azoulay, Ariella. *From Palestine to Israel: A Photographic Record of Destruction and State Formation, 1947–1950.* London: Pluto, 2011.

Azoulay, Ariella. "The Imperial Condition of Photography in Palestine: Archives, Looting, and the Figure of the Infiltrator." *Visual Anthropology Review* 33, no. 1 (2017): 5–17.

Azoulay, Ariella. "Photographic Conditions: Looting, Archives, and the Figure of the 'Infiltrator.'" *Jerusalem Quarterly* 61 (2015): 6–22.

Azoulay, Ariella. "Potential History: Thinking through Violence." *Critical Inquiry* 39, no. 3 (2013): 548–74.

Azoulay, Ariella. *Potential History: Unlearning Imperialism*. New York: Verso, 2019.

Bahn, Paul G. *Cambridge Illustrated History of Archaeology*. Cambridge: Cambridge University Press, 1996.

Baker, Rana. "Return to What? Against Misreadings of Gaza's Great March." *Mada*, October 14, 2019. https://madamasr.com/en/2019/10/14/opinion/u/return-to -what-against-misreadings-of-gazas-greatmarch/?fbclid=IwAR3sWF4qLQobH FRfK4lzkxE3XQqUKpnRQdIxtSz3pRfpPEI3Du4ak46rLqI.

Barakat, Rana. "Writing/Righting Palestine Studies: Settler Colonialism, Indig- enous Sovereignty and Resisting the Ghost(s) of History." *Settler Colonial Studies* 8, no. 3 (2018): 349–63.

Baram, Uzi. "Appropriating the Past: Heritage, Tourism, and Archaeology in Israel." In *Selective Remembrances: Archaeology in the Construction, Commemoration, and Consecration of National Past*, edited by Philip L. Kohl, Mara Kozelsky, and Nachman Ben-Yehuda, 299–325. Chicago: University of Chicago Press, 2007.

Baramki, Gabi. *Peaceful Resistance: Building a Palestinian University under Occupation*. London: Pluto, 2009.

Baron, Jaimie. "The Archive Effect: Archival Footage." *Projections* 6, no. 2 (2012): 102–20.

Barthes, Roland. "Theory of the Text." In *Untying the Text*, edited by Robert J. C. Young, 31–47. London: Routledge, 1981.

Beckles Willson, Rachel. *Orientalism and Musical Mission: Palestine and the West*. Cam- bridge: Cambridge University Press, 2013.

Benjamin, Walter. "Theses on the Philosophy of History." In *Illuminations: Essays and Reflections*, edited by Hannah Arendt, 253–64. Translated by Harry Zohn. New York: Schocken, 1968.

Benjamin, Walter. "The Work of Art in the Age of Mechanical Reproduction." In *Il- luminations: Essays and Reflections*, edited by Hannah Arendt, 216–53. Translated by Harry Zohn. New York: Schocken, 1969.

Benvinisti, Meron. *Sacred Landscape: The Buried History of the Holy Land since 1948*. Translated by Maxine Kaufman-Lacusta. Berkeley: University of California Press, 2000.

Benyamina, Renan. "Archive: Interview with Arkadi Zaides," Festival D'Avignon, 68th edition, 2014. Accessed April 20, 2020. http://www.festival-avignon.com /fr/spectacles/2014/archive.

Bergeson, Dylan. "The Biblical Pseudo-Archeologists Pillaging the West Bank." *The Atlantic*, February 28, 2013. https://www.theatlantic.com/international/archive /2013/02/the-biblical-pseudo-archeologists-pillaging-the-west-bank/273488/.

Bergstein, Mary. "Gradiva Medica: Freud's Model Female Analyst as Lizard-Slayer." *American Imago* 60, no. 3 (2003): 285–301.

Best, Stephen. *None Like Us: Blackness, Belonging, Aesthetic Life*. Durham, NC: Duke University Press, 2018.

Bhabha, Homi. "Of Mimicry and Man." In *The Location of Culture*, 85–92. New York: Routledge, 1994.

Bhandar, Brenna, and Rafeef Ziada. "Acts and Omissions: Framing Settler Colonialism in Palestine Studies." *Jadaliyya*, January 14, 2016. http://www.jadaliyya.com /pages/index/23569/acts-and-omissions_framing-settler-colonialism-in.

Bijstserveld, Karin, and José van Dijck, eds. *Sound Souvenirs: Audio Technologies, Memory and Cultural Practices*. Amsterdam: Amsterdam University Press, 2009.

Bishara, Azmi. "Bein makom le-merhav." [Hebrew] *Studio* 37 (1992): 6–9.

Boarini, Silvia. "Village Refuses to Be Wiped Off the Map." *Electronic Intifada*, November 11, 2015. https://electronicintifada.net/content/village-refuses-be-wiped -map/14993.

Bourdieu, Pierre. "Structures, Habitus, Practices." *The Logic of Practice*. Cambridge: Polity, 1990.

Boyarin, Daniel. "The Sea Resists: Midrash and the (Psycho)Dynamics of Intertextuality." *Poetics Today* 10, no. 4 (1989): 661–77.

Bradley, Harriet. "The Seductions of the Archive: Voices Lost and Found." *History of the Human Sciences* 12, no. 2 (1999): 107–22.

Bronstein Aparicio, Eitan. "Most JNF-KKL Forests and Sites Are Located on the Ruins of Palestinian Villages." *Zochrot*, April, 2014. https://www.zochrot.org/en/article/55963.

Brown, Wendy. "Resisting Left Melancholy." *Boundary 2* 26, no. 2 (1999): 19–27.

Brunner, Benny. *The Great Book Robbery*. Xela Films, Al Jazeera English, 2011.

Burris, Gregg. *The Palestinian Idea: Film Media and the Radical Imagination*. Philadelphia: Temple University Press, 2019.

Burton, Antoinette M. *Dwelling in the Archive: Women Writing House, Home, and History in Late Colonial India*. Oxford: Oxford University Press, 2003.

Busbridge, Rachel. "Israel–Palestine and the Settler Colonial 'Turn': From Interpretation to Decolonization." *Theory, Culture and Society* 35, no. 1 (2018): 91–115.

Butler, Judith. "When Gesture Becomes Event." Plenary Lecture, "Crossings and Transfers in Contemporary Anglo-American Thought," Theater Performance Philosophy International Conference, June 26–28, 2014. https://www.youtube .com/watch?v=iuAMRxSH--s.

Cadava, Eduardo. "Lapsus Imaginis: The Image in Ruins." *October* 96 (2001): 35–60.

Campt, Tina. *Image Matters: Archive, Photography, and the African Diaspora in Europe*. Durham, NC: Duke University Press, 2012.

Carter, Paul. *The Road to Botany Bay: An Exploration of Landscape and History*. New York: Knopf, 1988.

Cassirer Bernfeld, Suzanne. "Freud and Archaeology." *American Imago* 8, no. 2 (1951): 107–28.

Ceram, C. W. *Gods, Graves, and Scholars: The Story of Archaeology*. New York: Knopf, 1952.

Claeys, Gregory. *Dystopia: A Natural History*. Oxford: Oxford University Press, 2017.

Clare Murphy, Maureen. "1970s Film of Palestinian Struggle in Lebanon Restored." *Electronic Intifada*, November 17, 2013. https://electronicintifada.net/content /1970s-film-palestinian-struggle-lebanon-restored/12914.

Colman, Andrew. *A Dictionary of Psychology*. Oxford: Oxford University Press, 2001.

Comay, Rebecca, ed. *Lost in the Archives*. Toronto: Alphabet City Media, 2002.

"Communiqué Ministerial Strategic Dialogue on UNRWA," April 12, 2019. https:// www.unrwa.org/newsroom/official-statements/communiqu%C3%A9-ministeri al-strategic-dialogue-unrwa.

"Control and Becoming: Gilles Deleuze in Conversation with Antonio Negri." *Funam- bulist* (1990). Accessed April 15, 2020. https://thefunambulist.net/law/philosophy -control-and-becoming-a-conversation-between-toni-negri-and-gilles-deleuze.

Creatura, Isabella. "Digging for the Holy Land: The Politicization of Archaeology along the Israel-Palestine Border." *Brown Political Review*, November 6, 2015. http://www.brownpoliticalreview.org/2015/11/digging-for-the-holy-land-the -politicization-of-archaeology-along-the-israel-palestine-border.

Curtoni, Rafael P., and Gustavo G. Politis. "Race and Racism in South American Archaeology." *World Archaeology* 38, no. 1 (2006): 93–108.

Cvetkovich, Ann. *An Archive of Feelings: Trauma, Sexuality, and Lesbian Public Cultures*. Durham, NC: Duke University Press, 2003.

DAAR: Decolonializing Architecture Art Residency. "A Demolition." Accessed April 15, 2020. http://www.decolonizing.ps/site/a-demolition.

Darwish, Mahmoud. *Palestine as Metaphor*. Edited and translated by Amira El-Zein and Carolyn Forche. London: Interlink Pub Group, 2019.

David, Ariel. "Archeologists Recover Rare 9,000-Year-Old Mask Found by West Bank Settler." *Ha'aretz*, November 28, 2018.

Davis, Ruth. "Ethnomusicology and Political Ideology in Mandatory Palestine: Robert Lachmann's 'Oriental Music' Projects." *Music and Politics* 4, no. 2 (2010). Accessed April 20, 2020. https://quod.lib.umich.edu/m/mp/9460447.0004 .205/--ethnomusicology-and-political-ideology-in-mandatory?rgn=main;view =fulltext.

Davis, Ruth. *Robert Lachmann: The Oriental Music Broadcasts, 1936–1937: A Musical Ethnography of Mandatory Palestine*. Middleton, WI: A-R Editions, 2013.

Davis, Ruth. "Robert Lachmann's Oriental Music: A Broadcasting Initiative in 1930s Palestine." In *The Mediterranean in Music: Critical Perspectives, Common Concerns, Cultural Differences*, edited by David Cooper and Kevin Dawe, 79–95. Lanham, MD: Scarecrow, 2005.

Deleuze, Gilles. *Cinema 2: The Time–Image*. Translated by Hugh Tomlinson and Robert Galeta. Minneapolis: University of Minnesota Press, 1989.

Deleuze, Gilles. *Difference and Repetition*. Translated by P. Patton. New York: Colum- bia University Press, 1994.

Deleuze, Gilles. *Negotiations 1972–1990*. Translated by M. Joughin. New York: Co- lumbia University Press, 1995.

Deleuze, Gilles, and Félix Guattari. *A Thousand Plateaus: Capitalism and Schizophrenia.* [1987] Translated by Brian Massumi. Minneapolis: University of Minnesota Press, 2017.

Deleuze, Gilles, and Félix Guattari. *What Is Philosophy?* Translated by Graham Burchell and Hugh Tomlinson. New York: Columbia University Press, 1994.

Demerjian, Louisa Kay, ed. *The Age of Dystopia: One Genre, Our Fears, and Our Future.* Newcastle, UK: Cambridge Scholars Publishing, 2016.

Derrida, Jacques. *Archive Fever: A Freudian Impression.* Chicago: University of Chicago Press, 1995.

Dery, Mark. "Black to the Future: Interviews with Samuel R. Delany." In *Flame Wars: The Discourse of Cyberculture*, edited by Mark Dery, Greg Tate, and Tricia Rose, 179–222. Durham, NC: Duke University Press, 1994.

Diakonia International Humanitarian Law Resource Centre. "Occupation Remains a Legal Analysis of the Israeli Archeology Policies in the West Bank: An International Law Perspective," 2015. Accessed April 25, 2020. https://www.diakonia .se/globalassets/documents/ihl/ihl-resources-center/archeology-report-report .pdf.

Díaz-Andreu, Margarita. "Nationalism, Ethnicity and Archaeology: The Archaeological Study of Iberians through the Looking Glass." *Journal of Mediterranean Studies* 7, no. 2 (1997): 155–68.

Dib, Roy. "Emily Jacir Breaches Colonial Discourse." *Al-Akhbar*, November 25, 2014. https://al-akhbar.com/Literature_Arts/41961.

Doumani, Bishara. "Archiving Palestine and the Palestinians: The Patrimony of Ihsan Nimr." *Jerusalem Quarterly* 36 (2009): 312.

Du Bois, W. E. B. "The Ethics of the Problem of Palestine." ca. 1948. W. E. B. Du Bois Papers (MS 312), Special Collections and University Archives, University of Massachusetts Amherst Libraries. Accessed April 20, 2020. http://credo.library .umass.edu/view/full/mums312-b209-i090.

Enwezor, Okwui. *Archive Fever: Uses of the Document in Contemporary Photography.* New York: International Center of Photography, 2008.

Evans, Christopher. "'Delineating Objects': Nineteenth-Century Antiquarian Culture and the Project of Archaeology." In *Visions of Antiquity: The Society of Antiquaries of London 1707-2007*, edited by Susan Pearce, 267–305. London: Society of Antiquaries of London, 2007.

Ezer, Ben. *Courage: The Story of Moshe Dayan.* [Hebrew] Jerusalem: Ministry of Defense, 1997.

Fadda, Reem. "Not-Yet-Ness." In *Liminal Spaces 2006-2009*, edited by Eyal Danon and Galit Eilat, 223–31. Holon, Israel: The Center for Digital Art, 2009.

Fanon, Frantz. *Black Skin, White Masks.* [1952] New York: Grove Press, 1967.

Farge, Arlette. *The Allure of the Archives.* [1989, French] Translated by Thomas Scott-Railton. New Haven, CT: Yale University Press, 2015.

Feige, Michael. "Recovering Authenticity: West-Bank Settlers and the Second Stage of National Archaeology." In *Selective Remembrances: Archaeology in the Construc-*

tion, Commemoration, and Consecration of National Past, edited by Philip L. Kohl, Mara Kozelsky, and Nachman Ben-Yehuda, 277–98. Chicago: University of Chicago Press, 2007.

Finkelstein, Israel. The Archaeology of the Israelite Settlement. Translated by Daniella Saltz. Jerusalem: Israel Exploration Society, 1988.

Finkelstein, Israel, and Neil Asher Silberman. The Bible Unearthed: Archaeology's New Vision of Ancient Israel and the Origin of Its Sacred Texts. New York: The Free Press, 2001.

Foster, Hal. "An Archival Impulse." October 110 (2014): 3–22.

Foucault, Michel. The Archaeology of Knowledge and the Discourse on Language. Translated by A. M. Sheridan Smith. New York: Pantheon, 1972.

Foucault, Michel. Discipline and Punish: The Birth of the Prison. New York: Pantheon, 1977.

Fowler, Don D. "Uses of the Past: Archaeology in the Service of the State." American Antiquity 52, no. 2 (1987): 229–48.

Free, Joseph P., and Howard F. Vos. Archaeology and Bible History. Grand Rapids, MI: Zondervan, 1992.

Freud, Sigmund. "Constructions in Analysis." In The Standard Edition of the Complete Psychological Works of Sigmund Freud, Volume XXIII (1937–1939): Moses and Monotheism: An Outline of Psycho-Analysis and Other Works, 257–69. London: Hogarth, 1964.

Freud, Sigmund. "Further Recommendations in the Technique of Psycho-Analysis: Recollection, Repetition, and Working Through." [1914] In Collected Papers Volume II, 366–76. London: Hogarth, 1948.

Freud, Sigmund. "Mourning and Melancholia." The Standard Edition of the Complete Psychological Works of Sigmund Freud, Volume XIV (1914–1916): On the History of the Psycho-Analytic Movement, Papers on Metapsychology and Other Works, 243–58. London: Hogarth, 1917.

Freud, Sigmund. "The Uncanny." In Writings on Art and Literature, 193–233. Palo Alto, CA: Stanford University Press, 1997.

Freud, Sigmund. "The Uncanny." [1919] In Fantastic Literature: A Critical Reader, edited by David Sandner, 74–101. Westport, CT: Praeger, 2004.

Friedes Galili, Deborah. "Gaga: Moving beyond Technique with Ohad Naharin in the Twenty-First Century." Dance Chronicle 38, no. 3 (2015): 360–92.

Friedrich, Markus. The Birth of the Archive: A History of Knowledge. Translated by John Noël Dillon. Ann Arbor: University of Michigan Press, 2018.

Garcia, Pablo. "Ruins in the Landscape: Tourism and the Archaeological Heritage of Chinchero." Journal of Material Culture 22, no. 3 (2017): 317–33.

Gardi, Tomer, Umar al-Ghubari, and Noga Kadman, eds. Once Upon a Land: A Tour Guide. [Hebrew and Arabic] Tel Aviv: Zochrot/Pardes, 2012.

Gdoura, Wahid. "The Violation of Libraries and Books in Occupied Palestine: For the Safeguard of the Palestinian People's Cultural Heritage." In Libraries of Jerusalem, 36–38. Tunis: AFLI, 2003.

Ghalayini, Basma, ed. Palestine +100: Stories from a Century after the Nakba. Manchester, UK: Comma, 2019.

Giannachi, Gabriella. *Archive Everything: Mapping the Everyday*. Cambridge, MA: MIT Press, 2015.

Godard, Jean Luc, dir. *Notre Musique*. 2004.

Gopinath, Gayatri. *Unruly Visions: The Aesthetic Practices of Queer Diaspora*. Durham, NC: Duke University Press, 2018.

Gordon, Avery. *The Hawthorn Archive: Letters from the Utopian Margins*. New York: Fordham University Press, 2017.

Gordon, Joan. "Utopia, Genocide, and the Other." In *Edging into the Future: Science Fiction and Contemporary Cultural Transformation*, edited by Veronica Hollinger and Joan Gordon, 204–16. Philadelphia: University of Pennsylvania Press, 2002.

Gosden, Chris. "Race and Racism in Archaeology: Introduction." *World Archaeology* 38, no. 1 (2006): 1–7.

Grabar, Oleg, and Benjamin Z. Kedar, eds. *Where Heaven and Earth Meet: Jerusalem's Sacred Esplanade*. Austin: University of Texas Press, 2009.

Griffith, Phillip. "Basel Abbas and Ruanne Abou-Rahme's *And Yet My Mask Is Powerful*." *The Brooklyn Rail*, 2018. Accessed April 25, 2020. https://brooklynrail.org /2018/02/art_books/Basel-Abbas-and-Ruanne-Abou-Rahme-And-Yet-My-Mask -Is-Powerful.

Guggenheim, Katie. "Interview with Jumana Manna." Chisenhale Gallery London, September 2015.

Gutman, Yifat. *Memory Activism: Reimagining the Past for the Future in Israel–Palestine*. Nashville, TN: Vanderbilt University Press, 2017.

Habibi, Emile. *The Secret Life of Saeed: The Pessoptimist*. Translated by Trevor Le Gassick. London: Arabia Books, 2010.

Haddad, Katia. "Palestinian Artist Emily Jacir Presents Her Work in 'Europa' Exhibition." [Arabic] *Al-Arab Al-Yawm (ArabsToday.net)*, October 6, 2015. https://bit.ly /2G44g0i.

Haddad, Saleem. "Song of the Birds." In *Palestine +100: Stories from a Century after the Nakba*, edited by Basma Ghalayini. Manchester, UK: Comma, 2019.

Halabi, Zeina. "When Kamal Aljafari Erased Chuck Norris from Jaffa." *Jadaliyya*, May 31, 2015. https://www.jadaliyya.com/Details/32115.

Halaby, Samia. *Liberation Art of Palestine: Palestinian Painting and Sculpture in the Second Half of the 20th Century*. New York: H.T.T.B. Publications, 2001.

Halaka, John, dir. *The Presence of Absence in the Ruins of Kafr Bir'im*. 2007.

Hamdan-Saliba, Hanna. "Urban Planning and the Everyday Experience of Palestinian Women in Jaffa." *Documents d'Anàlisi Geogràfica* 60, no. 1 (2014): 115–34.

Hamilakis, Yannis. "Lives in Ruins: Antiquities and National Imagination in Modern Greece." In *The Politics of Archaeology and Identity in a Global Context*, edited by Susan Kane, 51–78. Boston: AIA, 2007.

Handal, Nathalie. "Kamal Aljafari: Unfinished Balconies in the Sea: Interview with the Filmmaker." *Guernica: A Magazine of Art and Politics*, February 18, 2016. https://www.guernicamag.com/kamal-aljafari-filming-ghosts-and-unfinished -balconies/.

Hartman, Saidiya. *Lose Your Mother: A Journey along the Atlantic Slave Road*. New York: Farrar, Straus and Giroux, 2008.

Hartman, Saidiya. "Venus in Two Acts." *Small Axe: A Caribbean Journal of Criticism* 12, no. 2 (2008): 1–14.

Hartman, Saidiya. *Wayward Lives, Beautiful Experiments: Intimate Histories of Social Upheaval*. New York: W. W. Norton, 2019.

Hawal, Kassem, dir. *Our Small Houses*. 1974 (24 minutes).

Heacock, Roger, and Caroline Mall-Dibiasi. "Liberating the Phantom Elephant: The Digitization of Oral Archives." Working Paper Series, Migration, and Refugee Studies Module, 2011.

Himada, Nasrin. "For Many Returns." *Feature #3*, January 21, 2018. https://contemptorary.org/for-many-returns/?auth=req.

Hirsch, Marianne. "Stateless Memory." *Critical Times* 2, no. 3 (2019): 416–34.

Hoagland, Ericka, and Reema Sarwal, eds. *Science Fiction, Imperialism, and the Third World*. Jefferson, NC: McFarland, 2011.

Hochberg, Gil. "Jerusalem, We Have a Problem: Larissa Sansour's Sci-Fi Trilogy and the Impetus of Dystopic Imagination." *Arab Studies Journal* 26, no. 1 (2018): 34–57.

Hoerth, Alfred J. *Archaeology and the Old Testament*. Grand Rapids, MI: Baker Books, 1998.

Hui Kyong Chun, Wendy. "Unbearable Witness: Towards a Politics of Listening." *Extremities: Trauma, Testimony, and Community*, edited by Nancy K. Miller and Jason Tougaw, 143–65. Urbana: University of Illinois Press, 2002.

"Interviews: Jumana Manna, as Told to Lara Atallah." *Art Forum*, September 18, 2015. https://www.artforum.com/interviews/jumana-manna-speaks-about-her-latest-feature-length-film-54890.

Israel Ministry of Foreign Affairs. "Culture: Archaeology." 2013. Accessed April 25, 2020. https://mfa.gov.il/mfa/aboutisrael/culture/pages/culture-%20archeology.aspx.

Israeli, Raphael. *Jerusalem Divided: The Armistice Regime, 1947–1967*. London: Routledge, 2002.

Jacir, Emily. "ex libris." June 9–September 16, 2012, in Kassel, Germany, at dOCUMENTA (13). https://universes.art/en/nafas/articles/2012/emily-jacir-documenta.

Jameson, Frederic. *Archaeologies of the Future: The Desire Called Utopia and Other Science Fictions*. London: Verso, 2005.

Jawabreh, Asma. "Films, Music and Seeds: Jumana Manna's Means of Preserving Palestinian Heritage." [Arabic] *Al-Fanar*, March 3, 2020. https://www.alfanarmedia.org/ar/2020/03/%D8%AC%D9%85%D8%A7%D9%86%D8%A9-%D9%85%D9%86%D8%A7%D8%B9.

Jones, Siân. *The Archaeology of Ethnicity: Constructing Identities in the Past and Present*. London: Routledge, 1997.

Judt, Tony. "Israel: The Alternative." *New York Review of Books*, October 23, 2003.

Kadman, Noga. *Erased from Space and Consciousness: Depopulated Palestinian Villages in the Israeli Zionist Discourse*. [Hebrew] Jerusalem: November Books, 2008.

Karpel, Dalia. "With Thanks to Ghassan Kanafani." *Ha'aretz*, April 14, 2005.

Karsh, Efraim. "Debating Israel's Early History." *Middle East Quarterly* 3, no. 2 (1996): 19–29.

Karsh, Efraim. *Rethinking the Middle East.* London: Frank Cass, 2003.

Katz, Ruth. *The Lachmann Problem: An Unsung Chapter Comparative Musicology.* Jerusalem: The Hebrew University Magnes, 2003.

Kelly, Robin. *Freedom Dreams: The Black Radical Imagination.* Boston: Beacon, 2002.

Kempinski, Aharon. "The Influence of Archaeology on Israeli Society and Culture." [Hebrew] *Ariel* 100–101 (1994): 179–90.

Kendon, Adam. "The Study of Gesture: Some Observations on Its History." *Semiotic Inquiry* 2, no. 1 (1982): 44–62.

Khalidi, Walid. *All That Remains: The Palestinian Villages Occupied and Depopulated by Israel in 1948.* Beirut: Institute for Palestine Studies, 1992.

Kholeif, Omar. "Focus Interview: Jumana Manna." *Frieze*, May 30, 2014. https://frieze.com/article/focus-interview-jumana-manna.

Kletter, Raz. *Just Past? The Making of Israeli Archaeology.* London: Equinox, 2006.

Kletter, Raz. "A Very General Archaeologist: Moshe Dayan and Israeli Archaeology." *The Journal of Hebrew Scriptures* 4, no. 5 (2003): n.p.

Kohl, Philip L. "Nationalism and Archaeology: On the Constructions of Nations and the Reconstructions of the Remote Past." *Annual Review of Anthropology* 27 (1998): 223–46.

Kohl, Philip L., and Clare Fawcett, eds. *Nationalism, Politics and the Practice of Archaeology.* Cambridge: Cambridge University Press, 1996.

Kourlasaug, Gia. "Twisting Body and Mind." *New York Times*, August 12, 2011.

Labocine. "Envisioning Future States with Science Fiction." *Journal of Labocine*, February 21, 2017. https://medium.com/labocine/envisioning-future-states-with-science-fiction-7a4ea54e00ca.

Lambert-Beatty, Carrie. "Make Believe: Parafiction and Plausibility." *October* 129 (2009): 51–84.

Langer, Jessica. *Postcolonialism and Science Fiction.* New York: Palgrave Macmillan, 2011.

Leigh Foster, Susan. "Choreographies of Writing." *Susan Foster! Susan Foster! Three Performed Lectures*, March 22, 2011. http://danceworkbook.pcah.us/susan-foster/choreographies-of-writing.html.

Lepecki, André. "Choreopolice and Choreopolitics: Or, the Task of the Dancer." *The DraReview* 57, no. 4 (2013): 13–27.

LeVine, Mark. *Overthrowing Geography: Jaffa, Tel Aviv, and the Struggle for Palestine, 1880–1948.* Berkeley: University of California Press, 2005.

Lezra, Esther. *The Colonial Art of Demonizing Others: A Global Perspective.* Oxford: Routledge, 2014.

L'Heureux, Antoine. "Art's Utopia: The Geography of Art against (Its) History." In *Art History after Deleuze and Guattari*, edited by Van Tuinen Sjoerd and Zepke Stephen, 255–74. Leuven, Belgium: Leuven University Press, 2017.

Limbrick, Peter. "Contested Spaces: Kamal Aljafari's Transnational Palestinian Films." In *A Companion to German Cinema*, edited by Terri Ginsberg and Andrea Mensch, 218–48. West Sussex, UK: Wiley-Blackwell, 2012.

Liosi, Marianna. "Speculations for Collective Transformations Farah Saleh in Conversation with Marianna Liosi." *IBRAAZ: Contemporary Visual Culture in North Africa and the Middle East* 10, no. 5 (2016). Accessed April 20, 2020. https://www.ibraaz.org/interviews/204.

Louis Mann, Justin. "Pessimistic Futurism: Survival and Reproduction in Octavia Butler's Dawn." *Feminist Theory* 19, no. 1 (2017): 61–76.

Lowry, James, ed. *Displaced Archives*. New York: Routledge, 2017.

Mafadleh, Ghassan. "Emily Jacir: A Lot from Palestine." [Arabic, 2020] *Al-Arabi Al-Jadeed*, January 18, 2015. https://bit.ly/33S8XlY.

Makdisi, Saree. "The Architecture of Erasure." *Critical Inquiry* 36, no. 3 (2010): 519–59.

Maliszewski, Lynn. "Basel Abbas and Ruanne Abou-Rahme's And Yet My Mask Is Powerful." *BOMB Magazine* (2017). Accessed April 25, 2020. https://bombmagazine.org/articles/basel-abbas-and-ruanne-abou-rahmes-and-yet-my-mask-is-powerful.

Manna, Jumana. "As Told to Lara Atallah." *Artforum*, September 8, 2015. https://www.artforum.com/interviews/jumana-manna-speaks-about-her-latest-feature-length-film-54890.

Manoff, Marlene. "Theories of the Archive from across the Disciplines." *Portal: Libraries and the Academy* 4, no. 1 (2004): 9–25.

Marks, Laura. *The Skin of the Film: Intercultural Cinema, Embodiment, and the Senses*. Durham, NC: Duke University Press, 2000.

Masalah, Nur. *The Bible and Zionism: Invented Traditions, Archaeology and Post-Colonialism in Palestine-Israel*. London: Zed Books, 2007.

Masalah, Nur. *The Palestine Nakba: Decolonising History, Narrating the Subaltern, Reclaiming Memory*. London: Zed Books, 2012.

Masalah, Nur. "Settler-Colonialism, Memoricide, and Indigenous Toponymic Memory: The Appropriation of Palestinian Place Names by the Israeli State." *Journal of Holy Land and Palestine Studies* 14, no. 1 (2015): 3–57.

Mauss, Marcel. *The Gift: The Form and Reason for Exchange in Archaic Societies*. London: Routledge, 1973.

Mazawi, Andre. "Film Production and Jaffa's Predicament." *Jaffa Diaries*, February 9, 1998.

Mbembe, Achille. "The Power of the Archive and Its Limits." In *Refiguring the Archive*, edited by Carolyn Hamilton, Verne Harris, Jane Taylor, Michele Pickover, Graeme Reid, and Razia Saleh, 19–27. Norwell, MA: Kluwer Academic Publisher, 2002.

McEwan, Cheryl. "Building a Postcolonial Archive? Gender, Collective Memory and Citizenship in Post-Apartheid South Africa." *Journal of Southern African Studies* 29, no. 3 (2003): 739–57.

Meador, Daryl. "A Cinematic Rejection of Gaza's Isolation." *Electronic Intifada*, July 20, 2017. https://electronicintifada.net/content/cinematic-rejection-gazas -isolation/21131.

Meador, Daryl. "Music Floats above Zionism's Barrier." *Electronic Intifada*, May 31, 2016.

Melhem, Ahmad. "Palestinian Museum's Digital Archive Project to Preserve Heritage." *Al-Monitor*, March 11, 2018.

Merewether, Charles, ed. *The Archive*. Cambridge, MA: MIT Press, 2006.

Milner, Andrew, ed. *Tenses of Imagination: Raymond Williams on Science Fiction, Utopia, and Dystopia*. Bern, Switzerland: Peter Lang AG, 2010.

Monterescu, Daniel. "The Bridled Bride of Palestine: Orientalism, Zionism, and the Troubled Urban Imagination." *Identities: Global Studies in Culture and Power* 16 (2009): 643–77.

Monterescu, Daniel. "Heteronomy: The Cultural Logic of Urban Space and Sociality in Jaffa." In *Mixed Towns, Trapped Communities: Historical Narratives, Spatial Dynamics, Gender Relations and Culture Encounters in Palestinian-Israeli Towns*, edited by Daniel Monterescu and Dan Rabinowitz, 157–78. Hampshire, UK: Ashgate, 2007.

Montgomery Byles, Joanna. "Archaeology and Psychoanalysis." *Maison de l'Orient et de la Méditerranée Jean Pouilloux* (2003): 59–64.

Moore, Niamh, Andrea Salter, Liz Stanley, and Maria Tamboukou. *The Archive Project: Archival Research in the Social Sciences*. London: Routledge, 2016.

Moorey, P. R. S. *A Century of Biblical Archaeology*. Louisville, KY: Westminster/John Knox, 1991.

Morelli, Naima. "New Directions for the Palestinian Museum: Interview with Director Dr. Adila Laïdi Hanieh." *Middle East Monitor*, June 26, 2019.

Morris, Benny. *The Birth of the Palestinian Refugee Problem, 1947–1949*. Cambridge: Cambridge University Press, 1987.

Morris, Leslie. "The Sound of Memory." *The German Quarterly* 74, no. 4 (2001): 368–78.

Moylan, Tom, and Raffaella Baccolini, eds. *Dark Horizons: Science Fiction and the Dystopian Imagination*. New York: Routledge, 2013.

Murray, Tim. *From Antiquarian to Archaeologist: The History and Philosophy of Archaeology*. Barnsely, UK: Pen and Sword Archaeology, 2014.

Nash, Aily. "Working With, and Through, Conflict: Interview with Basma Alsharif." *BOMB Magazine*, March 12, 2015. https://bombmagazine.org/articles/basma -alsharif/.

Nashif, Esmail. "Mawt al-Nas" (Death of the People). [Arabic] *Majallat al-Dirasat al-Filastiniyya* 96 (2013): 96–117.

Noland, Carrie, and Sally Ann Ness, eds. *Migrations of Gesture*. Minneapolis: University of Minnesota Press, 2008.

Nyong'o, Tavia. *Afro-Fabulations: The Queer Drama of Black Life*. New York: NYU Press, 2019.

Orrells, Daniel. "Derrida's Impression of Gradiva Archive Fever and Antiquity."
    In *Derrida and Antiquity*, edited by Miriam Leonard, 159–84. Oxford: Oxford
    University Press, 2010.
Ostoff, Simone. *Performing the Archive: The Transformation of the Archive in Contemporary
    Art from Repository of Documents to Art Medium*. New York: Artopos, 2009.
Pad.ma. "10 Theses on the Archive." April 2010. https://pad.ma/documents/OH.
Pappé, Ilan. "Israel's Latest Attempt to Erase Palestine." *The Electronic Intifada*,
    July 25, 2019. https://electronicintifada.net/content/israels-latest-attempt-erase
    -palestine/27941.
Peterson, Bhekizizwe. "The Archives and the Political Imaginary." In *Refiguring the
    Archive*, edited by Carolyn Hamilton, Verne Harris, Jane Taylor, Michele Pick-
    over, Graeme Reid, and Razia Saleh, 28–35. Norwell, MA: Kluwer Academic
    Publisher, 2002.
Petti, Alessandro. "Architecture of Exile IV.B." 2017. Accessed April 10, 2020. https://
    www.e-flux.com/architecture/refugee-heritage/99756/the-architecture-of-exile
    -iv-b.
Petti, Alessandro. "Introduction." *Refugee Heritage, Decolonizing Architecture Art
    Residency*, 2017. Accessed April 15, 2020. http://www.decolonizing.ps/site
    /introduction-4.
"Pictures of the Day: 6 April 2018." *The Telegraph*, April 6, 2018. https://www
    .telegraph.co.uk/news/2018/04/06/pictures-day-6-april-2018/group-palestinian
    -women-protester-guy-fawkes-masks-palestinian.
Rich, Adrienne. *Poems 1971–1972*. New York: W. W. Norton, 2013.
Rifkin, Mark. "Indigeneity, Apartheid, Palestine: On the Transit of Political Meta-
    phors." *Cultural Critique* 95 (2017): 25–70.
Roelstraete, Dieter. "The Way of the Shovel." *e-flux*, March 4, 2009. https://www
    .e-flux.com/journal/04/68582/the-way-of-the-shovel-on-the-archeological
    -imaginary-in-art.
Rouhana, Nadim. "Homeland Nationalism and Guarding Dignity in a Settler-
    Colonial Context: The Palestinian Citizens of Israel Reclaim Their Homeland."
    Borderlands 14, no. 1 (2015): 1–37.
Rouhana, Nadim, and Areej Sabbagh-Khoury. "Settler-Colonial Citizenship:
    Conceptualizing the Relationship between Israel and Its Palestinian Citizens."
    Settler-Colonial Studies 5, no. 3: 205–25.
"Ruanne Abou-Rahme and Basel Abbas in Conversation with Fawz Kabra." *Ocula
    Magazine*, January 18, 2018. https://ocula.com/magazine/conversations/basel
    -abbas-and-ruanne-abou-rahme.
Saadi, Yara. "Kamal Aljafari's 'Recollection': Tell Us, Tell Us about Jaffa." [Arabic]
    7iber, May 7, 2017. https://www.7iber.com/culture/recollection-review.
Sa'di, Ahmad H., and Lila Abu-Lughod, eds. *Nakba: Palestine, 1948, and the Claims of
    Memory*. New York: Columbia University Press, 2007.
Said, Edward. "Permission to Narrate." *Journal of Palestine Studies* 13, no. 3 (1984):
    27–48.

Said, Edward. *The Question of Palestine*. New York: Vintage, 1992.

Salaita, Steven. "American Indian Studies and Palestine Solidarity: The Importance of Impetuous Definitions." *Decolonization: Indigeneity, Education and Society* 6, no. 1 (2017): 1–28.

Saleh, Farah. "Archiving Gestures of Disobedience." *Contemporary Theatre Review* 27, no. 1 (2017): 134–48. Accessed April 20, 2020. https://hcommons.org/deposits /objects/hc:13884/datastreams/CONTENT/content.

Saloul, Ihab. "'Performative Narrativity': Palestinian Identity and the Performance of Catastrophe." *Cultural Analysis* 7 (2008): 5–39.

Sansour, Larissa, dir. *In the Future They Ate from the Finest Porcelain*. 2016 (29 minutes).

Sansour, Larissa, dir. *Nation Estate*. 2012 (9 minutes).

Sansour, Larissa, dir. *A Space Exodus*. 2008 (5 minutes).

Schalk, Sami. *Bodyminds Reimagined: (Dis)ability, Race, and Gender in Black Women's Speculative Fiction*. Durham, NC: Duke University Press, 2018.

Seikaly, Sherene. "Palestine as Archive." *Stanford University Press Blog*, August 1, 2014. https://stanfordpress.typepad.com/blog/2014/08/palestine-as-archive .html.

Sela, Rona. "The Genealogy of Colonial Plunder and Erasure—Israel's Control over Palestinian Archives," *Social Semiotics* 28, no. 2 (2018): 201–29.

Sela, Rona, dir. *Looted and Hidden—Palestinian Archives in Israel*. 2017 (46 minutes).

Sela, Rona. *Made Public: Palestinian Photographs in Military Archives in Israel*. Tel Aviv: Helena, 2010.

Sela, Rona. *Photography in Palestine/Eretz Israel in the Thirties and Forties*. [Hebrew] Tel Aviv: Muze'on Hertzliya le-omanut and Hakibutz Hameuchad, 2009.

Seroussi, Edwin. "Nostalgic Soundscapes: The Future of Israel's Sonic Past." *Israel Studies* 19, no. 2 (2014): 35–50.

Shai, Aron. "The Fate of Abandoned Arab Villages in Israel on the Eve of the Six-Day War and Its Immediate Aftermath." [Hebrew] *Cathedra* 105 (September 2002): 151–70.

Shams, Alex. "Interview: Nadia Abu El-Haj on Archaeology and the Zionist Project." *Ma'an News Agency*, April 9, 2014.

Sharrer, Eva. "Emily Jacir: ex libris." *Nafas, Universes in Universe*, 2012. Accessed April 25, 2020. https://universes.art/en/nafas/articles/2012/emily-jacir -documenta.

Shavit, Ari. "Survival of the Fittest: Ari Shavit Interviews Benny Morris." *Ha'aretz*, January 8, 2004.

Shavit, Yaacov. "The Bible as History and the Controversy over the Historical Truth in the Bible." [Hebrew] In *New Jewish Time: Jewish Culture in a Secular Era*, 129–34. Jerusalem: Keter, 2007.

Shihade, Magid. "Not Just a Picnic: Settler Colonialism, Mobility, and Identity among Palestinians in Israel." *Biography* 37, no. 2 (2014).

Shnirel'man, Victor A. "Nationalism and Archaeology." *Anthropology and Archaeology of Eurasia* 52, no. 2 (2013): 13–32.

Shohat, Ella. *Israeli Cinema: East/West and the Politics of Representation*. Austin: University of Texas Press, 1989.

Silberman, Neil Asher. "Promised Lands and Chosen Peoples: The Politics and Poetics of Archaeological Narrative." In *Nationalism, Politics, and the Practice of Archaeology*, edited by Philip L. Kohl and Clare Fawcett, 249–62. Cambridge: Cambridge University Press, 1995.

Silberstein, Laurence J. "Becoming Israel, Israeli Becomings." *Deleuze and the Contemporary World*, edited by Ian Buchanan and Adrian Parr, 146–60. Edinburgh: Edinburgh University Press, 2006.

Slyomovics, Susan. *The Object of Memory: Arab and Jew Narrate the Palestinian Village*. Philadelphia: University of Pennsylvania Press, 2000.

Smith, Joan. "I Find Myself Instinctively on the Other Side of Power." Interview with Edward Said. *The Guardian*, December 10, 2001. https://www.theguardian.com/books/departments/politicsphilosophyandsociety/story/0,6000,616545,00.html.

Stahl, Ziv. "Appropriating the Past: Israel's Archaeological Practices in the West Bank." Report by NGOs Emek Shaveh and Yesh Din, December 2017. Accessed April 25, 2020. http://alt-arch.org/en/wp-content/uploads/2017/12/Menachsim-Eng-Web.pdf.

Stanton, Andrea L. *"This Is Jerusalem Calling": State Radio in Mandate Palestine*. Austin: University of Texas Press, 2013.

Steedman, Carolyn. *Dust: The Archive and Cultural History*. New Brunswick, NJ: Rutgers University Press, 2002.

Stewart, Kathleen. *Ordinary Affects*. Durham, NC: Duke University Press, 2007.

Stoler, Ann Laura. *Along the Archival Grain: Epistemic Anxieties and Colonial Common Sense*. Princeton, NJ: Princeton University Press, 2008.

Stoler, Ann Laura. "Colonial Archives and the Arts of Governance." In *Archives, Documentation, and Institutions of Social Memory: Essays from the Sawyer Seminar*, edited by Francis X. Blouin and William G. Rosenberg, 269–71. Ann Arbor: University of Michigan Press, 2006.

Stoler, Ann Laura. "On Archiving as Dissensus." *Comparative Studies of South Asia, Africa and the Middle East* 38, no. 1 (2018): 43–56.

Strohm, Kiven. "The Sensible Life of Return: Collaborative Experiments on Art and Anthropology in Palestine/Israel." *American Anthropologist* 121, no. 1 (2019): 243–55.

Takahashi, Tess l. "The Imaginary Archive: Current Practice." *Camera Obscura* 22, no. 3 (2007): 179–84.

Tamari, Salim. "Treacherous Memories: Electronic Return to Jaffa." *Palestine-Israel Journal: Of Politics, Economic and Culture* 5, no. 1 (1998). Accessed April 15, 2020. https://pij.org/articles/435.

Tamari, Salim, and Issam Nassar, eds. *The Storyteller of Jerusalem: The Life and Times of Wasif Jawhariyyeh, 1904–1948*. Translated by Nada Elzeer. Northampton, MA: Olive Branch, 2014.

Tatour, Lana. "The Culturalisation of Indigeneity: The Palestinian-Bedouin of the Naqab and Indigenous Rights." *The International Journal of Human Rights* 23, no. 10 (2019): 1569–93.

Taylor, Diana. *The Archive and the Repertoire: Performing Cultural Memory in the Americas.* Durham, NC: Duke University Press, 2003.

Trigger, Bruce. *A History of Archaeological Thought.* Cambridge: Cambridge University Press, 1989.

Trigger, Bruce. "Romanticism, Nationalism and Archaeology." In *Nationalism, Politics, and the Practice of Archaeology,* edited by Philip Kohl and C. Fawcett, 263–79. Cambridge: Cambridge University Press, 1995.

Ulrike, Sommer. "Archaeology and Nationalism." In *Key Concepts in Public Archaeology,* edited by Moshenska Gabriel, 166–86. London: UCL Press, 2017.

UNESCO. Convention Concerning the Protection of the World Cultural and Natural Heritage, The General Conference of the United Nations Educational, Scientific and Cultural Organization meeting in Paris from October 17 to November 21, 1972, at its seventeenth session. https://whc.unesco.org/en/conventiontext.

Valluri, Gautam. "The Wanderer's Home Movies: An Interview with Basma Alsharif." *Projectorhead,* June 2016. Accessed April 25, 2020. https://projectorhead.in/an-interview-with-basma-alsharif/.

Vassileva, Biliana. "Dramaturgies of the Gaga Bodies: Kinesthesia of Pleasure/Healing." *Danza e Ricerca* 7, no. 8 (2016): 77–99.

Veracini, Lorenzo. "The Other Shift: Settler Colonialism, Israel and the Occupation." *Journal of Palestine Studies* 42, no. 2 (2013): 26–42.

Veracini, Lorenzo. "What Can Settler Colonial Studies Offer to an Interpretation of the Conflict in Israel–Palestine?" *Settler Colonial Studies* 5, no. 3 (2015): 268–71.

Walid, Salem. "Jerusalem: Reconsidering the Settler Colonial Analysis." *Palestine-Israel Journal of Politics, Economics, and Culture* 21, no. 4 (2016): 21–27.

Watson, Sir Charles Moore, and Palestine Exploration Fund. *Fifty Years' Work in the Holy Land: A Record and a Summary, 1865–1915.* London: Committee of the Palestine Exploration Fund, 1915.

Wazir, Burhan. "Palestinian Film Denied Oscars Entry." *The Guardian,* December 14, 2002. https://www.theguardian.com/world/2002/dec/15/film.filmnews.

Williams, Patrick, and Anna Ball. "Where Is Palestine?" *Journal of Postcolonial Writing* 50, no. 2 (2014): 127–33.

Winzen, Matthias, eds. *Deep Storage: Collecting, Storing, and Archiving in Art.* Munich: Prestel, 1998.

Wolfe, Patrick, and J. Kēhaulani Kauanui. "Settler Colonialism Then and Now: A Conversation." *Politica and Società* 2 (2012): 235–58.

Yaqub, Nadia. *Palestinian Cinema in the Days of Revolution.* Austin: University of Texas Press, 2018.

Yaqub, Nadia. "Refracted Filmmaking in Muhammad Malas's *The Dream* and Kamal Aljafari's *The Roof*." *Middle East Journal of Culture and Communication* 7 (2014): 152–68.

Zerubavel, Yael. *Recovered Roots: Collective Memory and the Making of Israeli National Tradition*. Chicago: University of Chicago Press, 1995.

Ziad, Fahmy. "Coming to Our Senses: Historicizing Sound and Noise in the Middle East." *History Compass* 11, no. 4 (2013): 305–15.

www.ingramcontent.com/pod-product-compliance
Lightning Source LLC
Chambersburg PA
CBHW051212170526
45166CB00005B/1865